ELY

THE HIDDEN HISTORY

DAVID BARROWCLOUGH AND KATE MORRISON

For James Morrison
and in memory of Zena Morrison

First published 2013

The History Press
The Mill, Brimscombe Port
Stroud, Gloucestershire, GL5 2QG
www.thehistorypress.co.uk

© David Barrowclough and Kate Morrison, 2013

The right of David Barrowclough and Kate Morrison to be
identified as the Authors of this work has been asserted in
accordance with the Copyright, Designs and Patents Act 1988.

British Library Cataloguing in Publication Data.
A catalogue record for this book is available from the British Library.

ISBN 978 0 7524 6555 5
Typesetting and origination by The History Press
Printed in Great Britain

CONTENTS

PREFACE

The concept for this book materialised over a lunch-time coffee in the Almonry Tearooms one sunny Wednesday in April 2011. Discussing the rich archaeology of the Isle found within the Ely Museum collections, we were struck by the fact that although there were numerous pictorial history books written about the Isle and various history books about Ely, these mostly focused on the cathedral and legendary figures. There was no book which solely covered the Isle's archaeology. This got us thinking and, over the course of the next week, our 'wouldn't this be a good idea?' had turned into a fully-fledged proposal. What we wanted was a book that not only provided the residents of, and visitors to, Ely with a readable and interesting archaeological perspective to the history of the Isle, but also one which could equally be of value to the scholar and student. We hope that, whether enthusiast, resident or visitor, you will find this an interesting and unique take on the history of the Isle of Ely that, as outsiders, we have come to regard as home.

The discussion draws on the published archaeological studies undertaken *inter alia* by the Fenland Project, University of Cambridge Archaeological Unit and Oxford Archaeology East, as well as many private individuals including excavations by Ann Holton Krayenbuhl, field-walking surveys by Michael Young and metal-detecting by Phillip Randall. We thank all of them for sharing the details of their finds with us and thus allowing us to tell the story of Ely and its origins.

This work is only possible because of the support and assistance that we have received from friends and colleagues in Ely and beyond. Thanks go in particular to the Chairman, John Marshall, the Trustees of Ely Museum and the President and Fellows of Wolfson College, University of Cambridge. To Dr Mary Chester-Kadwell our dear friend who has been enormously helpful, giving up much of her time to produce the maps as well as advising on the subject of the Anglo-Saxon Period, allowing us to use her research on the artefacts in Ely Museum and for her careful proofing of the text. We thank David Jacques, Ely resident and archaeologist, for his discussion of finds from Barway, for proofing the draft text and allowing us to not only take part in his excavations at Vespasian's Camp, but also to display the finds for the first time at Ely Museum. For his personal recollections of the discoveries made on his family farm at Barway we thank Phillip Randall, particularly for his advice on the discovery of the Roman coin hoard made when he was a young boy. The exquisite photographs which illustrate this volume were taken by Ely photographer Stephen Stanley Jugg, with additional pictures from the Ely Museum collection taken by members of Ely and District Photographic Society. We thank Dr Peter Hoare for his comments on the geology and Christina Barnes, Trustee of Ely Museum, for her wonderful insight into the history of Ely and for proofing the text. Likewise we thank Phillipa Wainwright for her painstaking proofing, comments and wonderful asides; Lorien Pilling for his friendship, support and countless cocktails and BCGs over the years, as well as his proofing of the text; Aiden Baker and the staff at the Haddon Library, University of Cambridge, for access to research material; Anna Jones the then librarian of the Lee Library, Wolfson College; the Sedgwick Museum of Earth Science, University of Cambridge, for access to their geology collections; and Penny Williams and the friendly staff at 3@3 for the endless hours we spent drinking coffee and hot chocolate whilst working on the book.

There are a few people that I (Kate) would like to give a special mention to. Firstly to say thank you to Doug Storey to whom I am indebted for his kindness and sage advice when it mattered. I hope that this book will, in some way, repay that debt. I would also like to thank Gillian Mason, Curator, Bletchley Park, for prompting me to apply for the position of Curator at Ely in the first place. If it hadn't been for her friendship, none of this would have been possible. To Bill Griffiths at Milton Keynes Museum, I would like to thank for entrusting me with his 'baby'. It is the most precious gift and I am humbled by his kindness. Finally I would like to thank David. I am so grateful to him for agreeing to write this with me. It has been a journey of discovery for both of us.

Finally we would both like to thank our dear friend Tim Jobling for his patience while his wife Mary laboured over the maps when she should have been helping him to plan their wedding, his pertinent questions about the book and the Friday night drinks that kept us all sane. We hope that you enjoy reading Hidden Ely as much as we enjoyed unearthing it. Any mistakes or omissions remain ours.

Kate & David
Milton Keynes and Ely,
June 2013

CHAPTER 1

INTRODUCTION

Most shudderingly entrancing of all was the Ancient Briton, who suddenly emerged from the peat in Burwell Fen, when the turf-diggers were at work. He stood upright in his dug-out canoe. His lank black hair dropped to his shoulders. The peat-dark skin was still stretched over the bones of his face. The eyes had gone but the eye-sockets were dark with mystery. He was clad in a long leather jacket, belted, with garter round his legs and the right arm was raised as though about to cast a spear.

Wentworth Day, 1970.

Encounters with our ancient forebears are rare, but when they occur they are powerful reminders that we are but the latest link in a chain that stretches back millennia connecting us to each other, to the land and to the louring fens. This book tells the story of the Isle of Ely (Figure 1) from its earliest geological beginnings to the seventeenth century. The approach is archaeological, to tell the story of life on the archipelago of islands known as the Isle of Ely through the monuments and buildings that people made, the objects they left behind, and just occasionally through discoveries of the people themselves. Archaeology is uniquely suited to tell this story of long-term social organisation because of its well-developed methodology for excavating and recording historical data.

We have been frustrated that there was no up-to-date account of the Isle's rich archaeological heritage. This concerned us as it has meant an over-reliance on histories, usually of near-mythic characters such as St Etheldreda and Hereward the Wake, which repeat unreliable older stories often based on fragments of text or without an authenticated source. These narratives rarely refer to the archaeological evidence and when they do, because of their age, lack discussion of more recent excavations. This has led to the proliferation of misconceptions about the island's history; in particular, that it began with the Anglo-Saxon princess, St Etheldreda, and the founding of what was to become Ely Cathedral, itself the subject of many accounts. This book therefore takes the opportunity to publish analyses of excavations that help to construct a

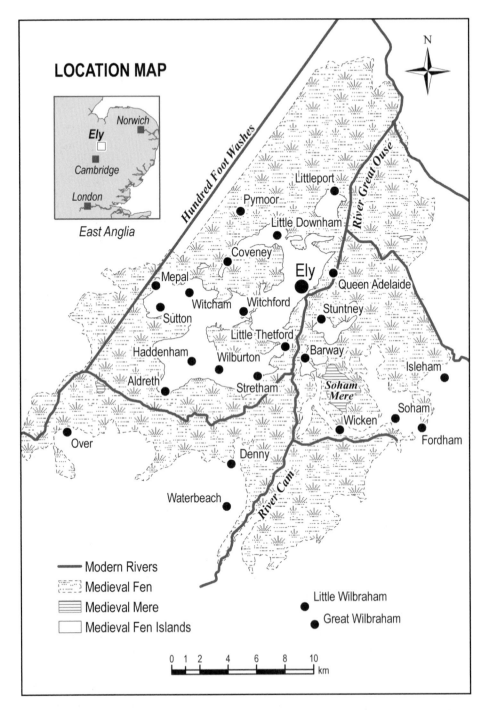

Fig 1. Location map showing the Isle of Ely in its physical setting. The main island of Ely is the largest in an archipelago which includes the smaller islands of Stuntney and Littleport. Map data © OpenStreetMap contributors, CC BY-SA.

narrative for the prehistoric as well as historical periods. Through this book we hope to reveal something of the richness and variety of the lives of the ordinary people who have preceded us in this corner of England.

SCOPE

Ely: The Hidden History spans the period from the Jurassic to the seventeenth century, a span of over 200 million years, although it is only in the last 8,000 years that humans have come to dominate the landscape. For convenience and ease of comparison the traditional terms for the divisions of time are used. The most distant, deep time of geological changes follows the conventional divisions of Jurassic through to Holocene (see Chapter 2), whilst the Prehistoric Period – Palaeolithic, Mesolithic, Neolithic, Bronze and Iron Age – has been adopted in Chapters 3, 4 and 5. Later periods follow their historic names, the Roman and Anglo-Saxon Periods cover the first millennium AD (Chapters 5 and 6), which are followed by a combined Norman, medieval and post-medieval one beginning at 1066 and ending in the seventeenth century (Chapter 7). The book ends with a discussion of long-term continuity and change, and the extent to which these contribute towards an expression of island identity. The discussion is, however, led by the archaeology, rather than terminology. It is felt that this retains clarity whilst also addressing the complexity of the archaeological record. The layout of what follows is therefore chronological.

Following this introduction, Chapter 2 deals with the Isle in deep time, setting out the geological background to the later human exploitation of the island. The Kimmeridge Clay of Ely contains fossils that can still be found today by the keen amateur. These fossils allow us to reconstruct the early Jurassic environment between *c.*200 and 145 million years ago, when the area was submerged by warm seas teaming with long-extinct aquatic species.

Chapter 3 begins with the Pleistocene, *c.*2.5 million to 11,500 years ago, when there is evidence that Ely and the surrounding areas were colonised by our now-extinct cousins, *Homo heidelbergensis* (the European cousin of the Asian *Homo erectus*) and *Homo neanderthalensis*, 'Neanderthals'. The Isle has produced a number of interesting finds from this period, the most impressive of which was the discovery of Acheulian hand axes at Shippea Hill, Little Downham, Isleham, Soham Fen and Sutton, which establish that a community of *Homo erectus*, an ancestor of modern humans, were living on the Isle (see Chapter 3). The discussion then moves from the Holocene, *c.*11,500 years ago to the present, and deals with the post-glacial colonisation of the Isle by humans and its Mesolithic exploitation. Evidence for the late Upper Palaeolithic, 40,000–10,000 years ago, is generally scarce in Britain because the ice sheets, which bordered the Wash, created a cold tundra-like environment around the Fens (Figure 2). Nonetheless a Soultrean blade, made by a Cro-Magnon, the first anatomically modern humans who co-existed with Neanderthals, c.20,000 years ago, was found at Littleport (see Chapter 3). During the Mesolithic the activities of mobile hunter-gatherer communities can be discerned from the many flints found on the Isle. Most of these finds consist of stray flints, collected rather than excavated from surface scatters. What is needed to develop our understanding of the way that these hunters lived their lives can only be provided by an archaeological context. The opportunity is taken here to review the local Mesolithic sites of Plantation, Peacocks and New Wold Farms, Primrose Hill and Back Drove. These contrasting locations, when considered in the context of research undertaken by the Fenland Survey (Hall 1996), make it possible to begin to understand the different types of activities undertaken and the extent of mobility among hunter-gatherer-fisher communities on the Isle of Ely.

Turning to the Neolithic, beginning c.4,000 BC, the evidence for occupation on the Isle still needs to be developed. What is most distinctive about the period in many parts of Britain are the communal monuments. Those that we have at Haddenham include a causewayed enclosure and long barrow and have provided unique insights into technology and burial practices due to their exceptional preservation. Importantly the long barrow has allowed us to study how local attitudes towards the dead changed over a period of several generations (see Chapter 3). Another feature of the Neolithic nationally is the adoption of polished stone axes, many examples of which are known on the Isle, allowing us to consider to what extent the Isle was connected to the rest of Britain through trade and exchange during this period. Overall, the evidence for the Neolithic has striking similarities with that of the Mesolithic, which suggests that the population remained relatively mobile.

This sense of continuity in the face of technological innovation is a theme that continues into the Early Bronze Age, the subject of Chapter 4. The earthworks and monuments are the most visible testament to the prehistoric occupation of the Isle of Ely and are widely spread across the island. Many barrows were destroyed at the end of the nineteenth century and the early part

Fig 2. During the last Ice Age Ely and the surrounding area resembled areas of modern Siberia and northern Canada, covered by a cold tundra vegetation of short grasses and shrubs. At this time mammoth herds roamed the landscape. This photograph shows a large molar tooth from a mammoth found from the fens around Ely. Source: the authors.

of the twentieth, and the literature has often bemoaned the lack of scientific excavation. We have therefore taken this chapter as an opportunity to present an analysis of the more recent excavations, those of Snow's Farm and Hermitage Farm at Haddenham and barrow SUT 7 at Sutton. We have also reviewed the older excavations. This data underpins a renewed analysis of the period, which includes consideration of the chronology, grave good assemblages, and demography in the context of what we know about settlement and domestic activity during this period. It is to the Bronze Age that we assign the origins of a distinctive island identity.

The latter half of the chapter progresses to the Middle and Late Bronze Age, and focuses on the deposition of metalwork (Figure 3). The break between Early and later Bronze Age is one of the more obvious disjunctures in the archaeological record. It is still not at all clear why the longstanding Early Bronze Age burial practices came to an end, although suggestions that it may have something to do with a deteriorating climate are supported by the local environmental evidence. The advent of popular metal detecting combined with more consistent reporting, thanks in part to the Portable Antiquities Scheme (PAS), has led to an increase in the number of finds of this period (see the online PAS catalogue: finds.org.uk). Using all the available evidence it has been possible to discern a distinct island flavour to metalwork deposits in Ely. Moving beyond simplistic observations about the presence of large hoards, and the presence or absence of certain weapon types, such as swords, it has been possible to identify particular local associations between certain types of deposits and particular types of location, such as prehistoric causeways, that point to the inhabitant's insular identity.

The Iron Age and Romano-British occupation of the area is explored in Chapter 5, with a particular focus on the evidence for settlement which builds upon important work undertaken by Christopher Evans and the Cambridge Archaeological Unit (CAU) in recent years. We attempt to dispel the myth that there were no Romans on the Isle. The hillforts are the best known evidence for the Iron Age Period and this chapter presents an overview of excavations that took place at Wardy Hill, Coveney, in the context of other settlements that have been excavated around Ely by the CAU and other archaeological units. We also introduce the idea of the Isle as a centre for religious and cult practices, tracing the emergence of an insular cult centre, focussing on the head, during the Iron Age.

Chapter 6 is concerned with the Anglo-Saxon Period c.AD 410–1066, which is marked by the introduction of distinctively Anglo-Saxon jewellery and weaponry. During this period St Etheldreda founded the monastery in AD 673 which may be seen as the origin of the settlement that we know today as Ely. This chapter focuses on the identification of the location of the sites of

Fig 3. Later Bronze Age chisel found by local metal detectorist Phillip Randall. Photo: Steven Stanley Jugg.

Cratendune and of the first monastery in Ely. The second half of the chapter is devoted to a discussion of the objects found locally, identifying those which are peculiar to the Isle and which suggest the existence of an island identity.

The islandness of Ely was made legendary as the last refuge of Hereward the Wake and his supporters in their opposition to William the Conqueror. Chapter 7 covers the period 1066 to 1660, beginning with the Norman Conquest and continuing through the Medieval Period. Following Hereward's defeat the importance of Ely as an ecclesiastical centre, which had begun in the Early Medieval Period, intensified with the building of the Norman cathedral. The Church dominated the town throughout the period with the street pattern of central Ely that is seen today having been established as early as 1200. Excavations since the 1990s have revealed much about the lives of the ordinary people which have allowed us to reconstruct the pattern of daily life for the medieval inhabitants of the town.

The book concludes with a consideration of changing attitudes toward Ely's island archaeology throughout history (Chapter 8). The focus is on an analysis of long-term continuity and change, and the extent to which these contribute towards an expression of island identity.

STUDY AREA: THE CONSTITUENT PARTS OF THE ISLE OF ELY

The Isle of Ely is best understood by considering each parish in turn (Figures 1 and 4).

Little Downham, otherwise known as Downham-in-the-Isle, lies on a north-western spur of the Isle of Ely; along with Coveney and Witchford, it encloses West Fen almost completely. The spur rises steeply reaching over 15m OD (above sea level) along its spine. In the fen there is a much lower continuation of the ridge northwards swelling out at the hamlet of Pymore north of which are two small islands: Primrose Hill and an unnamed one at Seventh Drove (Hall 1996, 12). The ridge is capped by boulder clay stretching from Ely and running to Pymore. Under the core of the modern village lies Glacial sand and gravel.

Fig 4. Location of the parishes, on and around the Isle of Ely, considered in this book. Map data © OpenStreetMap contributors, CC BY-SA.

The parish of Ely, which includes the city of that name, lies towards the east of the island of Ely on high ground. The hamlet of Chettisham lies north of the city and the deserted hamlet of Braham is to the south. On the east, protruding through the fen are, from north to south, the islands of Shippea, Quanea, Thorney, Stuntney and Nornea. Prickwillow lies in the fen on the roddon (the dried raised bed of a former watercourse) of the River Lark. The underlying bedrock of Kimmeridge Clay is capped with Lower Greensand on the high ground, lying mainly under the city (Figure 5). Small outcrops of Greensand lie on the top of Stuntney and along the lane to Nornea (Gallois 1980).

In the centre of the Isle of Ely, on a ridge running from Sutton in the west to Ely in the north-east, are Wentworth and Witchford. The ridge rises to about

18m OD and falls to Grunty Fen in the south and West Fen in the north. On the ridge is a capping of boulder clay, showing that it was suitable for habitation in preference to the heavier Jurassic clay, which is often waterlogged. Grunty Fen lies mainly in Wilburton parish and is a westerly-looking embayment between Sutton and Haddenham, which in the distant past was sealed off near Staple Leys Farm, closing off the Fen and allowing a Glacial lake to form in which peat built up to a depth of 3.5m during the Middle Ages. There would have been some small islands on slight rises in the West Fen, but by the late Saxon Period these would have been drowned.

On the western edge of the Isle of Ely, on a spur of high ground that has Sutton on the south-eastern edge, are Coveney, Witcham and Mepal. Mepal lies low by the fen on the north-western tip, looking towards Chaterris. Witcham is sited on high ground (21m OD) at the centre of the spur. Coveney is an island lying north of the spur, rising to 12.9m OD; the parish also includes Wardy Hill, another small island. The solid geology consists of Ampthill and Kimmeridge Clay, the division running in a line from the south of Mepal village to the middle of Coveney, with the Kimmeridge Clay lying to the south. A small amount of boulder clay lies under part of Witcham and a small area of Terrace Gravel runs from the south of Wardy Hill.

At a height of c.15m OD on the western edge of the Isle of Ely is Sutton, sited on a spur of Kimmeridge Clay and capped by boulder clay, which runs parallel to Haddenham. At the highest point, and also low in the south, are two small patches of Glacial sand and gravel. Haddenham in the south-west lies on a ridge which rises to 36m OD, the highest land on the Isle. The ridge is split into two spurs with the village of Haddenham at the junction, and the hamlet of Aldreth on the southern peninsula, where the spurs fall sharply to the fen. At the far west is slightly higher fen ground called the Upper Delphs, Adventurer's Fen lies nearer the village, and to the north-west is Foulmire. The West Water lies to the south, which marks the traditional boundary between the Isle of Ely and the rest of Cambridgeshire. Historically Haddenham was linked to the mainland by two routes; from Earith in the west, a winding road followed the top of a roddon, and from Willingham in the south there was a straight embanked road, the Aldreth Causeway, now a lane. Several excavations of prehistoric and Roman sites have been made, following the Fenland Survey, by the University of Cambridge and English Heritage (Evans 1984, Evans and Hodder 1987, Evans and Serjeantson 1988, Evans and Hodder 2006a, 2006b). The high ground comprises Ampthill and Kimmeridge Clays with a capping of Lower Greensand, and it is this permeable sand that has attracted the village to a hilltop site.

Wilburton, Stretham and Little Thetford parishes lie at the south-east of the Isle of Ely and form a ridge at Wilburton falling towards Stretham, with the

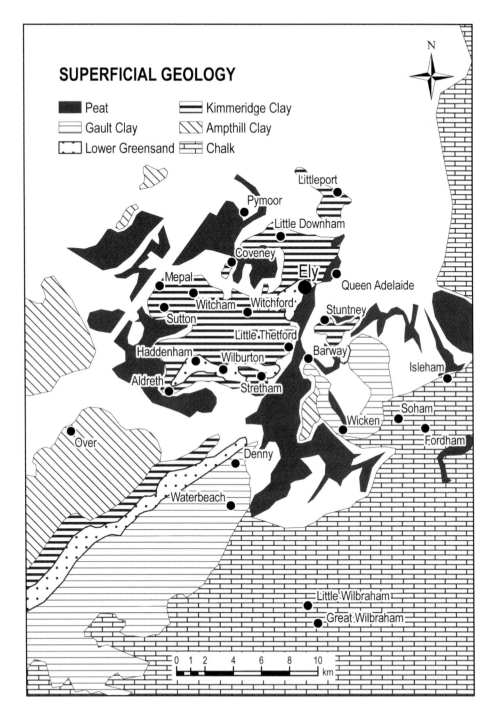

Fig 5. Superficial geology of the Isle of Ely showing the physical landscape of clays, sands and gravels. Map data © OpenStreetMap contributors, CC BY-SA.

West River as the southern boundary. To the north and west the ground falls from the ridge to Grunty Fen basin, most of which is in Wilburton parish. On the ridge is a narrow belt of Greensand where most of the known archaeology lies. Grunty Fen, also mentioned in discussion of Witchford, is a westward embayment of the fen between Haddenham and Sutton and has been blocked by a low ridge of Glacial deposit at Haddenham.

Further into the main fen, being on a peninsula that runs north-west from Fordham, are Soham and Wicken. This peninsula splits into two, each in the shape of an arc, with the low embayment of Soham Mere in between. The northern arm on which Soham is sited has three peninsulas on it, Soham Coates, Barcham, and Broad Hill. On the western arm is Wicken. The peninsula continues and splits to form a hammer-head, with Padney at the north and Upware at the south. At the mouth of the Soham Mere basin sit the two islands of Henney and Fordey. All the ground lies fairly flat reaching a maximum of only 12m OD (Figure 6). The bedrock of Soham is Gault Clay with Lower Greensand at the north-west. Coral occurs at the southern part of the Wicken peninsula where fossils are found from time to time. On the east is the edge of the sandy drift that lies beneath Isleham. Sandy soils also occur near Eye Hill and at Fordey, both at the north-west. Padney contains a little sand but is mostly Boulder Clay.

At c.18m OD lies Isleham on the south-eastern fen-edge, near the foot of the chalk ridge that runs along the south of the county. It is the furthest south-east of the parishes that we will consider, and is famous for the hoard of Late Bronze Age metalwork discovered in 1959, the largest single find made in the British Isles, comprising some 6,500 items and weighing 95kg (Britton 1960). At the foot of the chalk ridge on the River Snail is Fordham, with Fordham Moor to the north.

On the southern fen-edge is Waterbeach, which is separated by a broad low valley between the Isle of Ely and this part of the upland (c.6m OD). The valley is really a 'pass' because there is a watershed at Chittering, near where the A10 road crosses. North of the West River the ground of the Isle of Ely rises sharply, but on the south it is much gentler. To the north just rising out of the fen are the small 'islands' (really promontories) of Denny and Chittering.

Littleport consists of an island of about 400ha rising to 20m OD, the remainder being fen except for two small islands, Apes Hall and Butchers Hill, and an elongated extension of the main island called the Plains. The island is capped with Glacial sand and gravel. Apes Hall and Butchers Hill are Boulder Clay with small outcrops of terrace sand and gravel. Peacock's Farm in the south-east, and not far from Shippea Hill in Ely, was the site of important excavations in 1933–34 and 1962 by Clark and Godwin (Clark and Godwin 1962). These excavations provided the first dating evidence for the

Fig 6. View of a typical fen landscape around the Isle. In the foreground is one of the many artificial drainage ditches. Source: the authors.

Fenland Flandrian deposits. Clark and Godwin had previously investigated a Bronze Age site at nearby Plantation Farm (Clark *et al.* 1933) and Fowler undertook a small excavation on one of the Littleport Roman sites (site 36, Fowler 1949) whilst Smith *et al.* (1989) investigated Peacock's Farm and Letter F Farm (site 30). These important sites are discussed in further detail in the following chapters.

ISLANDNESS

Central to our approach is the notion of islandness and the ways that an island identity is constructed and maintained through time. The focus of this book is to question how the integrity of an island study area is maintained when its inhabitants are bound into a network of social and economic relationships. Recent studies have demonstrated that to a large extent isolation is a cultural phenomenon related to the construction of identity as much as to physical insularity.

In the 1970s, after Vayda and Rappaport's (1963) essay on island cultures and the work of John Evans (1973) on Malta, people considered islands as 'laboratories of culture change'; the nearest the archaeologist can get to putting a human community into an isolated setting to see what they do over several thousand years. Behind this lay an assumption that islands were both insular and isolated, defined by nice sharp edges, so that it is clear to the researcher where the boundaries are. Since Evans, a range of ideas and analytical techniques have coalesced around islands, island biogeography and island anthropology being the source of many ideas and approaches. Yet it is becoming clearer that cultural isolation is a phenomenon that rarely occurred on islands and thinking of them as laboratories can be misleading and inaccurate.

What is an island? Most people would probably identify insularity, a watery surround, as the defining feature. Australia would be excluded from consideration on the grounds that the landmass needs to be smaller than that of a Continent, whilst Malta would fit the definition. For Evans and others it was the geographical circumspection of islands, leading to a degree of physical isolation, which underpinned the notion of islands as laboratories. Island societies in general may give the illusion that they are easier to analyse because they exist within a sea-bounded landscape as opposed to a continental one, but this in no way assures them of isolation status. With few exceptions, island societies were never truly isolated. Thus even the most apparently straightforward categories of insularity are in fact fuzzy.

More recently cultural (psychological, socio-political and economic) factors have been shown to be important in determining isolation (Broodbank 1999, p.238) with Rainbird (1999, p.217) arguing that islands are social constructs insofar as they reflect feelings of isolation, separateness, distinctiveness and otherness. Nowhere is this truer than in the case of the 'dry' island, islands that although once surrounded by water have long since lost their physical isolation due to changes in sea level and drainage patterns (Barrowclough 2010, pp.27–46). Islandness is therefore open to cultural negotiation and thus variation in space and time, and it is this notion which forms the basis of this study of the Isle of Ely.

Dry islands are legion, although not always recognised as such (Figure 7). For example the Isle of Flegg on the east coast of Norfolk was a Viking stronghold in the late first millennium (Chester-Kadwell 2009, p.51, Fig.5.5) yet today many local inhabitants are unaware of its island status. Similarly Blackpool on the Fylde Coast of Lancashire was circumscribed by the Irish Sea during the Neolithic (Barrowclough 2008, pp.19–20, Fig.5), yet today little remains to remind the visitor of this fact. In contrast amongst the inhabitants of the Isle of Ely in Cambridgeshire, whose geographic isolation was ended when the peat fens were drained in the post-Medieval Period, an island mentality is still maintained. It is a place that has a remarkably strong sense of identity. Largely based upon Saxon and medieval associations, Ely identity hinges variously upon a series of near-legendary characters and the island's resistance to mainland authority (c.f. Darby 1940, pp.144–46). Focusing upon the exploits

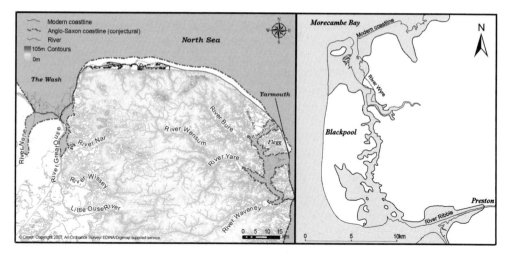

Fig 7. Examples of dry islands. Left: The Isle of Flegg in Norfolk. Right: the lost Fylde Island in Lancashire, were both once surrounded by a combination of sea and peat bog, a fact largely forgotten by the local populations. Courtesy Chester-Kadwell 2009, fig 5.5, and Barrowclough 2008, fig 5. Map data © OpenStreetMap contributors, CC BY-SA.

of Hereward the Wake (Keynes 2003, pp.29, 42–4), this ethos permeates, for example, Kingsley's *Hereward the Wake* (1866), MacFarlane's earlier *The Camp of Refuge* (1844), and most recently James Wilde's *Hereward* (2011).

There are therefore problems with Evans' approach. In the light of the intellectual shift in archaeology associated with post-processualism we need to rethink island archaeology, notably in approaches to landscape and material culture. Once we discard the assumption that islands are defined purely by physical insular isolation it becomes clear that we can no longer consider a single island as the ideal spatial unit of analysis; the history of islands is bound up with the mainland (Renfrew 2004, p.277). In order to understand Ely, we need also to look to the Cambridgeshire Fens and the rest of East Anglia and thence to the world beyond. Thus the once defined boundary of the Isle of Ely now seems to disappear off into the horizon. It is the interplay of isolation and interrelatedness that should be the focus of archaeological investigation in the future.

The problem we need to address is that of the polarity in island archaeology between isolation, 'islands as cultural laboratories', and interaction. For an islander the interactions with other members of the island community also have a quality of 'us' and 'them'. As Renfrew (Renfrew and Cherry 1986) pointed out, the island itself may be divided into polities, communities or even ethnicities, but they are more likely to hold affinities in common with their fellow islanders than with those in the world beyond. Island people need to be studied in relation to the network of social and economic relationships that bind them to each other and also to the outside world, moving between the local scale and the national and international (Sahlins 1987; Kirch 1986). As in the case of Malta, the relative isolation of Ely was a key factor in its development. In both cases isolation was a cognitive phenomenon where the reinforcing actions of the 'religious' polities of the island were of dominating significance, to the exclusion of extraneous social models.

Building on the work of archaeologists active in the county, and in particular those of the Cambridge Archaeological Unit, Oxford Archaeology East (formerly the Cambridgeshire County Council Archaeological Field Unit) and the Fenland Survey, it has been possible to begin to develop a narrative that stands for the past, that begins to answer the question which first brought us to the study of archaeology here: 'What was life like on the Isle of Ely in the past?'

LANDSCAPE

Before considering the archaeological evidence for the Isle of Ely we need first say something about the physical environment of the island. To do so is more than to set the scene, as the physical environment shapes and has been shaped by human activity in a complex series of interactions through the millennia. The changing environment is one important connecting thread between the people that inhabit it in different periods. Particularly in non-industrial, non-literate societies, inhabiting a landscape requires an engagement with the properties of that environment, and the constraints and opportunities that it presents. Those properties transcend the boundaries of world-view, language and culture that may separate the inhabitants of that landscape of one period from those that inhabited the same place in another. The physical environment is therefore an enduring, but not unchanging, frame of reference and holds considerable promise as a platform of shared understanding across time (Barrowclough 2005, pp.39–54; 2007).

During the last three decades there has been a growing recognition that the way that the landscape is perceived by past societies may be highly culture specific. Different ways of thinking about the landscape result in very different ways of organising it physically. This realisation led to a shift away from the generalising models of spatial organisation that had been sought in the 1970s. The new challenge has been how to retrieve these idiosyncratic cognitive elements from the material record. Christopher Tilley, Richard Bradley and Colin Renfrew have all suggested alternative approaches to the problem. One of us (David Barrowclough) has previously adopted a contextual approach to landscape studies that is multi-scalar and draws upon elements of these different approaches in order to construct an interpretation that, whilst grounded in empirical research, remains flexible enough to account for individual perception (Barrowclough 2007).

Many of the issues and questions that may be raised about life in prehistoric times are, to a large extent, tied to the relationship between the island's prehistoric inhabitants and this environment. A useful point to begin addressing these questions is to consider the key characteristics of the physical environment, and the processes that have changed it over time. A sound grasp of these processes is useful for two reasons. First, the physical environment defined the constraints and opportunities which faced its prehistoric inhabitants. An understanding of the processes that altered the environment over time, and the time-scales over which they took place, will make it clearer which elements of the environment may have been different from the conditions observable today, and which elements have remained largely unchanged. A second reason is that the dynamics of the physical environment, through human as well as natural agencies, may also determine which parts of the prehistoric material record are destroyed or preserved, as well as the circumstances in which they are discovered. This may in turn determine when patterns in the known evidence may be representative of the original distribution, and when they may be misleading artefacts of selective preservation or discovery.

LANDSCAPE CHANGE AND SITE PRESERVATION

Before we can begin to reconstruct something of life in the past using archaeological remains it is important to try to establish the extent to which the known finds may be considered representative of the total number of sites and objects that existed originally. The artefacts, sites and monuments known at present are the ones that have filtered through the processes of deposition, preservation and retrieval (Clarke 1973).

Deposition

Stone and copper-alloy tools are durable and both types have been preserved in large numbers, in part because of their intentional deposition which ensured they were protected for posterity. Monumental earthworks, such as long and round barrows, are by their very nature durable structures. The choice of raw material, location and size ensured their presence in the landscape was permanent. Cultural biographies of these monuments reveals that they were often multi-phased, with re-use in the Early Medieval Period not uncommon. The effect of such re-use is that throughout the period of their use, they tended to grow in extent and mass, and consequently to become more conspicuous. Domestic sites, with the exception of Iron Age defended enclosures, 'hillforts', present a sharp contrast. The evidence that excavation has revealed suggests ephemeral structures of light timber construction, which leave little impact on the landscape for example, thirty-five roundhouses excavated at West Fen Road (Mudd and Webster 2011).

Preservation, destruction and retrieval

A variety of different processes, both natural and anthropogenic, have the potential to destroy, change or hide sites and monuments (see Kristiansen 1985). Natural processes actively at work on the island include sedimentation and to a lesser extent erosion. Anthropogenic causes that have had a significant impact are urbanisation and mechanised agriculture. These will be considered in turn.

Sedimentation

Periods of glaciations and higher sea level led to the deposition of thick sediments, which mask the archaeological record (see Chapter 2). While sedimentation has the potential to preserve archaeological material, it also makes recovery by standard excavation techniques impossible. The formation of peat similarly preserves copper-alloy metalwork and also some organic remains, but again identification of remains is difficult. Peat is also strongly acidic and as a consequence whilst wooden artefacts and human skin preserve well, human bone does not. For example at Stuntney, a 'barrel' containing later Bronze Age metalwork was found (see Chapter 5) and a number (at least twenty-one) of 'bog bodies', Figure 8 (Briggs and Turner 1986, pp.181–82). The most interesting of these is that of a man found in a log canoe at Burwell sometime before 1970, the account of which is at the beginning of this chapter (Wentworth Day 1970).

Location	Date	Details
Burwell Fen	Before 1854	With jet necklace
	1884	Two male calvaria, jaw fragment and humerus
	1890	Lower jaw
	1898	Female skull with mandible
	1901	Six skull fragments
	Before 1911	Three mandibles
	Before 1971	Male stood upright inside a log canoe

Isleham Fen	1952	Two individuals
Isle of Ely	1874	Male skull
Reach Fen	1891	Lower jaw
	1901	Radius
Shippea Hill	1911	Crouched burial
Barway Fen	1918	Skull and lower jaw
Soham Fen	Before 1923	Skeleton with jet beads and socketed chisel
Upware	Before 1911	Male skull with mandible
Cambridgeshire	Before 1911	Male skull
	Before 1923	Unknown

Fig 8. Recorded finds of human remains of at least twenty-one individuals from the Fens of Cambridgeshire. Source: Briggs and Turner's *Gazetteer of Bog Burials* (1986, pp.181–182).

Erosion

Complementary to processes of sedimentation is that of erosion. The drainage of the Fens combined with intensive arable agriculture has led to the erosion of peat which dries out and then is carried away in the wind. This process is destructive of much archaeology and in many parts of the Fens the current ground surface has eroded to the former Bronze Age surface, with those above being lost.

Urbanisation

During the later twentieth century the Isle of Ely experienced a sustained period of urbanisation with the development of the City of Ely and the surrounding villages such as Haddenham, Sutton and Little Thetford all experiencing growth. The rapid building boom that took place around Ely in the last thirty years has revealed many new archaeological sites, such as the Iron Age to Anglo-Saxon site on West Fen Road, and the medieval site found below what is now Jubilee Gardens on Broad Street, both in Ely.

Agriculture

Retrieval is the third important filter between past activity and the known material record (Renfrew 1979, p.152; Fraser 1983, pp.235–61). The Fens have been the bread basket of England since Roman times when they were an Imperial Estate (Wilkes and Elrington 1978), but this increased significantly in the Post-war period. Increased mechanisation and intensification of agriculture mean that much of the island is now given over to arable agriculture. The effect of this is two-fold: first, archaeological remains are brought to the surface, especially by the increase in deep ploughing, with the potential for destruction or damage by the plough, or by the action of weathering processes that occur when remains lie on the surface. On the other hand, because the land is being ploughed, stray finds and crop marks, which often lead to the discovery of sites, are plentiful. Stone and metal objects have been regularly found for centuries by farmers and their labourers. The bias in favour of finding sites and artefacts on arable fields is further compounded by modern metal-detecting practices, which favour ploughed soil over pasture, reinforcing the bias found in existing records of archaeological distributions.

Site destruction and preservation: conclusions

It is certain that some monuments and artefacts have been destroyed and lost, but the total sample size is sufficiently large to enable us to use it to make some sort of interpretation of past human activity. It is clear that there exists a bias in the places where sites and artefacts have been found, with arable land and urban areas over-represented, whilst pasture and woodland tend to be under-represented. This bias should be remembered and taken into account when interpreting the distribution maps and analysis in the following chapters.

THEORIES OF TIME

Time is an essential element of our study. As a discipline, archaeology is uniquely positioned to deal with the interpretation of social reproduction through time. It is this temporality that separates it from other disciplines in the arts and social sciences such as history, social anthropology or sociology. Archaeology is suited to long-term studies of social organisation because it is an historical discipline with a well-developed methodology for excavating and recording diachronic data. Questions of temporality are avoided in other disciplines, such as anthropology and sociology, because they lack the methodology and data to address them, not because the issues are unimportant or inconsequential. It is in this area of social research that archaeology can make a unique contribution to our understanding of social processes, adding a time depth that other disciplines find difficult to match.

The traditional archaeological conception of time is that of a linear progression. Following the Greek philosopher Zeno (in Aristotle) it was argued that time passed in a linear way, rather like an arrow in flight, with time a succession of instants or moments. These instants are represented in the succession of layers that archaeologists excavate from the ground. This linear progression is expressed through chronology, the science of computing dates. Relative chronologies, such as the Three Age System of Stone, Bronze and Iron Ages, are based on relative order, and are the oldest in archaeology. They provide sequences of deposits and artefacts through the principles of stratigraphy (Harris 1989), seriation (Marquardt 1978) and typology (Gräslund 1987). Absolute chronologies are based on a time framework that is independent of the data being studied, for example radiocarbon analysis.

Although largely taken for granted, chronologies are theoretically problematic because they present time as a uniform linear phenomenon, which has tended to define the model for historical explanation in a similar uniform, linear way. In anthropology Durkheim noted that the way we conceptualise time is culturally specific, that the concept of time is embedded in social life (Durkheim 1915, pp.9–11). One of the most influential ethnographic accounts of time that illustrated Durkheim's views was Evans-Pritchard's (1939; 1940) study of the Nuer of East Africa. He showed how the Nuer time-reckoning was linked to cycles, such as the daily husbandry of cattle or seasonal cycles, and also to generational cycles and the descent system. The notion that time can be marked by events in the human life cycle, or by the natural phenomena of lunar or solar movements, which was revolutionary at the time, no longer seems controversial. There have been numerous archaeological studies, which have found that these ideas of temporality offer persuasive interpretations of archaeological data.

The challenge for archaeology is to find ways that combine the two approaches of long-term linear time and short-term cyclical time so as to be able to fulfil its role as the discipline that studies and explains social change over the long term.

THE *ANNALES* SCHOOL

The *Annales* school was critical of traditional history as a sequence of events. It was founded in 1929 by Febvre and Bloch, but for archaeology its most famous exponent was Fernand Braudel (1972; 1980). For them the core of the problem revolved around the duality of history as both continuity and change (Bloch 1954). A central aspect of *Annaliste* thought is structural history as elaborated by Braudel. He represented time in a linear way but proposed three different parallel timescales: the long, medium and short term (Figure 9).

Time Scale	Description
Evenements History of events	Short term – *evenements* Narrative, political history; events; individuals
Moyenne durée Structural history	Medium term – *conjunctures* Social, economic history; economic, agrarian, demographic cycles; history of eras, regions, societies; worldviews, ideologies (*mentalités*)
Longue durée Structural history	Long term – structures of the *longue durée* Geohistory: 'enabling and constraining'; history of civilizations, peoples; stable technologies, worldviews (*mentalités*)

Fig 9. Braudel's model of historical time: short-, medium- and long-term history.
Source: the authors.

By using more than one scale of time he was able to create a temporality that has the ability to combine long-term change and also short-term cyclical events. The long term, *longue durée*, covered very slow-moving processes such as the environment over several hundred or thousands of years; the medium term, *moyenne durée*, referred to social or structural history, such as persistent forms of social or economic organisation over periods of up to several centuries; and finally the short term, *evenements*, referred to events or individuals, usually the main focus of most traditional history. For Braudel each scale affected the course of the others and all were intertwined, although many have seen his main focus being on the long term. Given archaeology's long timescale and resolution, it is attractive to adopt the *Annales* representation of time to help us understand the story of the Isle of Ely. By using different scales in archaeological analysis a much richer representation of time is created.

This book represents the *longue durée*, measured in millions of years during which the geology of the Isle was formed and species were both born and fell extinct, topics covered in detail in Chapter 2. Each of the other chapters represents an example of the *moyenne durée* considering different archaeological periods, and within each chapter discussion of individual sites represents shorter events or *evenements*.

THE LIE OF THE LAND: TURNING MOLEHILLS INTO MOUNTAINS

Any fool can appreciate mountain scenery but it takes a man of discernment to appreciate the Fens.

Anon., in Godwin 1978, p.1.

INTRODUCTION

Growing up in the West of Scotland, with rolling purple and green hills and views of the Arrochar Alps and the Trossachs mountain range dominating the distant skyline, and in Lancashire with views overlooking the panoramic Morecambe Bay towards the Lakeland Hills, one is immediately struck by how flat and bleak the Fenland landscape is in comparison. For here, vast acres of remote, unending flat land stretch to the horizon and, on dull days, seem to merge with the great expanse of sky, broken only by a few trees surrounding scattered farms.

This view, however, belies the varied nature of the Fenland landscape which is not immediately apparent. If one were to look closely, one would slowly begin to appreciate the undulating nature of the landscape around them; the fertile black soils, the rivers meandering through the flood plains, and the shallow hills which have emerged as earth processes altering the underlying geology, eroding the overlaying deposits of the last 10,000 years, and giving rise to the fen islands, some only a few metres above sea level (OD). It is this microtopography which is important to the archaeologist when studying the ancient past. The flat landscape is thus deceptive, and these slight variations in the height of the land, where one area is slightly higher than the surrounding wetland, could prove to be a likely location for settlement and associated industry (Malim 2005, p.22). Thus, 'landscape is about the diversity of the marks that mankind has made on the world' (Pryor 2010, p.18) and this chapter will attempt to put the Fenland landscape into context, to show how the underlying geology is important in creating this island landscape and how this environment affects how people live and, in turn, how people have helped to shape the landscape.

THE FENLAND LANDSCAPE

The Fenland is an expanse of low-lying land that stretches 4,000km^2 over four counties: Cambridgeshire, Lincolnshire, Norfolk and Suffolk. From Lincoln in the north to Cambridge in the south; Peterborough and Huntingdon in the west; across to Boston and King's Lynn in the east (Figure 10), it is the largest area of former coastal wetland in Britain (Hall 1996, Malim 2005, Godwin 1978). The Fens form a vast, shallow basin drained by the rivers Cam, Nene, Ouse and their tributaries, and Defoe wrote in 1724, 'all the water of the middle part of England

Fig 10. Blaeu's 1648 map of the Fens and major drainage channels, with the Isle of Ely centre. Source: Blaeu 1648.

which does not run into the Thames or Trent comes down into these Fens' (Godwin 1978, p.1). Much of this land lies below 60m OD with the lowest parts of the Fens at, or just below, sea level. Without continued drainage, they would quickly become inundated (Sheail 2000) returning once again to its natural state of marshland with shallow meres. Wicken Fen, located 8km (5 miles) south of Ely, is one of four natural wild fens that still survive in East Anglia and provide a good example of what the Fens were once like prior to drainage.

It was the Romans who were the first to lay the foundations for the present drainage pattern in the Fens when they diverted the Ouse near Stretham (Galois 1988), but it wasn't until the seventeenth century, when drainage works began in earnest under the direction of Sir Cornelius Vermuyden, that the landscape was greatly altered by a series of long, narrow drains resulting in its present appearance as an rich area of intense agriculture providing nearly half of the grade 1 agricultural land in England.

Before drainage, the Isle of Ely (its highest point is in the west at Haddenham, 36m above sea level, and the lowest point 1.5m below OD at Shippea Hill), was a true island emerging from the surrounding marshland. Like other small islands and islets in the archipelago, such as Littleport to the north, Coveney to the west and Stuntney to the east, these were higher than the prevailing marshes and remained relatively safe from flooding, thus providing safe environments in which to settle, with a close proximity to the Fens where many resources could be exploited for food and building materials (French 2000). Some of these islands have a complex history and were continuously inhabited from Mesolithic times, but why was this? In order to put the Fenland landscape into context it is to the geology of this landscape that we now turn.

GEOLOGY IN ACTION

Geological processes happen around us constantly, from heavy rains and floods to wind and frost, but it is easy to think of the rocks beneath our feet as static. For some, who are lucky not to live in the shadow of an active volcano, and who reside in the same area for a period of time, they may never notice any significant, or otherwise, changes to the landscape around them. However, that does not mean to say that change does not happen.

If you ever drive along the back roads in the Fens you will be aware of the small changes that take place in the landscape. In Norfolk, for instance, a section of the road between Southery and Methwold Hythe is constantly being repaired, as deep folds regularly appear in its surface, in some cases it seems almost overnight. These form significant ripples along the road. The same process can be observed in Cambridgeshire on the back road leading from

Littleport to Queen Adelaide and through to Ely where the road appears to ripple. It is at such places that you become aware of the movement of the land beneath the surface that we travel on, and can see that the relationship of landscape to geology is still active (Pryor 2010, p.6).

The formation of the solid geology (bedrock) of Britain happened c.1,000 million years ago up until 2.5 million years ago as the result of complex interactions with the tectonic plates that together form the outer crust of the earth. The plates are less dense than the mantle on which they sit, which allows them to 'float' above it, and when they collided the 'energy released by their impact gave rise to the volcanoes and mountain ranges that have subsequently been worn down to form the hills and plains of our modern landscape' (Pryor 2010, p.7). These older rocks from the Cambrian (545-485 million years) and Ordovician Periods (485–445 million years) are harder sedimentary and volcanic, occurring towards the north and western parts of Britain and are more resistant to natural erosion (Figure 11). The underlying rocks found towards the south and east are formed from the younger Jurassic (200–142 million years) and Cretaceous Periods (142–65 million years). These softer sedimentary chalks, clays, sands and limestones are less resistant to natural erosion and over time have worn away into the downs, plains and valleys of the south and east of Britain.

The major events that shaped the British landscape, transforming it into an island, took place during the Quaternary era which spans from 1.8 million years ago to the present day, and includes two geological epochs (the Pleistocene and Holocene), the latter of which began about 10,000 years ago (Figure 12). During the Quaternary Period, Britain was dominated by a series of Glacial and Interglacial Periods, which have become known as the Ice Age. The Ice Age was in fact a number of ages when ice would cover the land during a cold (Glacial) spell and then retreat during the warmer (Interglacial) times when temperatures could be hotter than they are at present. This pattern of freeze-thaw induced a new series of superficial geological deposits, including gravels and boulder clays or 'till', which is known as Drift Geology. Drift Geology has affected and altered the landscape just as much as the Solid Geology and in many ways, as will be seen later, could be more important to our discussions of the development of the present Fenland landscape.

Throughout the Glacial Periods, in particular the Pleistocene Period (1.8 million years – c.10,000 years ago), huge slow moving rivers of ice covered the land with the power to move rocks and slowly grind away steep valley sides. It was during this period, known as the Paleolithic in archaeological terms, that the genus Homo evolved. The closest glaciers to Britain today are found in the French Alps. It is quite awe inspiring to stand overlooking the Mer de Glace at Mont Blanc and to witness first-hand the immense power of nature

Eon	Era	Period	Epoch		Date (millions of years)
Phanerozoic	Cenozoic	Quaternary	Holocene		
			Pleistocene	Late	0.01
				Early	1.8
		Tertiary / Neogene	Pliocene	Late	
				Early	5.3
			Miocene	Late	
				Middle	
				Early	
		Tertiary / Paleogene	Oligocene	Late	23.7
				Early	33.7
			Eocene	Late	
				Middle	
				Early	54.8
			Paleocene	Late	
				Early	65
	Mesozoic	Cretaceous	Late		
			Early		144
		Jurassic	Late		
			Middle		
			Early		206
		Triassic	Late		
			Middle		
			Early		248
	Paleozoic	Permian	Late		
			Early		290
		Pennsylvanian			
		Mississippian			
		Devonian	Late		354
			Middle		
			Early		417
		Silurian	Late		
			Early		443
		Ordovician	Late		
			Middle		
			Early		490
		Cambrian	D		
			C		
			B		
			A		543
Precambrian	Proterozoic		Late		
			Middle		
			Early		2500
	Archean		Late		
			Middle		3400
			Early		

Fig 11. Chronology of the major geological eons, eras, periods and epochs together with dates. Source: the authors.

Geological Period	Archaeological Period BP (Before Present)/BC (Before Christ)		Glacial Period	Sea Level
Holocene	Modern	(1800 to present)	Flandrian interglacial (12,000 BP to present)	High
	Post-Medieval	(AD 1500 – 1800)		
	Medieval	(AD 1066 – 1500)		
	Early Medieval	(AD 410 – 1066)		
	Romano-British	(AD 43 – 410)		
	Iron Age	(700 BC – AD 43)		
	Bronze Age	(2,400 – 700 BC)		
	Neolithic	(4,000 – 2,400 BC)		
	Mesolithic	(8,500 – 4,000 BC)		
Late Pleistocene	Palaeolithic	Late Upper Palaeolithic (12,000 – 10,500 BP = 8,500 BC)		
		Early Upper Palaeolithic (30,000 – 12,000 BP)	Devensian glaciation (70,000 – 12,000 BP)	Low
		Middle Palaeolithic (150,000 – 30,000 BP)	Ipswichian interglacial (130,000 – 70,000 BP)	High
Middle Pleistocene		Lower Palaeolithic (700,000 – 150,000 BP)	Wolstonian glaciation (380,000 – 130,000 BP)	Low
			Hoxnian interglacial (425,000 – 380,000 BP)	High
			Anglian glaciation (480,000 – 425,000 BP)	Low

Fig 12. Concordance of Geological, Archaeological and Glacial Periods for the Quaternary Period and their impact on sea level. Source: the authors.

(Figure 13). With a surface area of 32km², 7km long and 200m deep the Mer de Glace is the biggest glacier in France and moves about 90m per year, which equates to about a centimetre an hour. This gives some indication of what the landscape would have looked like in parts of Britain during this time when the glaciers that covered England were several thousand feet thick (Galois 1988). Half a million years ago an ice sheet covered East Anglia in its entirety, and it would be easy to think that the Ice Age landscape was inert but, all the while, the glaciers were shaping the landscape, bulldozing rocks and soil in front of them and crushing and grinding the material beneath them.

When the temperature increased the glaciers began to melt creating melt-water rivers. In the uplands of northern Britain the fast flowing water scoured out V-shaped valleys, but as the rivers moved into the lowlands, the flow slowed depositing flood-clay sediments (alluvium). In the last significant cold phase of

Fig 13. Europe's largest glacier, the Mer de Glace at Mont Blanc, France. Source: the authors.

the British Ice Age, known as the Devensian, 110,000–10,000 years ago, the Fenland basin was part of a large lake supplied by Glacial run-off (Pryor 2010, p.10). It is important to note that during this time, Britain was still connected to mainland Europe via a land bridge. The island as we know it today did not form until about 8,000 years ago. The last 10,000 years, which forms part of the Holocene Interglacial, is known as Flandrian and provides perhaps the greatest interest to archaeologists.

With a broad outline of Britain's geology now provided, let us examine the geology of the Fens and, in particular, the Isle of Ely and how this has affected, and in turn been shaped by, the people who have lived there.

GEOLOGY OF THE ISLE

The oldest underlying solid geology of the Isle of Ely is comprised of Jurassic and Cretaceous rocks laid down in horizontal layers 150-75 million years ago when this area had a tropical and subtropical climate and seas were shallow, warm and full of life (Figure 14; Galois 1988, p.4). The oldest Jurassic layer is Ampthill Clay, the main mass of which is almost black in colour. On top of this, sediments continued to be deposited to form the bluish-grey Kimmeridge Clay. Roslyn Hole (Roswell Pits) at Ely has the most famous section of Kimmeridge Clay in East Anglia where the clay has been extracted for more than a century to provide embanking and building materials.

Parts of the Isle were capped with Lower Greensand that formed in the Cretaceous Period, so named after the presence of the mineral glauconite

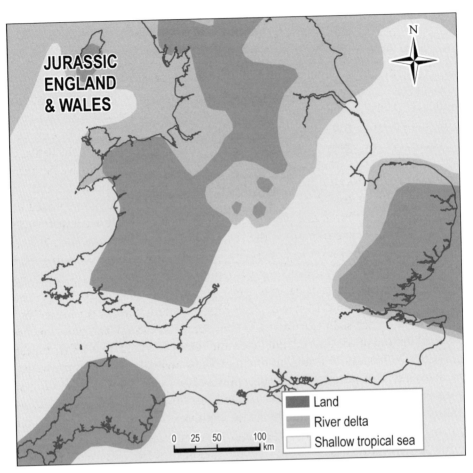

Fig 14. Map of Britain overlain by the physical geography of the Jurassic Period. During the Jurassic much of southern Britain was covered by a warm shallow sea adjacent to which were extensive river deltas with dry land confined to southern Norfolk, Suffolk and Essex, Cornwall, Wales, Northern Britain and Ireland. Map data © OpenStreetMap contributors, CC BY-SA.

which gives it a green colour. It was these sandy knolls that were favoured by prehistoric people when building settlements on the Isle. Most of this Greensand has now been 'covered by the Recent deposits of Fenland' (Galois 1988, p.45) and so in other words, the Quaternary Period has resulted in 'a thin but significant covering of drift deposits' (Sheail 2000) which concealed much of the solid geology. Interestingly, during this time, East Anglia was subject to earth movements that caused the land to warp, rise above sea level and tilt towards the east. The extensive eastward-flowing river networks that drained the area started to remove soil and create valleys, thus eroding the land back towards sea level. During the Quaternary, characterised by the series of Glacial (Anglian, Wolstonian and Devensian) and Interglacial (Hoxnian, Ipswichian and Flandrian) Periods (Figure 12 above), the dramatic climate swings resulted in the frequent slumping of valley walls. When the ice eventually began to melt about 10,000 years ago, Chalky Boulder Clay (Till) overlain with sands, gravels and Interglacial fluvial sediments were deposited when sea levels rose and the river valleys were inundated and filled with mud and peat (Malim 2001, p.23).

These Flandrian deposits make up the most important feature of the Fenland landscape, as they comprise the rich peat soils cultivated by successive farmers. Post-glacial amelioration saw the establishment of boreal forests, similar to those that can be found across parts of Canada and Russia, characterised by coniferous trees of birch and pine, later developing into deciduous forests, with the most common trees found in the Fens being lime and alder (French 2000).

As sea levels continued to rise, rivers burst flooding the surrounding area and forming marshland; the areas of higher ground remained proud of the marshes and formed true islands. Peat began to form 7–9m below OD at around 7,500 BC from evidence of Mesolithic tools found along the River Ouse (Malim 2005, p.25), so by the Neolithic, the Fenland landscape was one of partly wooded upland of willow and alder carr and lower areas of sedge fen with peat covering the lowland forests, out of which huge bog oaks are often ploughed. A carr is a type of waterlogged land, representing a stage between the original reed swamp and eventual succession of forest. The land is submerged with fresh water along a river or lake margin and when the reeds decay, the soil surface eventually rises above the water creating fens which allow sedges to grow. As this continues, riparian trees and bushes appear, such as alder, and a carr landscape is formed.

The original height of the peat was estimated to be about 3.5m above sea level during the Anglo-Saxon and Medieval Periods; whilst the present surface lies somewhere in the region of 2m below it. The Romans are credited with beginning the process of fen drainage (French 2000) which was continued on a vast scale in the seventeenth century, greatly altering the landscape and transforming it into the one that is recognisable today. The peat wastage, directly resulting from drainage, has resulted in the loss of the Iron Age, Roman and later organic levels. Generally speaking the current surface level equates to that present during the Bronze Age (Malim 2000, p.22).

FOSSIL HUNTERS

Archaeology is the study of the human past through its material culture. Often people misunderstand the role of archaeology, confusing it with the study of fossils. For the pioneers of archaeology in the nineteenth century, the line between archaeology, paleontology and geology was blurred. Only 200 years ago most educated people believed that the world had been created in 4004 BC (Ussher 1650), and all humans lived during the time described in Greek texts or in the bible. 'Everything which has come down to us from heathendom is wrapped in a thick fog; it belongs to a space of time which we cannot measure', wrote the Danish scholar Rasmus Nyerup (1759–1829). 'We know that it is older than Christendom, but whether by a couple of years or a couple of centuries, or even by more than a millennium, we can do no more than guess' (Klindt-Jensen 1975).

The nineteenth century was an era of invention and discovery, with significant advances in medicine and developments in science which would pave the way for the technological advances that would follow in the twentieth century. Many academic subjects such as archaeology, geology and palaeontology were in their infancy. Scottish geologist James Hutton (1726–1797) had studied the building up of layers of rocks (stratification) which later became 'the basis of archaeological excavation' (Renfrew and Bahn 1996, p.24). Hutton's work proved that this stratification of rocks was as a result of processes that were still taking place in lakes, rivers and seas, and this theory was argued further in the 1833 *Principles of Geology* by Charles Lyell who noted that geologically ancient conditions were essentially the same as those of our time (Figure 15). It was this concept which, when applied to the human past, 'marks one of the fundamental notions of modern archaeology: that the past was very much like the present' (Renfrew and Bahn 1996, p.24).

In 1841 Jaques Boucher de Perthes discovered in the gravel quarries of the Somme river, northern France, a number of stone implements, which archaeologists would call today 'bi-faces' or 'hand axes', along with the fossil bones of extinct animals. 'In spite of their imperfections, these rude stones prove the existence of man as surely as a whole Louvre would have done' (Stringer 2006, p.17) – thus, de Perthes argued, humans must have existed before the biblical flood. A ludicrous idea at the time: it wasn't until nearly twenty years later that this notion of the biblical creation of the world was challenged as scholars were growing to accept that human origins extended further back in time, to a pre-history, one that went before recorded history (Renfrew and Bahn 1996, p.24).

Sir John Evans (1823–1908) was one such scholar (Figure 15). One of the foremost scientific figures of his day, he was a pioneer in the field of prehistoric archaeology and geology, inspired by the 'unwritten history' revealed through the study of artefacts, archaeology and geology. He was one of the first in Britain to apply scientific rigour to the study of the human past and in 1859, along with geologist Joseph Prestwich, visited Boucher de Perthes and agreed with his initial findings. By studying the stratigraphic relationship between the

Fig 15. Portraits of nineteenth-century pioneers. Top left: Sir Charles Lyell. Top right: Boucher de Perthes. Bottom left: Sir John Evans. Bottom right: Joseph Prestwich. Sources: various.

stone tools and fossil bones, their scientific evidence established for the first time an extended antiquity for humans into geological time. 'Think of their finding flint axes and arrow heads ... in conjunction with bones of Elephants and Rhinoceroses 40ft below the surface in a bed of drift,' he wrote. 'It will make my Ancient Britons quite modern, if man is carried back in England

Fig 16. Roslyn Hole (Roswell Pits), Ely. The site was mined for its clay before being turned into a recreational area complete with freshwater lake. Although overgrown the photograph shows a surviving section through the Kimmeridge Clay, seen as a cliff face, within which fossils are deposited. Photo: the authors.

to the days when Elephants, Rhinoceroses, Hippopotamuses and Tigers were also inhabitants of the country...' (Stringer 2006, p.17). The early disciplines of archaeology, geology and palaeontology were therefore very much intertwined and it wasn't until much later that they became distinct fields of academia. To this end, this interrelationship of disciplines fits our narrative well, connecting the archaeology to the geology of the Isle and therefore also to the fossils found within it.

Roslyn Hole, also known as Roswell Pits, Ely, has the most famous layer of Kimmeridge Clay in East Anglia (Figure 16). Since 2008 it has been designated as a Site of Special Scientific Interest (SSSI) as the area represents the best fossil reptile locality in the northern outcrop of the Kimmeridge Clay. Fossils are abundant in these clay layers and provide palaeontologists with many clues as to what the Isle was like millions of years ago. Throughout the Mesozoic era, which encompasses the Triassic, Jurassic and Cretaceous Periods spanning 185 million years, the sea levels varied in height, flooding the Isle with deep water or retreating to form shallow seas. At the beginning of the Jurassic Period (200 million years) rising sea levels flooded much of southern Britain depositing a thick layer of mud which today forms clays and limestones of the Lower Lias (a sequence of rock strata). During this time, Cambridgeshire would have been under deep water and seas would have been full of life. Later, as the sea levels retreated, parts of East Anglia were covered with lush tropical forests cut by slow-moving rivers containing a diverse plant life with ferns, horsetails, cycads, conifers and ginkgos. On land, dinosaurs were the dominant group of vertebrates with flying reptiles (pterosaurs), small mammals, and the first birds and amphibians, while fish swam in the seas. When the Kimmeridge Clay was deposited between about 155–150 million years ago it marked the return to a deep water environment. Fossils found in this layer include: ammonites, bivalves, belemnites, crinoids, crustaceans, fish, foraminifera, gastropods, ostracods, serpulids and marine reptiles such as ichthyosaurs and plesiosaurs (Chatwin 1961) to name but a few.

Of the smaller marine creatures, ammonites, bivalves and belemnites are common fossil finds in these layers, and some may be seen in Ely Museum with a more extensive collection in the Sedgwick Museum of Earth Sciences, Cambridge. The name 'ammonite', derives from the spiral shape of their fossilised shells, thought to resemble ram's horns (Figure 17). Pliny the Elder (AD 23–AD 79) called such fossils *ammonis cornua,* 'horns of Ammon', after the Greek spelling of the Egyptian god Ammon who was typically depicted wearing ram's horns. These creatures, ranging in size from several centimetres to 2m in diameter, were molluscs and more closely linked to modern coleoids such as cuttlefish, squid and octopuses, than to the living nautilus that they visually resemble. From careful study of the fossils, it is known that the soft body of the creature filled the largest segments of the shell at the end of the coil, while the earlier, smaller, segments were walled off. It is believed that the animal could maintain its buoyancy by filling these segments with gas, thus the smaller sections of the coil would have floated above the larger sections. In medieval England, these fossils were called 'serpentstones' and thought to be petrified coiled snakes, believed to have healing or oracular powers.

Like the ammonites, belemnites belong to the same extinct group of marine cephalopod and were closely related to modern cuttlefish and squid (Figures 18 and 19). Like cuttlefish they contained an ink sac, but unlike squid they did not have tentacles, but ten arms of equal length. Belemnite fossils are usually made of the bullet-shaped shell which could reach up to half a metre long.

Fig 17. Fossilised ammonite found at Ely. Source: Trustees of Ely Museum.

Fig 18. A fossilised belemnite from Ely. Source: Trustees of Ely Museum.

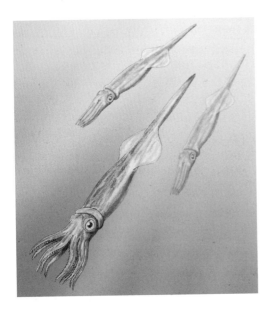

Fig 19. Reconstruction of a belemnite.

Fig 20. Fossilised Gryphaea, commonly called devil's toenails because of their distinctive shape. Source: Trustees of Ely Museum.

If you found the soft parts preserved it would make the creature 3m long. Myth surrounds these creatures and throughout Europe they were associated with thunder storms and known as thunderbolts, thunderstones or thunder arrows. It was a common belief that they possessed healing qualities and could cure rheumatism and sore eyes in both men and horses, the treatment of which involved grinding them into a powder and blowing that into the affected eye. While bivalves, such as the oyster Gryphaea, were known as devil's toenails, perhaps as a result of the thick, curved shape of the left valve, with prominent growth bands that resembled thick toenails (Figure 20). In the seventeenth and eighteenth centuries they were used to cure pain in the joints.

Of the marine reptiles, ichthyosaurs, the name derived from the Greek for 'fish lizard', were common fossil finds and resembled modern dolphins with a porpoise-like head and a snout like a crocodile, full of sharp teeth (colour plate 1). Represented by four families and a variety of species, the early ichthyosaurs of the Triassic Period looked more like lizards than fish with long flexible bodies and four paddle-like flippers, propelling themselves like eels (Figure 21). It was only later that they developed the more tuna-like shape with crescent tail. Built for speed, these creatures averaged a length of 4m, although some were as small as 70cm, while others could reach 15m in length. Ichthyosaurs were air-breathers and with their large eyes, were visual predators who lived in the lighter waters. Their diet, known from examining fossilised stomach contents, show, similar to whales today, one that was rich in squid, mostly (now extinct) belemnites. An ichthyosaur skeleton was also found by amateur fossil hunters in 2001 between Mepal and Sutton, 12km (8 miles) from Ely, on the western edge of the Isle on what was once the shore where the Fens met the higher ground (Figure 22).

Figure 21. Reconstruction of an ichthyosaur. Source: Dmitry Bogdanov.

Figure 22. Fossilised vertebra of an ichthyosaur. Source: Trustees of Ely Museum.

Fig 23. Pliosaur skeleton and reconstructions.

Fig 25. A fossilised plesiosaur head showing the jaw with short, sharp, pointed teeth. Source: the authors.

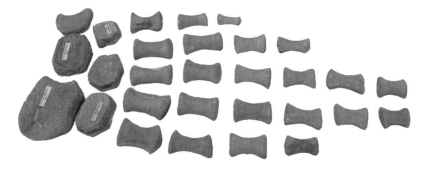

Fig 26. The fossilised paddle of a plesiosaur. Source: the authors.

The ichthyosaur contemporaries, Sauropterygia, meaning 'finned reptiles', are generally called plesiosaurs. Interestingly, it was the seventeenth-century antiquarian, William Stukeley (1687–1765), pioneer of archaeological invest-igation, who described the first plesiosaur skeleton in 1719. Stukeley, not aware that his partial fossil skeleton was an unknown animal, considered it might be part of a crocodile or porpoise. It was not until a century later that plesiosaurs were recognised as a distinct group of reptiles (Chatwin 1961). They comprised the short-necked pliosaurs (Figure 23) and larger long-necked plesiosaurs (Figure 24), and were among the largest marine predators of all time, reaching up to 20m long. The long-necked variety is best known for its mythical incarnation as the Loch Ness Monster. Their short, sharp, pointed teeth (Figure 25) were well suited to eating squid-like animals and they may even have preyed on smaller plesiosaurs and ichthyosaurs. Fossil evidence shows that, both the plesiosaurs and ichthyosaurs were viviparous, which means that like dolphins and whales today, they bore live young, rather than laying eggs. A small collection of fossils from Roslyn Pits can be seen at both Ely Museum and the Sedgwick Museum of Earth Sciences, Cambridge (Figure 26).

CONCLUSIONS: LIVING OFF THE LAND

The earliest inhabitants of Britain have been dated, through the discovery in the year 2000 of butchered bones and stone tools, to 800,000 years ago on the Norfolk coast at Happisburgh, providing the earliest evidence for human occupation in Northern Europe (Stringer 2006). As will be described in more detail in Chapter 3, evidence shows that during the warm Interglacial Periods, when Britain enjoyed slightly warmer weather than today, *Homo erectus* was also living on the Isle of Ely, hunting elephants, hippos and rhinoceros on the land, and in the rivers catching fish such as carp, pike and sturgeon.

As temperatures plummeted, the animals migrated across the land bridge to warmer climes followed by the hunter-gatherers in search of their food sources. Britain became uninhabitable: huge ice caps covered the north of the country and it was not until the end of the Devensian, about 10,000 years ago, that humans began to occupy Britain once again. At the end of the last Ice Age, about 8,000 BC, the land was vast open tundra, similar to that of Siberia, devoid of trees but not of life. Finds of bones reveal that reindeer and ox grazed on the meager covering of vegetation which included mosses, lichens, shrubs and sedges; wolves, arctic fox and stoat hunted lemmings and arctic hares (Pryor 2010, p24–25) while early humans were hunting mammoths.

Temperatures began to rise and certain animals such as the woolly mammoth and rhino became extinct while others, such as reindeer, left Britain and woodland species (aurochs, red deer and bison) appeared for the first time. Much of northern Britain and Scandinavia were still covered by ice and, as a result, sea levels were lower, but when the ice melted, sea levels rose by as much as 120m – a change noticeable within a human lifetime – and Britain became an island. The Mesolithic people would see huge upheaval in the landscape. Settlements, abandoned due to the loss of some of the richest hunting ground, were relocated on higher ground with the islands forming the Ely archipelago providing the perfect place to settle, where 'a varied and resourceful landscape was available all year' (French 2000; Holton-Krayenbuhl 2000, p.80). Archaeological evidence has confirmed that some of these islands have been continuously inhabited since Mesolithic times.

Today, despite drainage, the settlement pattern reflects that of the early inhabitants to Ely with most residing on the higher land and only a few scattered settlements surrounding farms in what were once the marshes, now given over to agriculture, providing the whole of the country with a plentiful supply of vegetables and cereals. Therefore, what can be seen is that the landscape, which is constantly being shaped through earth processes, has been further altered by the humans who have occupied the islands, adapting the landscape for their own benefit.

The covering of ice has removed many traces of the people inhabiting the area during the early Palaeolithic (Interglacial Periods). However, the Flandrian deposits have covered, and thus preserved, a large number of archaeological sites (Waller 1994) dating to the Mesolithic. For this reason our examination of the archipelago's hidden history begins c.500,000 years ago with the earliest known archaeological evidence found in the Isle.

CHAPTER 3

THE STONE AGE

LIVING OFF THE LAND: THE LATE UPPER PALAEOLITHIC, MESOLITHIC AND NEOLITHIC OCCUPATION

As these Fenns appear cover'd with Water, so I observ'd, too, that they generally at this latter part of the Year appear also cover'd with Foggs, so that when the Downs and higher Grounds of the adjacent Country were gilded with the Beams of the Sun, the Isle of Ely look'd as if wrapp'd up in Blankets.

Daniel Defoe, 1727.

Introduction

The term Stone Age is derived from a concept first described by Danish scholar C. J. Thomsen in 1848. Thomsen's Three Age System proposed that all collections could be divided into three: a Stone Age, a Bronze Age and an Iron Age. This classification was soon utilised by scholars throughout Europe and the Stone Age was later separated into three sections: the Old, Middle and New; or Palaeolithic, Mesolithic and Neolithic. The Palaeolithic was then further divided into Lower, Middle and Upper, whilst the Mesolithic and Neolithic were subdivided into early and late.

The earliest evidence for human occupation on the Isle of Ely dates to *c.*500,000 years ago from stone tools of the Lower Paleolithic. The evidence is sparse as the population would have been small and many of their shelters ephemeral. As a consequence it is impossible to reconstruct any meaningful pattern of occupation. What is clear is that they were concentrated on gravel beds, which marked an ancient coastline when the sea cut across from the Wash through to Oxford in the Jurassic and Quaternary as discussed in Chapter 2 (Figure 14).

The Ancient Human Occupation of Britain (AHOB) Project (Stringer 2006), through archaeological excavations, discovered that the first known inhabitants of Britain lived over 800,000 years ago in Happisburgh, Norfolk. That marks the earliest evidence for human occupation in northern Europe

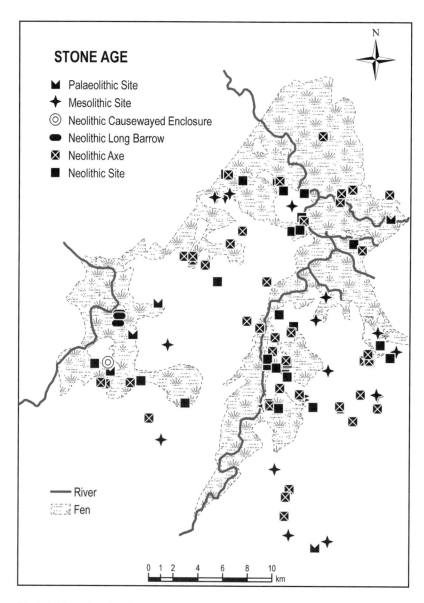

Fig 27. Map of major Stone Age sites mentioned in the text. Map data ©
OpenStreetMap contributors, CC BY-SA.

before the Anglian glaciation when the climate was similar to that of today.
The Happisburgh site is now on the coast, but at that time, Britain was
still connected to mainland Europe via Doggerland, which was a landmass
stretching from the east coast of Britain to the Netherlands and the west coast
of Denmark and Germany. This area, now lying under the English Channel,

has long been believed to have been inhabited since the discovery of a barbed antler point in 1931, dredged up by the fishing trawler *Colinda* 40km east of the Wash, Norfolk (Pryor 2010, p.26). Later finds of other prehistoric tools and animal remains, including mammoth and lion bones recovered in a similar way, confirmed the hypothesis.

The work undertaken by the AHOB project has shed new light on the Palaeolithic people who occupied Britain in the warmer stages of the last Ice Age, but as a result of subsequent glaciation and then erosion by ice and water evidence of their presence on the Isle of Ely is minimal. After the retreat of the ice, around 10,000 years ago, when the climate warmed, people began to live on the Isle once again. It is important to look at the lithic remains from the Isle in context with the wider area and when doing this to remember that Britain, as part of Europe, would exhibit the same cultural traits and affinities.

This chapter spans the *longue durée* c.494,000 years, from c.500,000 to 6,000 years ago (Figure 27). Archaeologists sub-divide this vast span into Palaeolithic, Mesolithic and Neolithic eras, each of which forms a *moyenne durée* (see previous chapter Figure 12).

The Palaeolithic

The Palaeolithic – literally meaning 'old stone' age (from the Greek words *palaios*, 'old' and *lithos*, 'stone') – is a term coined by archaeologist John Lubbock in 1865. The Lower Palaeolithic is the earliest part of the Old Stone Age and spans from when the first evidence of stone tools use by ancient humans (*Homo habilis* or 'handy man') appears in the archaeological record, roughly 2.5 million years ago until about 300,000 years ago with the emergence of *Homo sapiens* ('wise man') in Africa. It was during this time that stone tools first appeared on the African Continent in the form of flakes and pebbles. These tools were classified as the Oldowan Industry after Olduvai Gorge in Tanzania where they are well represented (Klein 1989, pp.165–70). This tradition continued for about 1 million years in Africa, the only place where our human ancestors existed up to that point.

By approximately 1.6 million years ago *Homo ergaster* had evolved in Africa, in turn fathering two lineages: *Homo erectus* ('upright man') in Asia and *Homo heidelbergensis* (descended from a precursor species, *Homo antecessor*) in Europe. Both were fashioning a variety of stone tools, different in appearance from the tools of the previous Oldowan tradition by c.1 million years ago in the case of *erectus* and c.500,000 years ago in the case of *heidelbergensis* (Lahr and Foley in Stringer 2006, p.51) living in Britain. Interestingly, in Europe the Oldowan tradition split into two parallel traditions that of the Clactonian flake tradition, named after Clacton-on-Sea, and the Acheulian (Figure 28). These new Acheulian tools were named after the archaeological site in St Acheul, near Amiens in the

Period	Date	Type	Mode	Tools	Characterisitics	Hominid	Key Sites
Lower Palaeolithic c.700,000- c.245,000 bp	c.700,000 years bp	Clactonian	1	Simple flake and pebble tools, chopping cores	Flakes with notches known as clactonian notches	Homo antecessor (no skeletal remains found in Britain, but artefacts from Pakefield are near in date). Homo heidelbergensis	Happisburgh (Suffolk), Pakefield (Suffolk), Swanscombe (Kent), Westbury-sub-Mendip (Somerset)
	c.500,000 years bp	Acheulian	2	Handaxes, scrapers and other retouched flakes	Elaborate, usually bifacial tools	Homo heidelbergensis	Boxgrove
Middle Palaeolithic c.245,000- c.40,000 bp		Levallois	3	Retouched flakes making points, side scrapers, notches, burins and flakes	Creation of tortoiseshell core	Homo heidelbergensis, Neanderthal	Aveley (Essex)
	c.60,000 bp	Mousterian	3	Points, Mousterian of Acheulian handaxes	Flat based handaxes known as *Bout Coupe*	Neanderthal	Pontnewydd Cave (Clwydd), Lynford (Norfolk)
Upper Palaeolithic c.40,700- 11,000 bp	c.40,700 bp	Leaf point industries	4	Blades from platform cores	Lanceolate-shaped tools and wood or bone hafts being used	Homo sapiens or Anatomically Modern Humans (Cro Magnon)	Beedings (Suffolk), Cheddar Gorge (Somerset)
	c.30,900 bp	Aurignacian Phase	4	Retouched and truncated blades, borers and piercers	Notched pieces and denticulates	Anatomically Modern Humans	Kent's Cavern (Devon)
	c.30,700- 25,100 bp	Gravettian Phase	4	End scrapers, burins, backed blades	Gravette points	Anatomically Modern Humans	Paviland Cave (Gower)
	c.15,400- 13,800 bp	Cresswellian Phase	4	Trapezoidal backed blades, points, needles	Long slightly curved blades	Anatomically Modern Humans	Cresswell Crags (Derbyshire-Nottinghamshire border)
	c.13,800- 12,500 bp	Pen Knife sub-phase	4	Backed blades, curve backed points and pen knife points	Straight backed blades	Anatomically Modern Humans	Hengistbury Head (Dorset)

Fig 28. Chronological table of different sorts of tool found on the Isle and the species of *Homo* that produced and used them. Source: the authors.

Somme Valley where some of the first examples of these were discovered in the nineteenth century (Berleant 2007).

The tool associated with this tradition is the tear-drop-shaped hand axe, which was flaked on two sides (bi-face) (Figure 29). Variously called the Acheulian hand axe, or *coup de poing* (from the French literally meaning 'blow with the fist'), it was the dominant tool in a variety of forms for the Lower Paleolithic and was potentially the 'Swiss army knife' of its day: an all-purpose tool used for woodworking and butchering, chopping, digging and scraping (White Howells 1997, p.124; Berleant 2007). This type of tool has by far the greatest representation on the Isle of Ely and shows the earliest inhabitants were *Homo heidelbergensis* living at Shippea Hill from evidence of five hand axes, Little Downham with two, and single stray finds from Isleham, Soham Fen and Sutton (Figure 30).

About 400,000–200,000 years ago, *Homo heidelbergensis* gradually became extinct with the emergence of *Homo sapiens*. The period from 300,000 to 30,000 years ago is referred to as the Middle Palaeolithic and it was during this time that the most famous of our human cousins lived: Neanderthals. Named after the Neander Valley in Germany, Neanderthals interbred with anatomically modern

Fig 30. Acheulian ovate hand axe from Eldon Hall, Byall Fen, Manea. Source: the authors.

Fig 29. Acheulian (*coup-de-poing*) tear-drop-shaped stone hand axe from Cambridge. Source: Salzman 1938, p.250, fig 1.

Fig 31. Levallois flake from South Park Street, Chatteris. Source: the authors.

Fig 32. Levallois tool from Shippea Hill. Source: Salzman 1938, p.254.

humans over 50,000 years ago, which has resulted in as much as four percent of the Eurasian human genome coming from Neanderthals (Rincon 2010).

Neanderthals are associated with a more advanced tool technology called Mousterian, named after a rock shelter in Le Moustier, France. Mousterian assemblages are comprised of hand axes, scrapers and points and are named after their perceived function (Stringer and Gamble 1995, p.145). One Mousterian find, from Littleport, proves that Neanderthals were living on the Isle. Following on from this, there was a more sophisticated technique known as Levallois, associated with both Neanderthals and *Homo sapiens*, which produced flaked tools (Figure 31). Triangular points, which could have been hafted, were commonly made using this technique, offering a development in hunting techniques with the possible use of spears or even arrow-like projectiles. A single Levallois type is known from Shippea Hill and suggests a continuous inhabitance from the Lower Paleolithic through to the Middle Paleolithic (Figure 32).

Between 40,000 and 10,000 years ago there was a shift from the Middle Palaeolithic into the Upper Palaeolithic. During this time the first anatomically modern humans (AMH), sometimes referred to as 'Cro-Magnons', appeared and co-existed with Neanderthals, until Neanderthals died out about 28,000 years ago (Lovgren 2005). This period saw the use of Solutrean tool technology, named after the type site at Solutre, France, which was more refined than seen before. It made use of antler or soft stone hammers to strike the flint producing much finer tools including tanged arrowheads. A single AMH Soultrean blade was discovered at Littleport and a rare leaf point at Hainey Hill, Barway (Colour plate 2).

Life on the Isle

The landmass that would later become the British Isles was subject to frequent and often dramatic transformations in climate, environment, ecology and topography during the Quaternary Period. Ice sheets repeatedly advanced and retreated, and the impact that this had on human populations would have been catastrophic. Although the AHOB project has done much to advance our knowledge of the subject – for example, the project has identified at least 400,000 years of occupation – this period in Britain, in terms of human habitation, is still little understood.

The Mesolithic

The last Ice Age ended *c*.10,000 years ago in about 8,000 BC. As we saw in the previous chapter, tundra landscapes that supported reindeer herds were colonised by birch and soon became thick deciduous woodland with dispersed fauna including elk, red deer, aurochs and wild pig. During the Mesolithic Period, between *c*.10,000–4,500 BC, sea levels were much lower than today so that Britain, as noted above, was joined to the Continent and the coast lay somewhere off Dogger Bank in the North Sea (Figure 33). As a consequence, the Fens were dry, standing at something over 30m (*c*.100ft) above OD but by *c*.6,000 BC, sea levels had risen so that Britain, formerly a peninsula of Europe, had become the island as we would recognise it today. In this rapidly changing environment people continued to live by hunting and gathering for several thousand years until agriculture became established.

Scatters of stone tools and the debris from their manufacture are the most abundant features of the record of the Mesolithic. The type artefacts from the

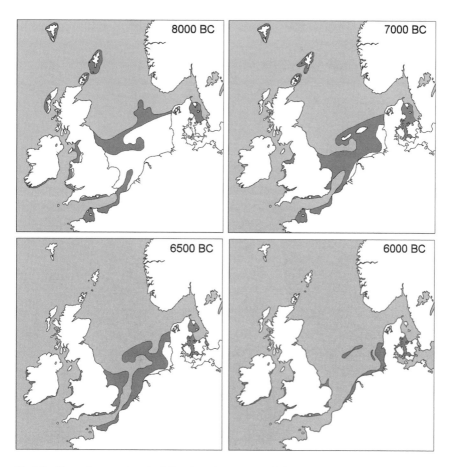

Fig 33. Changing sea levels following the retreat of the last ice sheets, showing the process of separation of Britain from the Continent. Source: after Bradley 2007, fig 1.4 based on Coles 1998; Shennan and Andrews (eds) 2000.

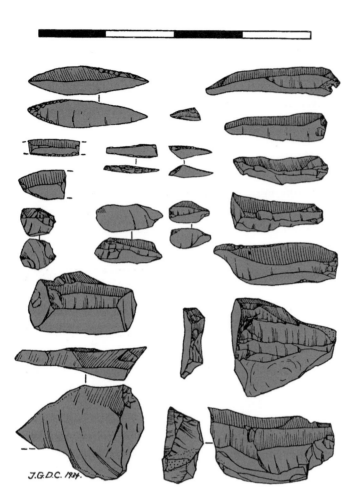

Fig 34. Tardenoisian flints from Peacock's Farm, Littleport (scale in inches). Source: Clark 1934.

period are microliths, which are small, retouched, flint blades, which occur in a range of shapes and sizes (Figure 34). Microliths are often found in hundreds, if not thousands, and were probably components of a wide range of tools including hunting equipment. The early Mesolithic, the period before 8,500 years ago, was dominated by 'broad blade assemblages', which are collections of relatively large microliths, either shaped like isosceles triangles or described as 'obliquely blunted points'. Later Mesolithic assemblages, after *c*.8,500 BP, are usually dominated by much smaller microliths in a wider variety of forms. These are termed 'narrow blade assemblages' and include needle points and scalene triangles.

The potential of Mesolithic evidence from the Isle of Ely is considerable given the protection afforded to sites by the later covering of peat, as shown by excavations at Plantation Farm (Clark *et al.* 1933). Mesolithic flint working is demonstrated by the finds from the Fens near to Shippea Hill, Ely, at Plantation and Peacocks farms. The flints were mainly cores and waste flakes, micro-burins and microliths. During this time, the landscape consisted of a sandy hillock with peat confined to river channels, a type of habitat favoured by Mesolithic hunter-gatherer people over a wide area of Europe. Smith *et al.* (1989) have argued for a pronounced Mesolithic impact on woodland, about 8,250 BP, at Peacock's Farm.

Nature of the Mesolithic Settlement

There is widespread evidence for Mesolithic activity across the Isle and in the surrounding area. At Little Downham all the sites found by the Fenland Survey lay on low islands or promontories rising out of the fens (Figure 35). Two of

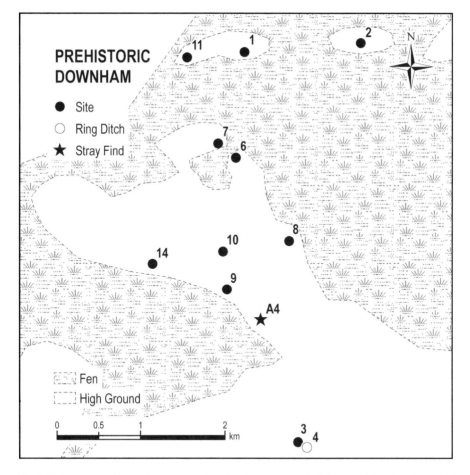

Fig 35. Close up of Downham map showing Sites 6 and 7, Primrose Hill Sites 1 and 11, and Seventh Drove Site 2. Map data © OpenStreetMap contributors, CC BY-SA.

these (Sites 6 and 7) lay close together on opposite sides of the neck of a Glacial basin at Pymore. On one side of the basin (at Site 6) two duck bills were found suggesting that the two sites actually formed a single site deliberately placed at the entrance to the basin to catch waterfowl and fish. Most of the flints consisted of blades and there was a lot of fire-cracked stone, which were the remains of cooking sites and hearths. A further flint patch occurred south of the basin and to the west on an outcrop of sand on the current peat edge were three areas producing Mesolithic blades, with the last having a large quantity of burnt and fire-cracked flint, which were the remains of a cooking pit site.

North of Pymore is the small elongated island of Primrose Hill (Figure 35). At its west end just emerging from the fen on a patch of gravelly sand lay a hunting site (Site 11) with large numbers of flint blades. Directly east lay another low elongated island at Seventh Drove consisting of gravelly Boulder Clay over almost all of which were scattered Mesolithic flints. The main concentration was at Site 2 where a tranchet axe fragment was found by the Fenland Survey along with flints and fire-cracked 'pot-boilers', the remains of a cooking hearth. Further south on the island of Pymore at Frith Head Drove (Site 9) sixteen microliths and sixty-eight blade cores were found by the Fenland Survey and close by (Site 14) a further four microliths and eighteen patinated blade cores were found.

At Ely, Mesolithic material is known from two sites at Shippea Hill (Wymer 1977, p.27). The sites lay low on sand partly exposed next to the peat fen. They were the westernmost outliers of the complex at Peacock's Farm. They produced early flints and one had fire-cracked 'pot-boilers', which indicate that cooking took place there (Hall 1996, p.30). Small quantities of Mesolithic flints came from other sandy areas. In the region of New Wold Farm, Nornea, there were blades and fire-cracked flint. These were outliers of the complex at Soham to the south (below).

In the area of Coveney, Witcham and Mepal the best evidence for Mesolithic activity is at Witcham where two sites were found by the Fenland Survey. Both lay on the tops of small sand hills or 'islands'. They found a range of blades, micro-blade cores, core tools, a microlith and fire-cracked flint. In a similar situation was a site at Coveney, which lay on a sandy rise and produced a large quantity of Mesolithic flints. At Sutton a Mesolithic site lay on a small, partly buried, hillock of sand only 200m by 60m. Nearby two sites had Mesolithic material and lay on small outcrops of sand. Similarly at Haddenham flints of the Mesolithic occured on a rise of gravel (Figure 36). Excavation at Back Drove in Foulmire Fen revealed activity in the late Mesolithic, with about 1,300 flints, mostly of this period, recovered.

Prehistoric activity at Soham was mostly limited to the sandy soils of the Greensand at the north and the drift sands to the east. North-west of Broad

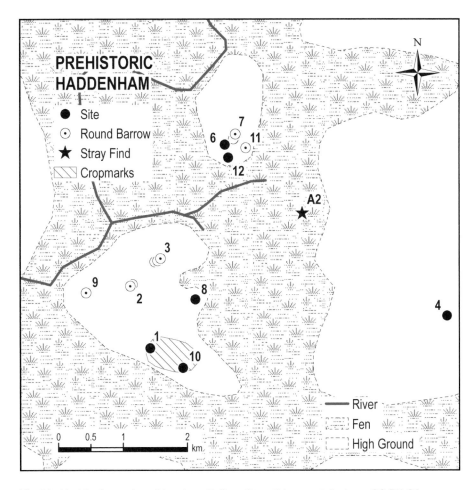

Fig 36. Haddenham sites. Map data © OpenStreetMap contributors, CC BY-SA.

Hill, Soham, was a remarkable complex of early prehistoric lithic sites lying close together on sand (Sites 6–7 and 10–14), all of them within a single square kilometre (Figure 37). They were quite similar in that they spanned the Mesolithic and Neolithic Periods, and all produced a profusion of lithics, including two Mesolithic axes found at Site 14, with many examples of knives, scrapers and other tools having been found at the complex.

At Isleham three sites had mixed Mesolithic and Neolithic finds, the most prolific being located on a small island next to the confluence of the Rivers Lark and Snail (Figure 38). The sites produced a mixture of flint tools, waste flakes and cores, whilst all of them had large quantities of white calcined flints (pot-boilers) representing cooking sites. The evidence from Waterbeach is less, although a Mesolithic axe has been found in the area (Hall 1996, p.119).

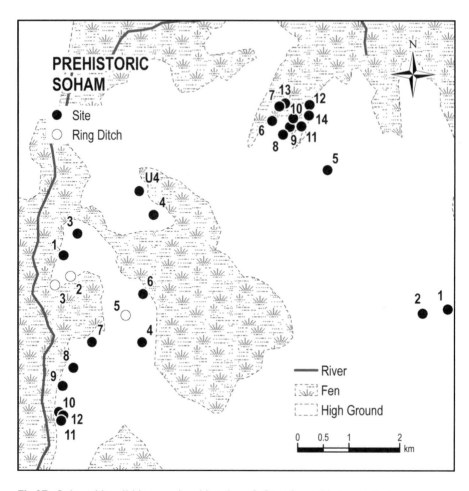

Fig 37. Soham Mesolithic complex. Map data © OpenStreetMap contributors, CC BY-SA.

Finally, at Littleport the most important early prehistoric sites lie at the south-east of the parish on small rises or islands of sand that were once probably dunes (Figure 39). Site 6 at Peacock's Farm was excavated in 1934 as part of the important investigations made by Clark and his colleagues (Figure 40; Clark, Godwin and Clifford 1935). Flints had been discovered at the nearby site on Plantation Farm in 1932 (Clark *et al.* 1933) and Godwin had discovered a flint at 2.26m below the then ground surface when taking peat samples. The fen deposits on the edge of the sand ridge at Site 5 were sectioned on the south-east. The excavation showed clearly that Mesolithic material occurred on the surface of the sand and spread out onto peat at a depth of -5.1m below sea level. Site 30 at Letter F Farm lies on a sandy knoll, which was excavated by

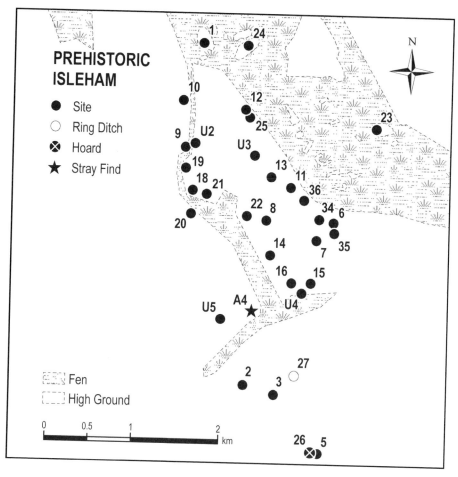

Fig 38. Isleham sites. Map data © OpenStreetMap contributors, CC BY-SA.

Whittle in 1983. Mesolithic flints were found on the sandy old ground surface underneath the early marine deposits. The remaining evidence comes from fieldwalking and stray surface finds with a total of fifteen sites on the island producing Mesolithic material including blade cores and waste flakes, for example at Sites 2, 3, 21, 26, and 32.

Discussion

The people of the Mesolithic, although basically continuing an Upper Palaeolithic hunting and gathering way of life, had to adapt to changes in the environment, which included the disappearance of large herds of

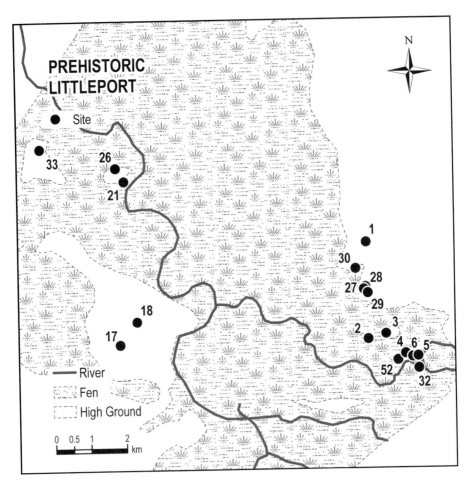

Fig 39. Map of sites at Littleport. Map data © OpenStreetMap contributors, CC BY-SA.

elk to be replaced by widespread forest cover. The most visible of these changes was the development of new types of tool. By the late Mesolithic, much of Ely was covered in mixed deciduous forest. This habitat was attractive to red deer who could browse on the shrubs, and also to aurochs, a type of wild cattle. Wild pig would also have been present in the woodland. Fish may have been another important element in the diet as we have seen from one of the sites at Isleham, located on the confluence of the rivers Lark and Snail, where salmon and trout would have provided a seasonal variation to the diet. Another important source of wild fowl, small mammals and fish would have been Site 6 at Little Downham on the periphery of the Isle. These would have been important sources of protein during the winter and early spring when

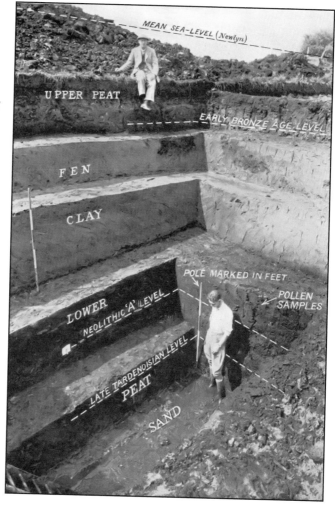

Fig 40. Stratigraphic sequence of fen deposits at Peacock's Farm, Littleport, showing the Mesolithic (Tardenoisian), Neolithic and the Early Bronze Age horizons of occupation. Source: Salzman 1938, plate facing p. 256.

plant food was at its scarcest. Grazing animals visiting sources of fresh water to drink would have provided the best hunting opportunities and may explain the site at Back Drove in Foulmire Fen and others elsewhere.

Whilst a hunting group would probably choose a readily available natural shelter such as a home base from which to exploit the resources of the surrounding area, the selection of a temporary location for a hunting camp would have been less influenced by environmental factors (Clark 1972). Even so certain locations were more attractive than others and may have been occupied on more than one occasion. Several locations, such as Seventh Drove and others at Witcham, may well fall into this category. People dependent on hunting and gathering normally range over a considerable area during the course of a year, exploiting the natural resources from season to season in different parts of their annual territory. During the winter they would have sheltered longest at one base, especially given that during the Mesolithic the climate was more extreme than now. Even in today's more moderate climate, red deer observe a seasonal rhythm in Northern Britain, sheltering on low ground during the winter and moving to higher ground in the summer (Chaplin 1975, p.41). The movements of individual herds would have followed the topography of the landscape, and this may account for the sites north-west of Broad Hill, Soham.

Conclusion

As Pryor (2010) notes, the impact on the land by bands of Palaeolithic hunters would have been slight and our knowledge of them on the Isle only exists from stray lithic finds. Nevertheless, although few in number, these nineteen finds are meaningful and firmly establish occupation on the Isle in the Palaeolithic. More easy to interpret on the Isle is the evidence from the Mesolithic. Here lithic assemblages indicate that many of its sites were temporary camps, the preferred location for these being on top of the sandy islands. The base camps, where larger groups may have congregated for longer periods of time, possibly in the winter, are harder to find (Bonsall 1981; Bonsall et al. 1986). Possible candidates are sites at Isleham, although it is more likely that these are favoured hunter/fisher sites that were visited seasonally, and that the base camps lay further afield in southern Cambridgeshire.

As inferred from the lithic evidence, the transition from the Late Mesolithic to the Neolithic began during the fifth millennium BC. The apparent lack of technological change between the flint assemblages of the later Mesolithic and Early Neolithic seen at sites in Soham and Isleham, which span the periods, suggests that many aspects of Neolithic lifestyle and economy were already in place by the fifth millennium BC. Evidence suggests that small-scale agriculture may have gradually become part of the Mesolithic repertoire, in addition to the established lifestyle of gathering, hunting and fishing.

NEOLITHIC

Introduction

An underlying theme of Neolithic studies has been a strong evolutionary assumption, that the pattern of cultural and other changes reflects an underlying process of steady, more-or-less linear progression to greater social complexity and differentiation, as well as to a larger population with a gradually more intensive economy (Whittle 1999, p.62). Traditionally narratives about the Neolithic, beginning around 4,500–4,000 BC, have therefore concentrated on the change from a transitory hunting, fishing and gathering lifestyle typical of Late Mesolithic groups to an increasingly settled agriculture. This change is marked by the appearance of a new artefact assemblage containing leaf-shaped arrowheads and pottery, together with ceremonial and funerary monuments. The cultivation of cereals has been seen during the Late Mesolithic, whilst it has been suggested that the Neolithic was less settled than previously thought, and that people maintained a significant degree of seasonal or transitory movement, blurring the distinction between the two periods (e.g. Barrett 1989; 1994; Topping 1997; Whittle 1997). Subsistence was based on a broad spectrum of cultivation, gathering, herding, hunting and fishing (Whittle 1999, p.61). Neolithic introductions were domesticated cattle, pigs, sheep and/or goats and cultivated cereals: wheat and barley (Whittle 1999, p.59).

Contemporary interpretations also stress the regionality of this transition (e.g. Barrowclough 2007; 2008; 2010) with authors noting that whilst there are many shared elements of material culture and architecture across Britain, the manner and timing of the introduction of domesticated plants and animals, and the use of particular monumental forms may have varied considerably across different regions. Rather than a single model that explains the British Neolithic we need to consider the variety of different ways in which a Neolithic package was adapted to local conditions. The Late Neolithic, c.3,000–2,500 BC, is regarded as marking a phase of intensification of settlement, land use and artefact production, and has been associated with the first indications for the existence of social hierarchies (Bradley and Edmonds 1993). There is evidence for long-distance communication and interaction, particularly in the realm of ritual and ceremony. On the Isle of Ely, however, the period is also seen as one where distinctive regional characteristics become apparent.

The Neolithic Package

The transition from the Mesolithic to Neolithic on the Isle of Ely was a gradual process. Lithic scatters remain the most abundant source of evidence for human activity in the Early Neolithic, c.4,000–2,800 BC, as they were in the Late Mesolithic, and as we have already seen, sites such as Isleham and Soham span the Late Mesolithic and Early Neolithic. There is some evidence that indicates that Neolithic settlement on the Isle followed a shifting pattern, possibly of seasonal occupation, often in the same locations as Mesolithic sites (Brown and Murphy 1997, p.12). Plant remains indicate that wild plant resources were at least as important as cultivated ones (Wilkinson and Murphy 1995). The remains of numerous pits on higher ground can be interpreted as resulting from repeated reoccupation of the same general location (Healy 1988, Brown 1988).

The shift from the Mesolithic to the Neolithic may be identified in the archaeological record by the introduction of a characteristic new Early Neolithic technology: round-based pot styles; chipped and polished stone and flint axes; leaf-shaped flint arrowheads; long barrows and causewayed enclosures. Absent from Britain are the great timber longhouses of the first Neolithic of Central Western Europe, known as the *Linearbandkeramic* (LBK) cultural tradition, of the mid-sixth millennium BC onwards (Whittle 1999, p.63). The later Neolithic is identified by more profusely decorated round-based pots in the Peterborough tradition and flat-based Grooved Ware pots; waisted, partially polished and other variant stone axes; asymmetrical and transverse flint arrowheads and other portable artefacts including stone and antler maceheads, bone pins and stone balls.

Leaf-shaped arrowheads, which replaced Late Mesolithic microliths, are most often found in isolation, perhaps as casual losses from hunting and related activities (Figure 41). Although many of the widely accepted typological or chronologically diagnostic forms for the Neolithic are represented, the most common of which is the scraper, assemblages are often characterised by informal or multi-use forms suggesting the expedient use of available raw materials. Mesolithic traits continue throughout a large part of the Neolithic, and in turn Neolithic types are found in Early Bronze Age assemblages.

Another characteristic of the Early Neolithic are polished stone axes, part of the economic changes associated with the adoption of agriculture and the domestication of animals (Figure 42). Most have been smoothed or 'polished' by rubbing or grinding on another stone. The rounded end of the axehead would have been set in a wooden haft, with the wider end forming the cutting edge. Complete, or near complete, axes have been found throughout the Isle of Ely in a range of different locations. For example, at Wilbraham four chipped and partially polished stone axes of pointed oval section were found in unused

Fig 41. Leaf-shaped arrowhead from the Isle of Ely. Source: Trustees of Ely Museum.

condition tightly packed together (Figure 43; Fox 1923, p.6). The axes should be interpreted as a cache and their deposition into the ground understood as a means of returning minerals to their natural state. Gabriel Cooney (1998) described clear evidence that material associated with the working of stone during the Neolithic in Ireland was deliberately placed back into the earth during the course of activities that likely involved both placation of, and dedication to, the earth. A similar motivation may have driven the people of the Isle, and if so, then caches of stone axes, especially those partially polished and/or chipped, may represent related types of activities.

A number of the axes found on the Isle have flattened sides, a typical feature of examples produced and found in the Lake District, and where thin-sectioning has been undertaken, the results confirm

Fig 42. Polished stone axe from the Isle of Ely. Source: Trustees of Ely Museum.

that many originated at Great Langdale in Cumbria (Clough and Cummins 1988, pp.219–221). Most of the axes date to the period c.2,750–2,000 BC, when agriculture was already established. From about this date the production of axes in upland areas of Britain, the Lake District and North Wales, was highly organised and products from these 'factories' travelled hundreds of miles into areas such as the Isle that do not contain these rocks.

Axes were also made of flint: for example at Burwell Fen, two flint axes 11.5cm (4.5in) and 12.7cm (5in) long, and of pointed oval section were found (Evans 1872, p.263). The nationally significant flint mine of Grimes Graves in neighbouring Norfolk was an important source of high-quality flint, but was not the only source. Flint was also collected from the surface of the ground where it occurs in Breckland and transported to relatively flint-poor areas such as the Isle (Healy 1991). Particular flints were consistently selected for the manufacture of axes, many of which come from surface till rather than flint mines. Many of the Fenland axes are made from a tortoiseshell-like mottled orange flint (Healy 1991) including examples from the Isle of Ely, such as the flint axe found at Barway (Colour plate 3).

The consistent selection of these materials from the tills may be related to

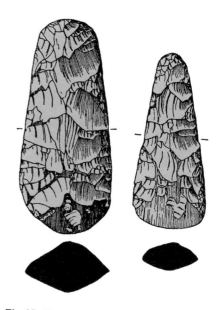

Fig 43. Two partially polished flint axes from a hoard of four found at Wilbraham. Source: Salzman 1938, p.261, fig 11.

Fig 44. Pebble hammer/macehead from Willow Grange Farm, Chittering. Private collection. Photo: Steven Stanley Jugg.

the use of non-flint erratic boulders deposited during the last Ice Age for stone axes, as well as for objects like pebble hammers (Figure 44), rubbers and querns (Green 1988).

The other major new technological advance at the beginning of the Neolithic was the introduction of pottery, augmenting the earlier use of organic containers by Mesolithic communities. Early Neolithic pottery is characterised by round-based pot styles, some decorated, of the Grimston pottery type. Grimston ware is widely found in the Ely area and throughout Britain as a whole (Figure 45). Decorated assemblages of Middle Neolithic Mildenhall style

Fig 45. Neolithic pottery sherds from Peackock's Farm, Littleport. Source: Salzman 1938, p.260, fig 10.

(c.f. Cleal 1992) are widespread (e.g. Clark *et al.* 1960, Hedges and Buckley 1978, Healy 1988). Later Neolithic pottery takes the form of more profusely decorated round-based pots in the Peterborough tradition and flat-based Grooved Ware pots. Pottery finds, although small in absolute terms, are widespread across the Isle of Ely from burial and settlement contexts, and both Peterborough Ware and Grooved Ware are found. Neolithic pottery has been found at Peacock's Farm, Shippea Hill, -4.5m (*c.*15ft) below the modern sea level, an indication that in the Neolithic the sea level was much lower than today.

The consensus is that the indigenous Mesolithic population became Neolithic by adopting new material culture, incorporating new subsistence staples, and developing a new world view, rather than this being a case of movement of large numbers of people from the Continent to Britain displacing, and perhaps replacing, an indigenous Mesolithic people (Whittle 1999, p.63).

The most visible legacy of the Neolithic is its monuments, in particular the long barrows (tombs in elongated mounds), dating to the earlier Neolithic. These tombs echo the form of the great timber longhouses constructed by the first farmers on the continent, and contain collections of assorted human bones. Also visible are the remains of ditched enclosures that defined special places used for a variety of purposes including gatherings and rituals, the commemoration of the dead and for feasts (Whittle 1999, p.58).

Characteristics of the Neolithic Occupation

As with the Mesolithic there is evidence for widespread occupation of the Isle and its surroundings during the Neolithic. At Little Downham, to the north on low islands, are Sites 6 and 7 where Mesolithic flints have been found (above) as well as Neolithic material: three sherds of Neolithic pottery together with flints (Figure 35). Immediately to the south of Site 6 a polished Neolithic axe has been found. North of Pymore lies the small elongated island of Primrose Hill which seems to have been settled during the Neolithic. At its west end (Site 11) Neolithic flints, mainly blades, were found by the Fenland Survey. Previously, an axe made of igneous rock was discovered sometime before 1949 on the edge of the island, and in the vicinity more flints including fire-cracked ones, suggesting cooking, were found. Further evidence for settlement came from the discovery of a saddle quern related to Site 11. Stone querns, being heavy, tended to be located at permanent settlements and thus strongly suggest that the island was home to a small local population. East of Primrose Hill lies the elongated island of Seventh Drove where a leaf-shaped arrowhead has been found. Further south on the island of Pymore at Frith Head Drove (Site 8) blades and a knife with one sherd of Neolithic pottery have been found. Site 9 (Figure 35) produced a large number of Neolithic blades, blade cores and a variety of arrowheads: laurel leaf (one), leaf-shaped (four) and thirty-three transverse arrowheads (out of a total of 1,832 flints). There were also forty-five pieces of pottery of Mildenhall type and Site 14 produced 465 Neolithic flints and one sherd of pottery.

Around Ely Neolithic finds are scarcer, but include polished axes. However, no scatters of stone tools were found by the Fenland Survey, suggesting that the area was only sparsely occupied (Hall 1996, p.30). There were several areas with a few flints: one lay south of Nornea and included blades and a scraper as well as a concentration of burnt flints that probably represent temporary cooking sites, and another area of low density flint was found south of Stuntney (Hall 1996, p.30). Equally thin distributions occur around Witcham where finds include a flint scalene triangle, a piece of polished Neolithic flint axe, a sherd of Neolithic pottery and a piece of bone, as well as flints. More activity

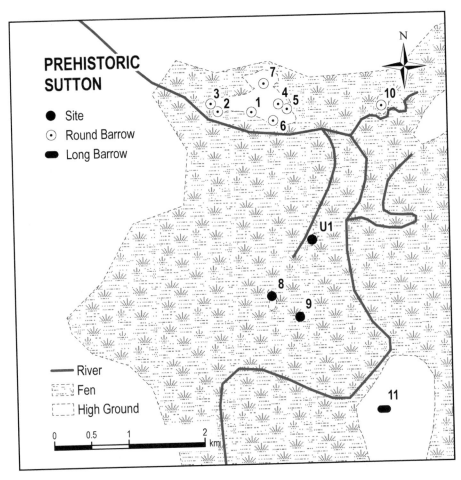

Fig 46. Map of sites around Sutton. Map data © OpenStreetMap contributors, CC BY-SA.

seems to have taken place around Coveney where several Neolithic axes have been found including two made of flint and two of greenstone. A sandy rise produced large quantities of flint tools, mostly blades, and a rim sherd from a Neolithic vessel. At Way Head there was a finely worked tool and a leaf-shaped arrowhead worked on one face only, and near Wardy Hill, again on a small sandy rise, a few blades and cores of Neolithic date have been found. At Mepal in addition to four stone axes there is a wide and fairly dense scatter of flint that includes scrapers, two polished knives and fire-cracked flint.

The Neolithic sites at Sutton lie in North Fen and Sutton Meadlands, and are all found on rises or islands of light soil left by the Ouse (Figure 46). Sites 1, 2, 8, 9 and 11 belong to the Neolithic. Site 1 lies on a sandy gravel island, which has a tongue of sandy soil running westwards, from which a large quantity of flint and several sherds of pottery have come. Site 2 yielded blades and blade cores, a tanged arrowhead and two plain pottery bodysherds. Most significant of all is a long barrow burial monument (Site 11), which lies close to the old Ouse channel and is nearly buried by peaty alluvium. The monument is c.50m long, 21m wide with the top protruding 0.38m above the field. It is aligned north-east/south-west, on an axis parallel to that of the nearby Haddenham long barrow (below), but the Sutton example is likely to be even better preserved. Geophysical survey showed that there may be a chamber at the north-east end of the monument (Hall 1996, p.58). Analysis of pollen from the site shows that the barrow was constructed in an open landscape where there had been arable farming in the Early Neolithic Period (4505–4000 cal. BC, Q-2814). There was later abandonment of the area with formation of lime woodland before peat formed over which was laid marine clay dated to 2860–2135 cal. BC, Q-2813. A second probable long barrow lies south of Site 11 towards the long barrow at Haddenham (Hall 1996, p.58).

Equally rich evidence for Neolithic occupation comes from nearby at Haddenham (Figure 36). At Back Drove in Foulmire Fen, Haddenham (Site 12), flints were found with a few sherds of Neolithic plain and decorated pottery. The site lay on terrace sands buried 1.1m below the present land surface. Preservation was exceptionally good and the bones of cattle and red deer, several clusters of nutshells and a spread of bark have been found. A nearby area of burnt flint was interpreted by the Fenland Survey as a source of temper, possibly for pottery production, but may have been debris from a cooking pit. Taken together the evidence indicates that there was human occupation on the River Ouse terrace (Evans and Hodder 1987, pp.185–86).

Two rare monuments of the Neolithic Period occur in the Haddenham Fens, a long barrow burial site (Site 6) and a causewayed enclosure communal site (Site 10), making the fen important at both a regional and a national level. The long barrow lay on an island near the River Ouse channel almost surrounded by

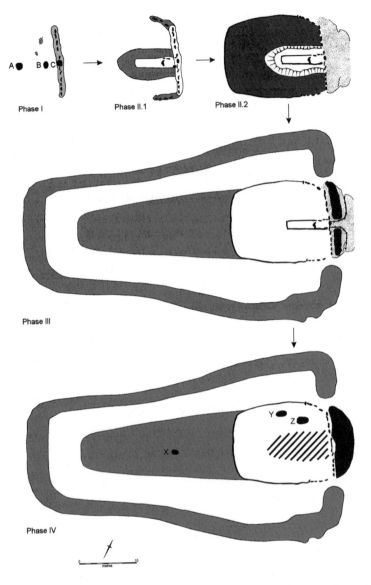

Fig 47. The phased construction sequence of Haddenham long barrow. Phase I consisted of three substantial upright posts (A, B, C), one of which was incorporated into a façade. In phase II.1 the wooden burial chamber was constructed behind the facade, to which curved terminals were added. In phase II.2 an earthen mound was heaped over the tomb and a gravel forecourt added in front of the facade. Phase III was marked by the elongation of the earthen mound and the addition of a ditch around the barrow enhancing the forecourt entrance. The final phase, IV, saw the closure of the entrance, marked by the construction of a bank across the façade. Later, secondary burials (X, Y, Z) were inserted into the top of the barrow mound. With the passing of time the wooden chamber collapsed under the weight of the earth above, leaving a surface depression in the mound. Source: Evans and Hodder 1987, fig 3.30.

marine clay, and was first discovered as a long low mound protruding through the fen by *c.*1m with apparent dimensions 18m by 49m on a north-east/south-west axis with the north-east being broader than the other (Evans and Hodder 1987, p.183). Excavations revealed that, at the scale of *evenements*, the tomb was the result of a sequence of four phases of construction (Figure 47). At the north-eastern end of the mound was a burial chamber made of large oak timbers, which were preserved in the waterlogged fen. The mortuary structure measured 2m by 7m, and the roof, floor and walls were constructed of a horizontal arrangement of large oak planks each up to 25cm thick, 1.4m wide and 4m in length, made by splitting timber the full diameter of the original trunk. The walls were enclosed with earthen banks on all sides except for the north-eastern entrance, and held in place by upright split trunks at the four corners, and by another massive upright placed about a third of the way along from the entrance. The inner upright divided the structure into a vestibule, in which red stones were left, and an inner chamber. The general construction is similar to that of the stone megalithic tombs found elsewhere in Britain.

A facade 12m long was placed at right-angles in front of the mortuary structure with the ends curving to the south-west to flank the burial chamber. A gravel surface ran the length of the façade and stretched out 5.5m eastwards. On it was a post-and-panel structure making a funnel-shaped false entrance to the façade. A palisade with an external bank ran 18m from the façade to revet a primary subrectangular mound. The inner chamber only contained partly articulated human bone from at least five individuals and on the forecourt were placed complete pottery vessels, perhaps containing offerings. A turf mound was built in the eastern end of the mortuary structure, over which, and to the west, the final barrow was built. It had a clay silt core capped by turf and was finally completed with gravel. It was 1.2m high, 50m long, and surrounded, except at the east end, by a ditch 2.5m wide and 1.5m deep (Hodder and Shand 1988).

The Neolithic causewayed enclosure, a type of communal gathering place, covers 8.5ha forming an ovoid shape and is one of the largest causewayed enclosures known in Britain. The enclosure was constructed from a ring of interrupted ditches within which was set a wooden palisade. Crossing the ditches were several causeways which allowed access to the interior via gaps in the palisade (Figure 48). An unusual feature of the enclosure, not normally found in eastern England, is that there is only one ring of interrupted ditches, whereas elsewhere in England two are commonly found. This, and its unusual size, give a sense that the island builders wanted to imprint their own identity, by way of a local articulation of an established design, on the enclosure.

There were two main phases of ditch construction, the first being irregular and the second a recutting of extended ditch segments that was probably contemporary with the construction of the palisade. Apart from its regular

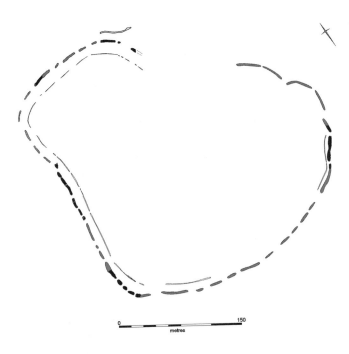

Fig 48. Plan of the causewayed enclosure at Haddenham. The enclosure was formed of a series of segmented outer ditches within which was a timber palisade, interspersed with gaps allowing passage into the enclosure via specific routes (e.g. the gap at the bottom of the plan where the causeway in the ditch aligns with that of the inner palisade.) Source: after Hodder and Shand 1988, fig 5.1.

causeway interruptions, evidence of more formal entranceways, marked by extended circuit gaps, complex ditch-terminal recutting sequences, intentional deposits of human skulls and other 'placed' artefacts, have been discovered (Evans and Hodder 1987, pp.186–91; 1988, pp.12–13). Little evidence for structures was found in the interior of the enclosure and preservation of organic remains was poor as this was a dry land site at its height. The density of artefacts discovered inside the enclosure was low (only 0-8.5 flints per square metre). No bank survived in association with the ditches and this is ascribed mainly to destruction by Iron Age ploughing.

The monument probably had a communal or ritual function, there being no evidence of interior settlement. Evidence for associated settlement in the form of substantial post-built houses is absent. Instead the settlement record is mainly in the form of artefact scatters and pits, the latter having been found in large numbers in the vicinity. Similar settlement evidence was found at Hurst Fen, Suffolk, to the south of the Isle of Ely, where a large group of pits were excavated, and smaller numbers were found locally at Peacock's Farm, Littleport (below). Shelter is likely to have consisted of skin tents or other light structures that have left little trace rather than timber framed houses.

Elsewhere on and around the Isle the evidence for Neolithic activity relies on finds of stone tools. A bifacially worked flint sickle and a Neolithic flint axe came from Little Thetford parish. The Mesolithic site north-west of Broad Hill, Soham, also includes Neolithic artefacts suggesting a *long durée* of occupation.

An outlier of this complex is Wicken Site 1, a linear scatter on the sandy edge of Fordey (Figure 37). Site U1 is a cooking site consisting of a calcined flint area used for heating water and there are more indeterminate flints in the area north of Fordey at Soham U2, probably Neolithic. Many single finds of flints and later prehistoric artefacts have been found at Barway, the Soham part of this peninsula. On the east, near Isleham parish, is Soham Site 1, which produced flints of Neolithic date. Neolithic axes have also been reported from the area. Six calcined flint or pebble areas, most of them small and near the fen edge, occur at various parts of Wicken peninsulas (Sites U2-7). All are without finds and are probably early from their low situation. A few flints occured at Padney and a background scatter occurred around Ash Tree Farm (Hall 1996, p.75).

At Isleham calcined flints occurred as individual concentrations on their own, often in very large numbers, and most commonly on the fen edge at 0–2m OD (Figure 38). The Isleham sites had a very similar appearance to each other. The earlier Neolithic sites were Sites 1, 25, 18, 21 and 22, the last three being on the fen edge, with a further site, Site 23, on a small island. Sites 16 and 5 also date to the earlier Neolithic and lay further upstream. The later Neolithic sites are Sites 24, 20, 19, 14 at the fen edge; and Sites 13, 34, 7, 6, 15, 12 on the higher ground. Of the earlier Neolithic Sites 1 and 11 are located on a small island next to the confluence of the Lark and Snail. Site 25 is in a similar situation on the eastern side of the peninsula; Sites 18, 21 and 22 are on the west next to the Snail, all producing worked flints, with pottery and a large quantity of calcined flint. Sites 16 and 5 lie on the upland, Site 5 being of interest because it is coincident with the findspot of a Late Bronze Age Hoard (discussed in the following chapter). The distribution of early pottery (Plain Bowl and Peterborough style), Late Neolithic (Grooved Ware) and Beaker forms fits with the flint distribution, and endorses the finding that the earlier sites are located mostly at the periphery of the dry land, but most of the later sites are on the higher ground of the peninsula. The only Beaker site, Site 8, is placed on a high spot at 1.5m OD. This fits with changes in the environment, which saw rising fen levels at that time (Hall 1996, p.86).

At Fordham two Neolithic sites are known. They lie fairly close to each other, one against the river and the other a little higher up. Both yielded large flints and calcined material. Several axes, both flint and stone, are known (Clough and Green 1972, p.145; A2, A8–14 and five others). A fine axe (A15) was found in 1988. The gravelly fens north-east of Waterbeach have produced several Neolithic axes, found by chance over the years. There are nine polished flint axes and three of stone as well as a flaked stone chisel; most of the discoveries were made in Joist Fen. A small site with fire-cracked flint was found by the Fenland Survey near Denny Abbey (Hall 1996, p.119). It is believed to be a prehistoric cooking area.

At Littleport the excavations by Grahame Clark *et al.* at Peacock's Farm (Site 6), discussed in the context of the Mesolithic occupation (Figure 39 above), produced an Early Neolithic Bowl and other pottery at a depth of -4.2m (Clark *et al.* 1935). Site 1 yielded a polished Neolithic axe as well as flint, including a transverse arrowhead. To the south of Site 1 lies Site 30, separated by an inlet from Sites 27–29 which also lie on an outcrop of sand. Further south still are Sites 2 and 3, again on areas of sand. Each produced an unusual mixed culture of Mesolithic and Neolithic flint and fire-cracked material associated with hearths or cooking pits (Hall 1996, p.20). These sites represent camps or bases, of varying duration, which have been visited repeatedly during the Neolithic. At Peacock's Farm, lithic scatters spread across a ridge of sand, set beside a small river, have been found associated with small pits of rubbish down the side of the ridge (Smith *et al.* 1989). Peacock's Farm was probably a temporary camp for pastoral people. At Gilgall Farm in the south-east of Littleport island Kerridge found Neolithic blade cores, waste flakes and a triangular flake which was perhaps in the course of being prepared to become a leaf-shaped arrowhead. Several Neolithic axes have been found in the Plains area. Indications of agriculture come from a flint sickle-blade from Burnt Fen, Littleport (University Museum of Archaeology and Ethnology 1906, p.173).

Conclusion

In this rapidly changing environment people continued to live by hunting and gathering for several thousand years until agriculture became established in the Neolithic. Evidence of life during the Palaeolithic Period rests mainly on the stone tools with the different types of evolving people identified mainly through relatively minor technological changes in tool production techniques. Against this backdrop the Neolithic stands in contrast not only because of the more specialised use of stone but also through manipulation of plants and animals. The domestication of plants and animals is significant in our understanding of Neolithic attitudes towards life and death, displayed in their burial monuments and causewayed enclosures. It is in the Neolithic Period that we can shift the focus of our analysis from the *longue durée* of the Stone Age to the *moyenne durée*, where we start to identify ritual/religious ideology (*mentalités*), and even the lives of individuals, *evenements*, when we can analyse individual burials.

CHAPTER 4

THE BRONZE AGE

A mile distant from the town is a little hamlet from which I decended from a steep hill and so cross a bridge over water which enters into the Isleand of Ely, and so you pass a flat on a gravel Causey which way the Bishop is at the charge to repair else there would be no passing in the Summer ... In the winter this Causey is over flowed and they have no way but boates to pass in.

Celia Fiennes, 1698.

INTRODUCTION

Traditionally the Bronze Age, as defined by Thomsen as part of his Three Age System (see Chapter 3), covers the period c.2600 to 700 BC nesting it and its sub-divisions at the level of the era, *moyenne durée*. The period exhibits marked internal contrasts in burial, ritual, monument building and material culture, which have variously led to its subdivision into Early (2600–1600 BC), Middle (1600–1200 BC) and Late (1200–700 BC) phases, or just earlier (c.2600–1400 BC) and later (c.1400–700 BC), where 'earlier' corresponds roughly with the Early phases and 'later' with the Middle and Late phases combined. Within these broad period divisions it is possible to further sub-divide the period into numerous phases (Burgess 1979; Burgess 1980; Burgess 1988; Needham 1996; Needham *et al.* 1997). The names used for these various phases often derive from the place names of major archaeological finds, for example the Wilburton phase, which took its name from Wilburton village where a major hoard of bronze metalwork was found (see below). For the purposes of our discussion a concordance, which reconciles the different sequences with a timeline in both years cal. BC (used for calibrated radiocarbon dates) and bc (uncalibrated), is illustrated in Figure 49 (Barrowclough 2007). Figure 50 shows an estimated prehistoric fen edge with the key Bronze Age sites mentioned in the text marked, many of which were located on high spots of larger islands. The monuments shown represent clusters of burial barrows, for example in the Haddenham-Sutton area where there was a large barrow cemetery, discussed in further detail below. During the Early Bronze Age there would have been

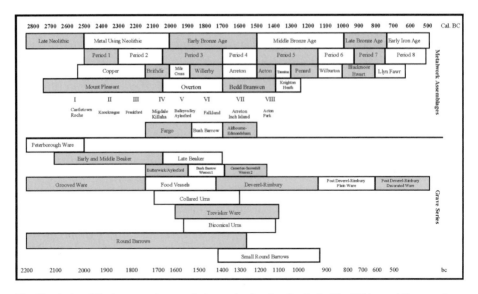

Fig 49. A simplified concordance of chronologies for the Late Neolithic and Bronze Age periods. Source: Barrowclough 2007 based on Burgess 1979, 1980, 1988; Needham et al. 1997; Gibson and Kinnes 1997; Garwood 1999.

active watercourses, tributaries of the River Ouse, creating a dendritic pattern of twisting streams and rivers across the Fens, whilst later in the Bronze Age the whole area would have been peat covered (Hall 1996, p.58).

EARLIER BRONZE AGE OCCUPATION

Nationally the earlier Bronze Age is marked by technological and ritual innovation. Archaeologically this is seen in the adoption of copper-alloy (bronze) metalwork, the introduction of new pottery styles and the construction of new forms of earthworks. On the Isle of Ely, and the neighbouring areas, the innovations that are seen at a national level in the latter half of the third millennium BC are reflected in changes in both social and religious practices. Equally there is considerable evidence for a continuity of practice between the Late Neolithic and Bronze Age. Many sites occupied in the Bronze Age had also been occupied during the Neolithic, and continued to be occupied into the Early Iron Age. An example of this *longue dureé* across periods has been observed at Isleham where calcined flints dating to the Mesolithic and Neolithic continued into the Beaker Period at Site 8, a place located on a small spur of higher ground, 1.5m OD, which represents a cooking site and, which judging from finds of Early and Middle Bronze Age pottery, continued to be used into the Middle Bronze Age (Clark 1937).

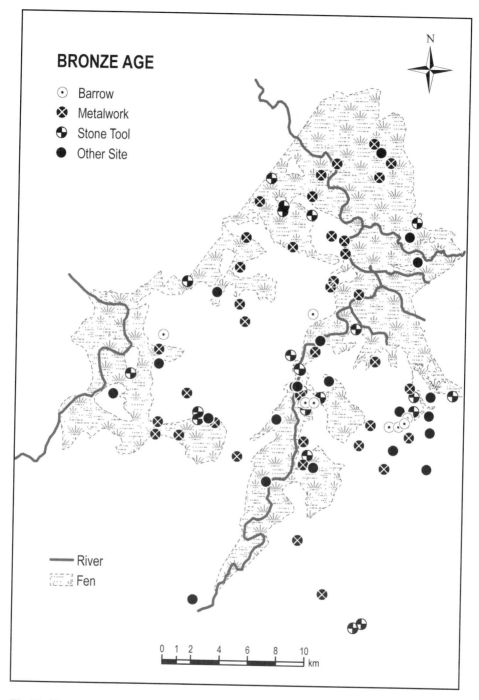

Fig 50. The Bronze Age fen edge together with the location of key Early Bronze Age burial monuments (round barrows) and stone tools, together with later Bronze Age metalwork finds. Map data © OpenStreetMap contributors, CC BY-SA.

Fig 51. Perforated stone implement, axe-hammer, from Willow Grange Farm, Chittering. Private collection. Photo: Steven Stanley Jugg.

Stone utilised in the Late Neolithic continued to be exploited for the production of axe-hammers (Figure 51) during the third millennium BC, and there is a suggestion that the population retained a degree of mobility in their lifestyle.

The distinction between 'Late Neolithic' and 'Early Bronze Age' is therefore somewhat artificial as others have pointed out (Burgess 1976; Whittle 1980) and for this reason there will be an inevitable overlap between the two. During both the Neolithic and earlier Bronze Age locally available flint sources appear to have been exploited extensively, whilst better quality flint material was sourced from areas close to the Isle in the flint mines of Norfolk, for example at Grimes Graves. Although many of the widely accepted typological or chronologically diagnostic forms for the earlier Bronze Age are represented, such as the barbed-and-tanged arrowhead (colour plate 4), assemblages are often characterised by informal or multi-use forms which suggest the expedient use of available raw materials where these were easily available.

Many of the later Neolithic and earlier Bronze Age burial monuments were excavated in the nineteenth and early twentieth centuries, but analysis of more recent excavations, for example at Haddenham and Sutton (below), along with radiocarbon dating means there is secure dating evidence for a large number of them. It is therefore possible to begin to understand something of the fine-grained chronology of these sites at the level of *evenements*, where individuals and events, such as a burial or even separate stages in a burial sequence, may be identified.

The transition from Neolithic to Bronze Age is marked in southern England by the Beaker Period. This period is defined by burials where the body was placed in a crouched position under a round barrow often with grave goods, typical of which are Beaker pots, barbed-and-tanged arrowheads, blades and flakes, bone awls and flint daggers (colour plate 5). Less common, but of the same period, are stone wrist guards, which would have been used by an archer to protect their wrist from injury (Figure 52). For example, at Isleham, stray finds include a flint dagger from near Windy Hall (probably from Site 1; Lethbridge and O'Reilly 1933, p.165), an early flint dagger from Lammas Ground (Paterson 1948), a large flint flake and a 'battle axe' (Roe 1966). In a sandpit at Little Downham a Beaker burial was found consisting of a Beaker vessel, flint dagger, Kimmeridge shale button, pulley ring and flint knife (Figure 53, Lethbridge 1930)

Fig 52. An Early Bronze Age, Beaker period, archer's wrist guard. Made of stone, it would have been strapped with leather or cord to the wrist to protect the lower arm when using a bow and arrow. Source: Trustees of Ely Museum.

Fig 53. Early Bronze Age Beaker period burial group. Ceramic Beaker, Kimmeridge shale button and pulley-ring, flint knife and flint dagger. Source: Lethbridge 1930.

Earlier Bronze Age sites and monuments are found on light soils, continuing the pattern of occupation found in the Neolithic. During the Bronze Age the mudflats receded and the Fens became dominated by peat which slowly spread over marine clay, burying the rodons, and up the landward edges of the Isle. At Little Downham two arrowheads, one tanged and the other barbed-and-tanged, were discovered as chance finds. These may either have been dropped from boats or were lost in watercourses when hunting for fish or fowl, and indicate that the roddons were still open streams during the Late Neolithic and at the start of the Early Bronze Age, but that they were buried during the Early Bronze Age (Hall 1996, p.17). Only the major drainage channels survived. Our main evidence for boats during this period comes from the accidental discovery of a boat or 'canoe' at 'North Fen', Haddenham, in 1843. It was 8m long and not less than 0.75m in breadth, and carved out of a single oak tree. There were grooves in which a sternboard would have been placed (Evans 1881, Fox 1926). No precise location is available, but since it was 'covered by peat' there is every chance that it could be Bronze Age. In the account of finds made in Grunty Fen in 1844 reference is made to this boat as being 'half a mile up the valley in line' (von Hugel 1887) which may indicate a find spot not in North Fen, but north of Haddenham in Grunty Fen, Wilburton. Similar boats are known from excavations at Must Farm, Whittlesey Mere. The removal of the sternboards at both sites suggests deliberate scuttling of the vessels (Figure 54).

Fig 54. A Bronze Age log boat excavated at Must Farm, Whittlesey, Cambridgeshire in winter 2011/12. The boat was carved from a substantial single oak log. At the stern (right-hand side of the photograph) a separate sternboard could be inserted and packed with clay to make the boat watertight, but as in the description of the boat found at 'North Fen', this had been removed, suggesting that the boats had been deliberately scuttled. Photo: the authors.

Settlement Evidence

Evidence of settlement is sparse, although some early lithic sites have been found, some of them producing pottery, which is indicative of settlement. At Primrose Hill Site 1, Little Downham (Figure 35), a flint scatter of the Bronze Age may represent a settlement (Hall 1996, p.17). On Littleport island there are two sparse flint scatters that are assigned to the Bronze Age, Sites 17 and 18 (Figure 39). They produced a few rough flints, and there is a thin background of flint over the higher sandy ground of the island. At Apes Hall a few Bronze Age flints were recovered from Site 21, whilst Sites 28 and 29 near the Little Ouse produced small scapers of Beaker date. The Early Bronze Age sites at Plantation Farm, Littleport (Site 32, Clark *et al*. 1933), and Peacock's Farm Site 6, Littleport (Figure 39, Clark *et al*. 1935, pp.298–99) were both excavated by Clark in the 1930s. The range of finds is demonstrated by the illustration of some of those from Plantation Farm (Figure 55). At Peacock's Farm, Beaker and Early Bronze Age material occurred immediately on top of the marine clay, the lowest deposit being at -1.6m (Figure 56). Occupation lay on a sand ridge with debris spreading out into peat lying 0.05–0.15m above marine clay. On the sand there was occupation debris of pottery sherds, bone, charcoal and calcined flint. Among the worked flints were plano-convex knives and barbed-and-tanged arrowheads. Studies of a human skeleton found in 1911 just above the marine clay (Figure 57, Clark *et al*. 1933) suggest a date towards the end of the Early Bronze Age (Hedges *et al*. 2007, pp.194, 358). Generally the water table was too high during the Bronze Age to support settlement on anything but the highest islands, and the area of these was very small.

Some of the best evidence for settlement on the Isle comes from excavations north of Lancaster Way Business Park, Witchford, in 2011 where two Late Neolithic/Early Bronze Age pits were found spaced 14m apart (Atkins 2011, pp.47–66). The pits were located on the northern edge of the knoll plateau overlooking the valley to the north. The first pit contained forty sherds of domestic Beaker pottery from four vessels, along with worked flint, hazelnut shell, charred grains of cereal and charcoal. In the vicinity thirty-three pieces of worked flint (five blades, seven flakes and twenty-one chunks) were found. The flint indicates small-scale activity in the Neolithic and Bronze Age. The Beaker pottery from the second vessel was decorated and has parallels with two vessels from Ely (Figure 58, Clarke 1970, Fig.885 and 994). That of vessel four, was a rusticated (fingernail decorated) example similar to one found at North Fen, Sutton (Webley and Hiller 2009). Sherds from each vessel were analysed for presence of lipids (fats and waxes). Analysis showed the presence of ruminant fat, which fits with research elsewhere on Early Bronze Age pottery that shows the presence of fats (lipids) from various food sources, mainly animal meat or

dairy products (Soberl and Evershed in Atkins 2011). A bronze awl was found
c.25m to the south of the pits, it has a square section and was used to punch
stitch holes into leather (Crummy in Atkins 2011). The pottery vessels had been
used for food preparation. The fabric and poorly executed decoration of the
Beaker pottery from the Witchford pits are similar to vessels found within

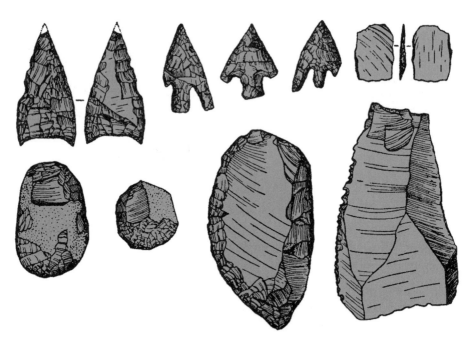

Fig 55. Early Bronze Age flint implements from Plantation Farm, Littleport. Top row,
left to right: hollow-based arrowheads, barbed-and-tanged arrowheads, petit tranchet
arrowheads. Second row: knife, thumbnail scraper, knife, scraper. Source: Salzman
1938, p.270, fig 15.

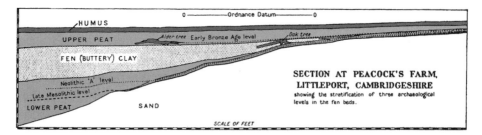

Fig 56. Section at Peacock's Farm, Littleport, showing the stratification of the
Mesolithic, Neolithic and Early Bronze Age occupation levels in the fen beds. Source:
Clark et al. 1935.

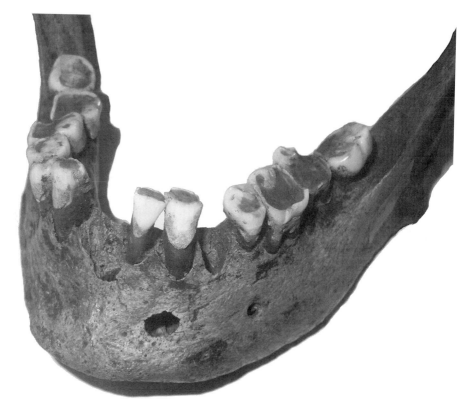

Fig 57. Lower jaw from an Early Bronze Age burial found at Shippea Hill. The jaw displays evidence of a large abscess that has left a large hole in the jaw (centre of the photograph). Photo: the authors.

burials elsewhere on the Isle. Beaker sherds and perforated deer antler butts were discovered in a pit at Burnt Fen, Littleport, in c.1965. There were parts from at least eight different vessels (Edwardson 1966). Interpretation of the site was difficult at the time, but in the context of the Witchford pits, it seems unlikely that these are 'chance' finds. Instead they may have been a 'formal' deposit. It has been argued by Gibson (2000) that the depositing of sherds from many vessels denotes rituals designed to ensure the fecundity of the earth and its resources (Atkins 2011).

One of the main reasons for the lack of evidence for Early Bronze Age domestic occupation on the Isle may be due to the topography. As Atkins (2011, pp.47–66) points out, in the Early Bronze Age the water levels were lower and most Early Bronze Age domestic occupation may have lain at c.0m to 2m OD. At this low level, there is presently little building development and thus

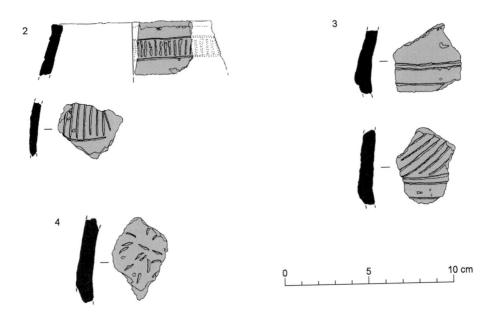

Fig 58. Early Bronze Age Beaker pottery from pits north of Lancaster Way Business Park, Witchford. Vessels 2, 3 and 4. Source: after Atkins 2011, fig 8 (top).

little archaeological excavation. This theory is borne out by the excavations of settlement activity at North Fen, Sutton (Webley and Hiller 2009, pp.11–36). Activity straddling the Late Neolithic and Early Bronze Age was found at *c*.0.5m OD on a small 'island' of river terrace gravels and sand. Excavation revealed evidence of hearths and pits together with pottery sherds and two large waterholes, one with a wooden revetment structure, suggesting that it was dug for use by humans rather than cattle. These remains suggest that people had begun to settle in fixed places by the Early Bronze Age (Webley 2009, p.35), and they shed light on the lives of the people who were buried in the barrows at Haddenham and Sutton discussed below.

Burial Evidence

The chief monuments are burial barrows which occur across the Isle. At Little Downham an Early Bronze Age cremation cemetery, Site 4, was discovered in 1929. Workmen found two complete Collared Urns in a pit *c*.0.6m in diameter. The vessels were empty but may have originally contained food and drink. Nearby another pit contained a cremation with a mass of partially burnt bones and charcoal. Two more pits, with a similar arrangement of deposits, one containing two complete Collared Urns on top of each other, and the other a cremation, were later found. The finds included a dagger and scraper made of flint, and a ring and button made of Kimmeridge shale (Lethbridge 1930, plate xvii).

A large hilltop barrow cemetery existed in the north of Ely in the area of Springhead Lane. Human bones had been found by workmen in the area over a period of at least fifty years, and in 1914 workmen found two Beaker vessels, skulls, at least eleven jaw bones and a stone axe-hammer (O'Reilly 1928). The cremation of a child aged about nine years was found placed in a finely decorated beaker (Trump 1959) 1km away buried in a barrow measuring c.20m in diameter (Salzman 1948, pp.264, 266). The evidence points to the higher ground north of the city being chosen as the burial site for a small population that lived on this part of the Isle. Field survey of this sandy landscape by the Fenland Survey, and by Mike Young along the route of the A10 bypass during its construction, found a widespread but thin background scatter of flint (Hall 1996, p.35). The sandy lower slopes of the island edge at Ely were favoured spots in the Early Bronze Age with more flints, blades, blade cores, and some fire-cracked flint, being found by the Fenland Survey (Hall 1996). Late Neolithic and Early Bronze Age monuments are often associated with water and in particular springs which inspired particular ritual and mythic meaning.

Elsewhere barrows and groups of barrows can be found on isolated peninsulas in the fen. For example, there are four Early Bronze Age barrows in the parish of Wicken (Figure 37), at Fordey, Sites 2 and 3 (13.5m and 18m across), and at Padney, Site 5 (Hall 1996, p.75). There is also a ring ditch near Padney Farm. At Soham two mounds of barrows within ring-ditches occur in the Greenhills area. Two more ring-ditches occur which are probably to be associated with the earthwork barrow in Fordham Moor (Site 5) making a small group. Two Bronze Age sites lie north-west of Broad Hill, Soham, Sites 8 and 9. In both cases they lie on the highest locally available ground, about 1.8m OD. They produced considerable quantities of typical rough flints and waste of the period, as well as barbed-and-tanged arrowheads. It is possible that the two sites form a single large one (Hall 1996, p.75). At Fordham an Early Bronze Age barrow 22m in diameter is known along with an important unprovenanced Beaker burial found in c.1905. It was an inhumation accompanied by an unusual handled beaker vessel (Clarke 1970, pp.476, 550). Only thirty-seven handled beakers are known of which eighteen are from East Anglia and the Fens indicating that this is a regional type.

Most of the monuments discussed so far were either accidentally 'excavated' during building work in the early twentieth century or else found by the Fenland Survey and left unexcavated. As a consequence our knowledge of these barrows is sketchy, consisting of poorly recorded memories and boxes of finds held in museum stores. What is lacking from them is a scientific analysis of the monuments and their contents. Fortunately a small number of more recent excavations, for example Snow's Farm barrow (HAD III, Evans and Hodder 2006a, pp.18–38) in the south of the Isle, help us understand the chronology and ideology behind the construction of barrows across the Isle.

A concentration of twenty-four barrows can be found in the south-west of the Isle on the Ouse valley where it widens into the fen basin. They form the Haddenham/Over group, which continues on what was the north side of the Ouse Valley in Sutton and Chatteris (Hall 1992, p.88). Within this group is the extensive barrow cemetery found in Haddenham and Over Fens (Figure 36). From north to south the cemetery consists of seven different sites with eleven round barrows in total lying on gravel 'islands' near where the river enters the fen. These barrows produced a range of burials and associated objects that reflects the pattern already described on the Isle. Thus, the central barrow of Site 3 revealed a cremation, possibly secondary, with bone fragments, a barbed-and-tanged arrowhead, a calcined plano-convex flint implement and a damaged whetstone. Underneath was another cremation without grave goods. The barrow was about 30m in diameter and was originally *c.*2m high. Also at Site 3, the south-western mound, a Collared Urn cremation group was excavated with the bones of an adult male, aged about thirty, and two small vessels placed in a large vessel. The bones represented a selection from most parts of the skeleton and had been placed in the urn in an ordered manner and sealed with pyre sweepings. The small vessels were on top. Modern excavation techniques made it possible to hone in on the level of the individual, *evenements*, and even to obtain a radiocarbon date for this site accurate to within fifty years: 3360±50 BP, 1800–1520 cal. BC (BM-2497) (Evans and Hodder 1984; 1987).

The barrow at Snow's Farm (HAD III, Fenland Survey Site 1) was complex with a bank revetment encircled by a ditch 27m in diameter (Figure 59). No central grave was discovered but the primary context had sherds from an intentionally broken Collared Urn lying in an area of scorching. Within the revetment bank were remains of a cremation pyre with fragments of burnt human bone and charred split-plank timbers. Two secondary inhumations and a cluster of ten urned and loose cremations in the secondary fills of the ditch, showed a considerable period of activity (Evans 1984, Evans and Hodder 1987, p.190).

Consideration of one of these sites, the Hermitage Farm barrow excavation (Evans and Hodder 2006a, pp.38–50), will help us understand some of the other less well recorded early Bronze Age barrow burials. The Hermitage Farm barrow consisted of a central mound, 13.5m in diameter encircled by a ditch 23m in diameter (Evans and Hodder 2006a, p.39). Within the barrow was the burial of an infant (aged under six months) that had been placed in a crouched

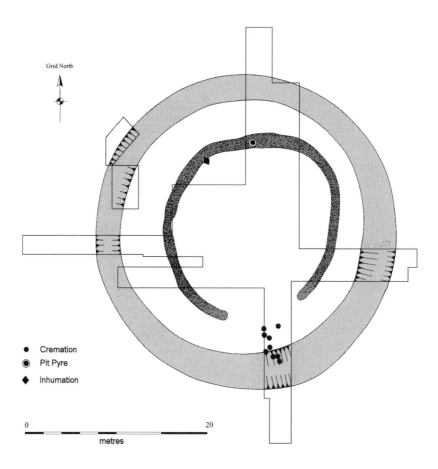

Fig 59. Site plan of the Early Bronze Age burial barrow (HAD III) at Snow's Farm, Haddenham. The plan shows the circular structure together with the location of the burials. Source: after Evans and Hodder 1987, fig 2.8.

position. There was also a large collared urn, within which had been placed two smaller vessels, set upright, and a cremation (Figure 60). The careful excavation of this urn and its contents by specialists from the University of Cambridge Archaeological Unit allows us to reconstruct the detail of the burial sequence, and focus on a process of short-term time *evenements* that lasted only a few hours. The large collared urn was first partially filled with black, almost pure charcoal. This charcoal was so pure that it is thought likely that it was sieved in water to remove impurities before being placed in the urn (Evans and Hodder 2006a, p.43). The charcoal inside the urn had then been shaped to form a 10cm deep hollow into which had been placed fragments of skull surrounded by upright vertebrae, and above this had been placed fragments of long bone. Amongst, and up to 7.5cm above, this layer was a dark grey 'ashy' horizon containing small pieces of charcoal and burnt fragments of bone. Into the upper part of this layer had been set a second smaller urn placed upright and packed into the larger urn by material from the funeral pyre that must have been swept into the urn whilst still hot, judging by the discolouration of the urn's rim. The top of the sweepings lay flat at a depth of 12cm below the rim of the main urn, and embedded within the surface of this material was a third urn, which had also stood upright, its mouth level with that of the main urn. The third vessel was found empty but may well have originally held food or drink (Evans and Hodder 2006a, p.46). The space around the third vessel, at the mouth of the main larger urn had been left empty, with its mouth sealed, probably by a piece of cloth tied under the collar of the urn (Evans and Hodder 2006a, pp.45–6).

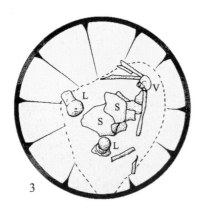

The sequential filling and placement of infill within the main urn, A, has been considered by Christopher Evans and Ian Hodder (2006a, p.50) to reflect an intentional and structured succession of acts, with the main urn symbolically acting as if it were a burial pit. The first stage of the burial began with the funeral pyre where the remains were sorted by hand. Pure charcoal from the pyre was collected and carefully placed in the bottom of the main urn. A shallow was scooped out in the centre into which cremated bone was set. These

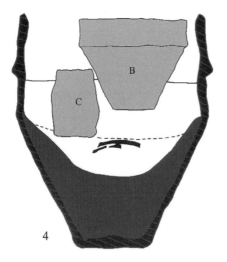

Fig 60. Early Bronze Age Collared Urn burial from Hermitage Farm barrow, Haddenham. Reconstruction sectional drawing through the primary collared urn showing pure charcoal at the bottom (dark grey) which has been hollowed in the middle to allow for the skull fragments, ribs and long bones. Secondary vessels B (Collared Urn) and C (Plain Ware vessel) were placed above in the sweepings from the pyre. Source: after Evans and Hodder 2006a, p.43, fig 2.25.

were the long bones, which tended to survive the cremation process, which once removed from the pyre were broken into smaller pieces in order to fit in the hollow. This was followed by the addition of mixed charcoal and bone, which appear to have been swept from the pyre. Into this layer the second urn was inserted, with more pyre debris packed around and over it. This layer was then levelled to form a floor onto which the third urn was placed; after this the main urn was sealed. Clearly a lot of time and care went into this process. Preparation for the burial included not only the cremation ceremony itself but following this the reduction of the bone, probably by pounding with stones, into small pieces. This process may, by making the individual bones less identifiable, symbolically represent the de-individualization of the dead (Evans and Hodder 2006a, p.50).

On the northern side of the Ouse Valley at Sutton six round barrows form a loose cluster with five of them on the North Fen island and the 6th not far away to the east, at Blockmoor Fen (Figure 46). Topographically they form the southern extremity of the Chatteris prehistoric complex. The island would

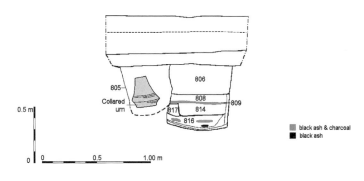

Fig 61. Excavation of inverted collared urn burial and associated deposits, barrow SUT III, Sutton. Top: photograph of the *in situ* urn. Bottom: section through the burial. Source: after Connor 2009, fig 4.

have been isolated in the Bronze Age, and for this reason favoured as a burial ground. Excavation of one of these barrows (SUT 7) revealed two central pits, one of which contained an inverted Collared Urn within which were the cremated remains of an adolescent aged twelve to eighteen years (Dodwell in Connor, 2009, p.43) accompanied by a flint knife of plano-convex type (Bishop in Connor, 2009, pp.41–2). An unusual feature of the burial is that the upturned Collared Urn had a hole in the base through which the cremated remains, dated to between 1880–1670 cal. BC (SUERC-19125: 3440±30 BP), appear to have been poured. The second pit contained one or more organic containers within which were ashy deposits, probably the debris from the cremation pyre (Figure 61, Connor 2009, pp.38–41).

The site was excavated by Aileen Connor who found good evidence for structured deposition, just as at the Hermitage Farm site. She identified two or possibly three distinct episodes of activity (Connor 2009, pp.40–1, 45). The first ashy deposit, numbered 816 on the plan, appears to have been contained within a now-decayed basket or wooden bowl. Lying above this was another ashy deposit (814) forming a flat-based, vertical-sided interface with deposit 817, another probable organic container. A horizontal layer of black ash (809) sealed the fill numbered 814, and was in turn, sealed by a final layer of ashy organic silt (808). The upper half of the pit was filled with a homogenous mid-grey silty clay (806) that was indistinguishable from the fill of the cremation pit (805) (Connor 2009, pp.40–1). The absence of cremated bone may suggest that the pyre material was carefully separated into its constituent parts, as at Hermitage Farm.

Interpretation of Burials

As we have seen, containing the dead was a preoccupation of Early Bronze Age society, as it is in many cultures. What we see in the cremated remains of the carefully packed funerary urns may be the final stage in a process of containment that began when the deceased first passed away. This is because the transition from the world of the living to the world of the dead, when the corpse is 'betwixt and between', is a particularly unsettling time for society (Douglas 1966; also Leach 1976; 1977, pp.171–73). At this time the living are confronted by the danger, brought about by death, of a torn social fabric: it is a time when long-standing social relations have to be renegotiated. The living also have to confront the physical contamination of a decaying body, which the anthropologist Mary Douglas (1966) demonstrated is considered unclean in many cultures, and therefore polluting, and perhaps socially dangerous. This liminal period is therefore the most dangerous in the human life-cycle and must be contained.

The inversion of urns may also have a specific ritual significance. The performance of actions backwards, and of things being inverted or turned inside out, are common ritual elements in funerary practices. Ucko considers the case of Zulu ceremonies in which the coffin bearers walk backwards, a hole in the house wall is used instead of the door and 'yes' is used to mean 'no' and vice versa (Ucko 1969). The eschatology is that of a world of the dead inverted to that of the living. Turning the clothing on the corpse inside-out is a common practice in many societies; among the Lo Dagaa the smock worn by the corpse was turned inside out. Reversal reinforces the normality and naturalness of everyday practices by defining their opposite in ritual time. It also serves to separate the dead and their realm from the living.

The provision of accessory vessels in the Hermitage Farm and Sutton barrow burials were there to facilitate the smooth transition of the living to the world of the dead, their contents, various food stuffs, were there to sustain the deceased in the afterlife. Grave goods placed with the dead may have served a similar role and may have been items that were possessions of the deceased, or they may have been mourners' gifts to the dead. They may have been placed with the burial to equip the dead for the world of the afterlife, or to prevent the dead coming back to haunt the living. Parallels drawn from anthropology may assist us to explore the range of possibilities. What is interesting about the selection of knives, such as that placed in the urn at Sutton, and daggers, often placed with Beaker burials, is that they are artefacts associated with the act of cutting, with separation of one thing from another. One possibility is that the placing of a knife or dagger on or in their grave by their survivors may represent the dead's severance from the living. The aim of placing the object with the burial may serve to prevent the deceased from remaining in the world of the living. For example, among the Iban of Borneo, a knife may be included in burials to symbolise the cutting of those ties (Uchibori 1978). Hunting equipment such as barbed-and-tanged flint arrowheads, flint blades and scrapers often accompany the dead. These may have been accoutrements to feed the dead in the afterlife, or complex symbols that expressed the values, aims, and attitudes of mourners.

Conclusion

A Neolithic to Early Bronze Age continuity is demonstrated in the Isle's archaeological record. Evidence for Early Bronze Age occupation consists mainly of burial monuments, their associated grave goods and lithic implements, the same classes of evidence that were used to construct an understanding of the Neolithic. The origins of the practices that have been identified in the Early Bronze Age may likewise be traced back to the Neolithic. In particular surviving Neolithic traits in urns demonstrate a close relationship between the two periods. The Early Bronze Age was also a time of increasing diversity, seen in the variety of burial monuments, interments and grave assemblages, accelerating a pattern that began in the Late Neolithic.

Indications are of a largely pastoral economy supplemented by some cereal cultivation. Pollen evidence suggests widespread but irregular and spasmodic forest clearances during the period, although generally small scale in character. From these findings it may be inferred that there was a larger population in the Early Bronze Age than in the Neolithic Period. The presence of many barbed-and-tanged arrowheads presumably means that hunting remained a means of food gathering, reflecting the continuing disturbance of the forest cover on the clay inland. Hunting was possibly a seasonal activity carried on from settlements of more lasting status on the fen 'coast' of the island.

THE LATER BRONZE AGE METALWORK

Introduction

The burial barrows that were such a visible feature of the earlier Bronze Age cease to be built in the later part of the second millennium and thereafter

Fig 62. A reconstruction of a Bronze Age round house at Flag Fen, near Peterborough. Houses of the period were typically circular in plan and made of light wicker-work panels covered in mud mixed with a variety of locally available materials, such as animal hair and dung. Less is known about the roof, but most likely it was some form of thatch, using locally available grasses, perhaps covered in turf to give strength and stability, as in this example at Flag Fen. Photo: the authors.

ritual focuses increasingly on the deposition of bronze metalwork, often in rivers and bogs. There is little evidence of settlement: at Way Head, Coveney, there was a dark occupation area yielding some flints and sherds of Late Bronze Age pottery along with fire-cracked flint used for cooking, and at Ely a Bronze Age food vessel was found near Shippea in 1942 (Bushnell 1951). Examples of Bronze Age houses have been found elsewhere in the region, for example at Flag Fen where there is a reconstruction of a typical round house of the period (Figure 62). On the Isle it is instead the bronze (copper-alloy) metalwork that gives meaning to the term 'Bronze Age', the one category of data that crosses boundaries between the Early, Middle and Late stages of the Bronze Age giving coherence to the period.

The availability of affordable metal detectors has led to a dramatic increase in the number of bronze finds in the last thirty years. Although many finds have not been reported a significant number have, and it is thanks to local metal detectorists such as Phillip Randall, whose finds are on display in Ely Museum, that we have been able to write this study. Finds are rare in settlements, but single finds or collections of items, hoards, often without any archaeological context, are plentiful in and around the Isle of Ely. The metalwork of the later Bronze Age was varied with many new types of object, the most common of which are axes, spears, daggers, rapiers, swords, and various horse-harness fittings (Figure 63).

The Later Bronze Age Occupation

In the fen at Little Downham a socketed axe and some spearheads were found (Salzman 1938, pp.273, 302; Lethbridge and O'Reilly 1936, p.163) and on the island of Pymore an early rapier was reported in 1985 (Cambridgeshire Archaeological Records (CAR)). At Site 1 at Primrose Hill (Hall 1996, p.17; Figure 35) a looped and socketed bronze axe was found before 1949. Bronze axes and other objects are known as chance finds from Littleport. In the fens around Ely several pieces of bronze metalwork have been recorded as stray finds including a Late Bronze Age socketed axe that came from Prickwillow (CAR 1956). This is in addition to the Stuntney hoard discussed below and a socketed bronze axe found in Wentworth on a gravelly Boulder Clay spur (Lucas in Hall 1996, p.41).

A number of poorly provenanced finds found before 1861 are described as 'from Coveney'. They include two shields found together (Figure 64), a palstave and two swords; a socketed axe and looped spearhead are preserved in the Ashmolean Museum, Oxford (Brown and Blin-Stoyle 1959, Trump 1962, Coles 1962). A Bronze Age palstave was recorded by the Fenland Survey (Hall 1996, p.50 plate II) and another axe was reported to have been discovered c.1973. The only known chance find from Sutton is an unprovenanced Late Bronze Age sword of the Wilburton type, so named after two significant hoards of

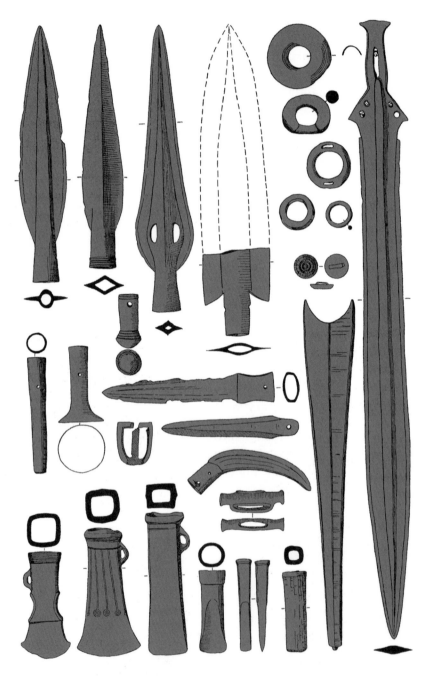

Fig 63. Examples of some of the more commonly found later Bronze Age artefacts from the region. From top left to right: spears, rings used for harness fittings, sword. Middle row, left to right: spear shaft ferrules, daggers, sword chape. Bottom row, left to right: socketed axes, socketed gauge, socketed chisels, socketed hammer. Source: Salzman 1938, p. 281, fig 20.

metalwork found in 1844 and 1882 in Grunty Fen (see below). A further two unprovenanced hoards of Late Bronze Age metalwork are known from Wicken. In 1850 an unusual curved blade with an outside cutting edge and a spiked macehead were recorded (Boilean 1850). In the British Museum is a group of Late Bronze Age metalwork that includes five swords, one chape, a ferrule and two socketed spearheads (Salzman 1938, p.279). Several poorly provenanced pieces of metalwork come from the east and south of Soham (Trump 1962, pp.80-103). A bronze axe was discovered in 1930, and at Down Field a gold flanged torc was ploughed out in *c*.1954. From Ely parish a looped socketed spearhead of golden colour with brown mottling was found by Issac Taylor at Wood Fen Farm in 1932 (Figure 65). The patina and colour suggest that the spear had been deposited in water, perhaps as a ritual offering to the gods. This is because in non-oxidising circumstances the process of corrosion cannot take place and bronze objects retain their golden colour. Wet locations usually provide this condition and so wet-context finds still have their original colour (Fontijn 2002, p.40).

Fig 64. A pair of bronze metalwork shields found at Coveney before 1861. The shields, which are in poor condition with damage to the edges, date to the later Bronze Age, and are displayed at the Museum of Archaeology and Anthropology, University of Cambridge. Photo: Salzman 1938, pl. VII.

Fig 65. Looped socketed spearhead from Wood Fen Farm, Black Bank, Ely. This type of object is typical of the Middle Bronze Age, Period 5 (Penard), c.1300–1150 cal BC. Photo: Norfolk County Council/Portable Antiquities Scheme.

At Isleham, a bronze dagger and palstave have been reported (Hall 1996, p.88) in addition to the Isleham Hoard, the largest hoard of Bronze Age metalwork found in Britain, which is considered below with the other hoards. Late Bronze Age metalwork is also known from Fordham where a spearhead, and a socketed and looped axehead were found in the village. Finally, four pieces of bronze metalwork were discovered in the 1850s 'from Waterbeach': a palstave and three rapiers (Trump 1962).

Hoards

The most significant finds of metalwork are the later Bronze Age hoards recovered from the fen edge (Figure 66). A Late Bronze Age hoard found in the fen near Stuntney, Ely, in c.1939 was first discovered by ploughing and then later excavated. There were over eighty objects in a cylindrical wooden tub made in two parts (colour plate 6). Among the artefacts were three looped palstaves, socketed axes, a socketed gouge, sword fragments and ingot cakes. The typology of the implements indicate a date late in the Wilburton phase of the later Bronze Age (Clark and Godwin 1940, Brown and Blin-Stoyle 1959, Trump 1962).

Further south lies Wilburton, which is well known for its hoards of later Bronze Age metalwork. The first was discovered in Grunty Fen in 1844 in an area used by the poor for digging turf. At about a metre depth three looped axes, known as 'celts', were found and 0.3m below them a fine gold torc made of a twisted 'rod' coiled into a helix (von Hugel 1887, Taylor 1980). The metalwork

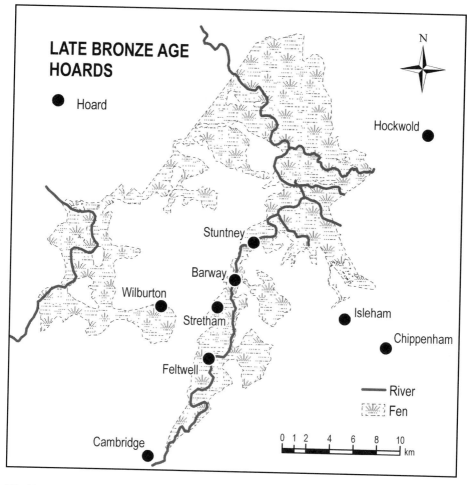

Fig 66. Map showing the distribution of later Bronze Age hoards around and close to the Isle of Ely. Map data © OpenStreetMap contributors, CC BY-SA.

is dated to the Middle Bronze Age (Brown and Blin-Stoyle 1959, p.66). Another hoard, sometimes described as a founder's hoard or metal-smith's stock, was discovered in 1882 (Figure 67). The site, occupying an area of 1.8m by 0.9m, was found in *c*.0.7m of peat lying on clay. It contained 163 pieces that included 115 spearheads, of which eighty-seven were complete and twenty-eight broken; there were also one looped palstave, two socketed axes, swords, and scabbard ends (Evans 1885). Founder's hoards were defined by Evans as 'the stock-in-trade of some bronze-founder of ancient times, as they comprise worn out and broken tools and weapons, lumps of rough metal, and even moulds in the accumulation of bronze was destined to be recast' (Evans 1881, p.457).

The Wilburton hoards lend their name, as we saw in the case of the Stuntney hoard, to the Wilburton Phase of the Bronze Age dated between 1150 and 1000 BC (Figure 49). Metalwork of this period is highly innovative and contains a range of new elaborate types, including extremely long and thin cast tongue chapes, hollow-bladed spearheads, cauldrons and varied accoutrements (Bowman and Needham, 2007, p.96). Another radical innovation of the Wilburton smiths was their extensive use of lead as an additive to bronze.

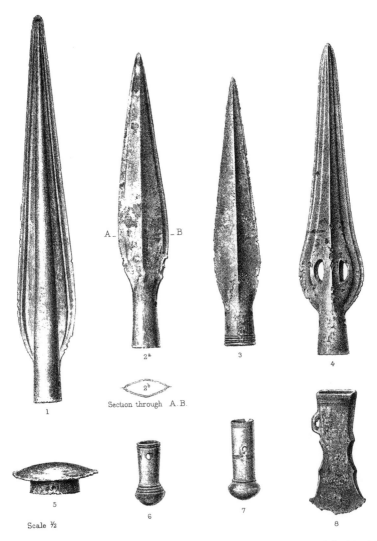

Fig 67. Illustration of some of the artefacts from the Wilburton hoard first published in 1884. The finds illustrated include several spears and spear ferrules, and also a 'waisted' socketed axe of Ulleskelf type, similar to one found in the Barway-Little Thetford hoard. Source: Evans 1885.

Fossilised skull of an ichthyosaur from the Isle of Ely. Source: the authors.

Solutrean leaf point, c.40,000 years old, from Hainey Hill, Barway. Source: Trustees of Ely Museum.

Characteristic tortoiseshell-like mottled orange flint axe from Barway, Ely. Private Collection. Photo: Steven Stanley Jugg.

Early Bronze Age barbed and tanged arrowhead from Little Thetford. Private collection. Photo: Steven Stanley Jugg.

Early Bronze Age Beaker period flint dagger, from Willow Grange Farm, Chittering. Private collection. Photo: Steven Stanley Jugg.

Bronze metalwork from the Stuntney hoard, found close to the causeway connecting Stuntney and Ely. From left to right: ingot cakes, socketed axes, and the remains of the wooden tub within which the metalwork was found. Source: the authors.

Some of the metalwork from the Barway-Little Thetford hoard. Fragments of broken rapier, peg-socketed spearhead, dagger and Ulleskelf type socketed axe (extreme right), together with a complete chisel and socketed axe (rear). Private collection. Photo: Steven Stanley Jugg.

Photograph of the lower half of a broken Uleskelf type socketed axe from the Barway-Little Thetford hoard. Private collection. Photo: Stephen Stanley Jugg.

Roman brooch found by a metal detectorist,
one of many votive objects found on the Isle.
Photo: Trustees of Ely Museum

Coins from the hoard of Roman
coins found at Barway in 1958.
Source: the authors.

Great square-headed brooch decorated with animal and bird designs. Photo: Steven Stanley Jugg.

Amber and glass beads found at 'Cratendune', Little Thetford, c.AD 530–580. Five amber beads of various shapes, and one blue glass melon bead, a continental import, all in fair condition. The combination of amber beads and the single melon bead suggests a mid-sixth century date. Photo: Steven Stanley Jugg.

Anglo-Saxon gold finger-ring. The ring is decorated with two rows of horseshoe-shaped stamps. Photo: Steven Stanley Jugg.

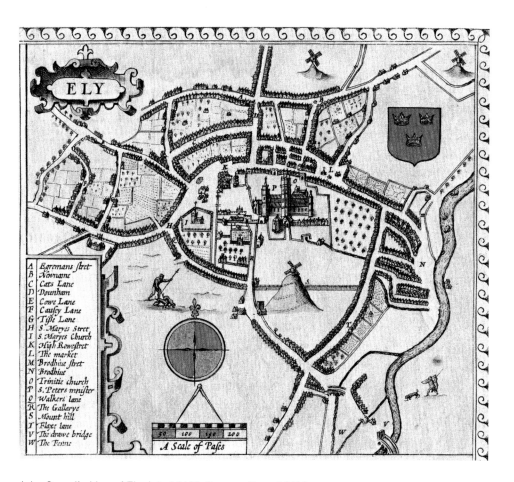

John Speed's Map of Ely dated 1610. Source: Speed 1610.

Glass fragments, evidence of
stained glass window manufacture.
Photo: Steven Stanley Jugg

Babylon ware manufactured in
the Babylon area of Ely. Photo:
Trustees of Ely Museum.

This produced alloy compositions contrasting completely with the preceding Penard phase of metallurgy, and at times with rather excessive proportions of lead. Clearly lead was coming into circulation much more widely and this provides the background to more frequent use of lead alone or in lead-tin mixes for specialised purposes, such as seen in the construction of flesh-hooks discussed below.

Not far away a disturbed hoard has been identified (Barrowclough forth-coming) alongside a wooden causeway of later Bronze Age and possibly Early Iron Age date (Colour plate 7). Discovered in 1932, the causeway ran between Barway and Little Thetford (Figure 68, Lethbridge 1935, Lethbridge and O'Reilley 1936). Stakes were caught by the plough and upon excavation the track was found to be constructed of timber posts supporting brushwood with sand placed over the top. It was 9m wide and 800m in length. Along with the metalwork there were sherds of Middle Bronze Age Deverel-Rimbury type pottery, much of which had been disturbed by plough action. Metalwork includes many types found in the Wilburton hoard, including socketed axes of the relatively rare Ulleskelf type, which are typical of Wilburton phase metalwork, being of a particularly elaborate shape (Colour plate 8).

Other finds include the first complete flesh-hook found in England (Figure 69). Evidence suggests that during feasts meat was cooked in large cauldrons, and that these unusual objects were used to hook cooked meat out of the cauldrons. 'It was found this year [1929] about nine feet from the surface in digging a dyke on reclaimed fen-land at Little Thetford, Isle of Ely' (Bowman and Needham, 2007, p.63). It has a wooden shaft 'in the lower socket or ferrule, with a wooden peg through it'. The flesh-hook from Little Thetford has two prongs, fixed to a wooden haft at one end, with a bronze ferrule at the other end, and thus falls into the later more elaborate Class 3 type, dated to the Wilburton Phase of the Late Bronze Age c.1100–800 BC (Bowman and Needham, 2007, p.81). Flesh-hooks are rare, with only around thirty-six examples known; but they have a widespread distribution from the Caspian Sea to the Atlantic (Bowman and Needham, 2007, p.56 and Fig.22). Two concentrations are known, one in Northern Ireland and the other around the Fens (Figure 70). Local examples include three Class 2, single-pronged, types found at Eriswell, to the east of Ely; Flag Fen, to the west on the fen edge; and on the fen edge at Feltwell, a few miles north-east of the Isle in Norfolk. The Eriswell and Feltwell examples were both found with Class A bronze cauldrons. As well as the Class 3 type, double-pronged, Little Thetford flesh-hook a Class 4 type is known from the Isleham hoard (below), which also contained fragments of Class A cauldrons, a class first developed in the previous Penard phase. The combination of flesh-hooks and cauldrons is evidence of an active Bronze Age feasting ritual in this region (Bowman and Needham, 2007, p.53).

Fig 68. Photograph of the causeway that ran between Barway and Little Thetford, taken in the 1930s. The picture shows the surviving timbers that had been found by the farmer Stanley Randall at New Fordey Farm, Barway. After he had dug them up, he turned them upside down and replanted them in the place he had found them. Note the pointed ends of the posts, which were shaped to allow them to be hammered into the ground more easily. Since this photograph was taken the surface of the field has fallen by c.3 m. Photo: courtesy of Phillip Randall.

Fig 69. Drawing of the flesh-hook from Little Thetford. Source: Karen Hughes.

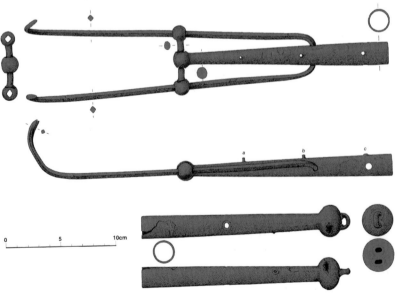

The Little Thetford flesh-hook is unusual suggesting that it was an experimental piece made by smiths working within the Wilburton tradition (Figure 71). At least one other unusual flesh-hook emerged from this tradition, with some otherwise unidentified fragments of shaft in the Isleham hoard suggested to be from a solid-shaft flesh-hook (Bowman and Needham, 2007). Found by a farmer in December 1959 when ploughing, the Isleham hoard is the largest in Britain with *c.*6,500 bronze pieces, of which 2,500 items are from weapons and martial equipment, and 2,600 are ingots (Britton 1960). Much of the material was similar to that in the Stuntney, Wilburton and Barway-Little Thetford hoards, and included broken swords, socketed axes, palstaves, double-edged knives, decorated fittings and fragments of bronze vessels. This led to an

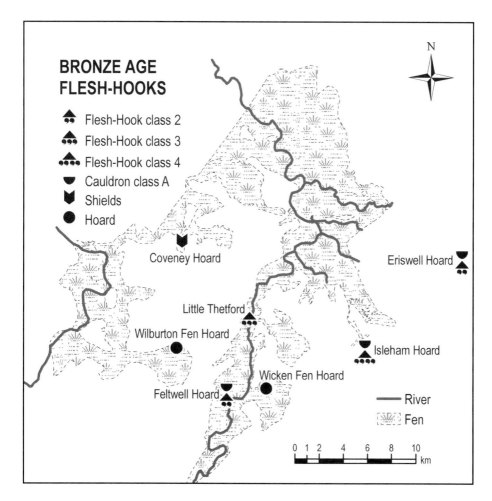

Fig 70. Map of the fens showing find spots of flesh-hooks and cauldrons. Map data © OpenStreetMap contributors, CC BY-SA. After Bowman and Needham, 2007, p.64.

interpretation of the hoard as having belonged to a founder or smith (Britton 1960, Malim 2010), much like the Wilburton hoard (above), a view supported by the presence of casting jets and pieces of moulds, although there was no evidence of casting or working on the site.

A study of pollen from the site shows that the Late Bronze Age landscape was relatively clear of woodland, and was used for pasture and arable agriculture (Malim 2010, p.120). Other material included horse harness fittings and tools, as well as the cauldron and flesh-hook fragments already discussed.

The hoard had been placed in a very large ceramic Post-Deverel-Rimbury (PDR) Plainware pot dug into a pit within a Bronze Age ditch on the edge of

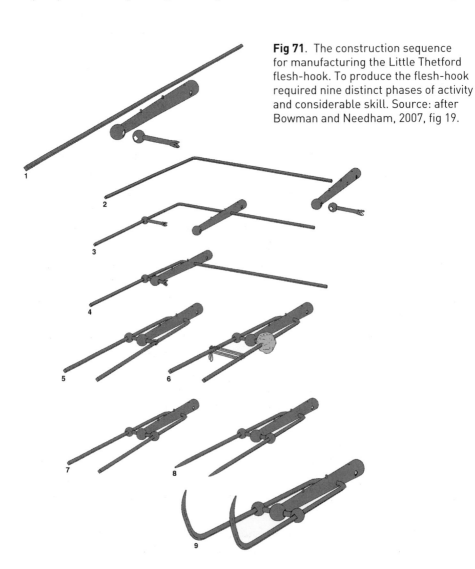

Fig 71. The construction sequence for manufacturing the Little Thetford flesh-hook. To produce the flesh-hook required nine distinct phases of activity and considerable skill. Source: after Bowman and Needham, 2007, fig 19.

the fen next to a rectangular house (Malim 2010, p.73). This type of pottery is dated to between *c*.1150 and 800 BC and fits well with typological analysis of the metalwork and radiocarbon dating of the site, which suggests that it is of Wilburton type and dated between 1150 and 1000 BC. Analysis of the artefacts' metallurgy shows much is of continental origin, a characteristic of Wilburton hoards, with Central Europe the probable source (Malim 2010, p.74).

In addition to these, two more contemporary hoards lie within 10km of Little Thetford, one with broken-up weapons from Wicken Fen, and the other a pair of sheet-bronze shields from Coveney Fen. Further away, on the western fen edge another Wilburton stage hoard has been excavated at Bradley Fen, near Peterborough (Bowman and Needham, 2007, p.96). Taken together these hoards represent an unrivalled concentration of Wilburton stage metalwork incorporating the most prestigious of objects, much weaponry, and the Isleham hoard, which can be seen at West Stow Anglo-Saxon village in Suffolk, and is the largest hoard yet found in Britain.

Discussion

Much of the literature on later Bronze Age metalwork in the area focuses on the classification of different artefact types with surprisingly little detailed analysis of the landscape environment of the deposits. Observations usually differentiate between items deposited in watery places, rivers, meres and bogs, and those deposited on dry land. Those in watery places have been interpreted as ritual offerings and those on dry land as either 'founders hoards', that is, as raw material to be melted down in a metal worker's foundry, or as valuables lost or hidden in time of crisis. Such interpretations are overly simplistic. Our study of the findspots, made possible by detailed study of metal detectorists' finds and the fieldwork of the Fenland Survey, and facilitated by the detailed records of the Cambridgeshire Historic Environment Record and the Portable Antiquities Scheme, reveals that particular sorts of artefact were associated with particular places in the landscape. Following similar work elsewhere, in Ireland (Needham 1989), the Netherlands (Fontijn 2002), and in the Fens (Yates and Bradley 2010), we argue that this approach allows for a more nuanced understanding of a complex practice.

Our analysis of the data for the later Bronze Age Period combines the distribution of different metalwork types with reconstructions of the landscape to identify different patterns of deposition that move away from a simplistic wet-dry dichotomy. Through this contextual approach we have identified four different patterns of deposition on the Isle.

First is a strong association between finds of complete weapons and the River Great Ouse. This pattern of deposition in flowing water has been observed by

Richard Bradley here and elsewhere across north-west Europe, for example in the River Thames, suggesting that it marks a common wide-ranging belief (Bradley 1998, pp.99–109; Yates and Bradley 2010, pp.405–15).

A second pattern that emerges is that hoards, especially those of weapons, are in contrast most often found in bogs, pools and meres. This pattern of deposition in still, rather than flowing, water indicates a grammar of deposition that we are only just beginning to understand.

Thirdly the data reveals that broken weapons were treated differently from complete examples. Thus, whilst complete weapons are found in wetlands, broken fragments of the same types of weapons, especially swords, occur as single finds on dry land. Once again this is a pattern observed across much of north-west Europe where collections of broken fragments are interpreted as founders hoards (Bradley 1998, pp.114–29; Yates and Bradley 2010, pp.405–15). As we saw (above) the collection of fragments found at Isleham have been interpreted this way.

A fourth, and to our mind the most intriguing, pattern is that of concentrations of finds alongside causeways connecting different parts of the island of Ely to each other and to the mainland. Our identification of a hoard associated with the causeway leading from Little Thetford to Barway adds to pre-existing knowledge of deposits associated with causeways, including the hoard at Stuntney, which lies on the route that to this day leads to Ely. Similar collections of metalwork are associated with Bronze and Iron Age causeways elsewhere in Britain and northern Europe. This observation suggests that this may be another widespread pattern of behaviour (Field and Parker-Pearson 2003, pp.179–88).

Our interpretation is that the Fens around the Isle of Ely represented a boundary between the Isle and the outside world, and an important aspect of these carefully selected hoard locations is that they all lie on points where that boundary is transgressed. In addition to those placed directly alongside causeways we note that Wilburton, the site of two hoards, lies on the isthmus that still connects the Isle with the Cambridge mainland, while similarly, the Isleham hoard lies on a route from Ely, via Quanea, that passes via the rivers Lark and Gipping to the east coast and a sea route to the Continent (Malim 2010, p.125).

The anthropologist Mary Douglas (1994) has described how the transgression of boundaries is both powerful and dangerous. As such the Fens, and in particular, crossing places may have been thought of as liminal locations, which would account for the care taken in choosing the places where deposits were made. For example, that of Isleham was only 5m from the fen edge and placed in a boundary ditch separating the domestic cultivated world of the house from the natural and uncultivated world of the fen. Douglas emphasised that the transgression of such boundaries is often circumscribed and should be maintained with ritual action. Although impossible to prove, it might not be too far-fetched to believe that deposition of the hoards was related to a belief in an 'under-world'. Such a belief is widespread among many religions (Bradley 2000, pp.28–32). If such a world was thought to exist, then the peat bogs of the Fens might have been seen as the openings and gaps in the land by which to communicate with it. For the participants deposition represented a final loss, and whether or not those making the deposit believed in the notion of sacrifice to the supernatural or not, the different characteristics of the various types of wetland contributed to the dramatic impact of the act of deposition at Stuntney, Wilburton, Coveney and Barway-Little Thetford: the total disappearance of these objects under the black liminal waters of the Fens.

Conclusion

In the long term, the most fundamental development that takes place in the landscape during the Late Neolithic to Early Iron Age seems to be the formation of a structured cultural landscape (Fokkens 1999). Throughout the Bronze Age, the landscape became increasingly characterised by signs aimed at making the ancestral past tangible. Barrows represented the most important and lasting intentional act of the inhabitants to shape their landscape, but to the inhabitants the ancestral nature of the landscape also came to the fore in other signs of former occupation. In the course of the Bronze Age relocating a farmstead was less a matter of entering areas that were not yet marked by previous phases of habitation, cultivation and burial, and more a matter of returning to named places with historical ancestral meaning.

The deposition of metalwork in both watery and dry places intensified throughout the later Bronze Age, a practice found throughout northern Europe at this time (Bradley 1990). It is suggested that the significance of different types of locations, especially different watery ones, is based on widely shared religious beliefs. Whatever their precise religious motivations may have been, the presence of flowing water in rivers and still water in bogs and meres may have been circumstances that gave significance to deposits (Richards 1996, p.317). The qualities for which different types of water were valued may have been various: purity, pollution, regeneration, fertility (discussed further in the next chapter; Douglas 1994, p.162), and the finer details of this for the prehistoric people of Ely may be inaccessible to archaeologists. What archaeology does show is that different types of watery environment were imbued with different elemental significance. This led to the differential selection of locations for the deposition of single finds and hoards, with particular places in the landscape, especially causeways, being locations of intensive deposition.

CHAPTER 5

THE IRON AGE AND ROMANO-BRITISH OCCUPATION

The numerous natives live in thatched cottages, store their grain in subterranean caches and bake bread from it. They are 'of simple manners' and are content with plain fare. They are ruled by many kings and princes who live in peace with each other. Their troops fight from chariots, as did the Greeks in the Trojan War.

Pytheas the Greek.

INTRODUCTION

The third and final phase of Thomsen's Three Age System is known as the Iron Age, so defined because of the belief that it represented the first use of iron. The Iron Age typically dates from *c*.800 BC to the Roman invasion in AD 43, although there was some overlapping with the Late Bronze Age traditions and in most of the country, outside of the south-east of England, the Iron Age way of life continued long after the Roman invasion, particularly in Scotland (Carroll and Lang 2008, p.95). In many cases, the evidence for Iron Age occupation overlaps with that of the Roman Period and at places such as Watson's Lane, Little Thetford, excavation has shown that Iron Age traditions continued for half a century into the Roman occupation (Evans 2003, p.70), evidence for an insular identity. For this reason, it is best to address both the Iron Age and Romano-British occupation on the Isle in the same chapter.

The Romans' first foray into Britain was under Julius Caesar in 55 and 54 BC, but it wasn't until the Emperor Claudius invaded a century later in AD 43 that they made any significant impact on the local archaeological record (Figure 72). Aerial photography is of little use in identifying these sites due to the nature of the clay subsoil around the Isle, making identification of Iron Age and Roman sites difficult. Until recently, with the work undertaken by the Fenland Survey, it was supposed that there was little or no Roman occupation around the Isle of Ely. As this chapter will show, this is far from true.

THE PERIOD DEFINED

The Iron Age spanned about 800 years and, like all periods described in Thomsen's Three Age System, can be further subdivided into Early (*c*.800–*c*.400 BC), Middle (*c*.400–100 BC) and Late (100 BC–AD 43). The people who lived in Britain at this time have come to be known as Celts and they possessed a distinct cultural and artistic character (Pryor 2010, p.118). In the 1880s a cemetery of cremation burials and grave goods dating to the first century BC was discovered in Kent, which was interpreted as the burial place of immigrants from Belgic Gaul who had fled to Britain in advance of the Roman army. A second site was excavated in the 1920s, and these two cemeteries at Aylesford and Swarling have become the type-sites for that culture in South-East England. Innovations associated with these people included the introduction of coinage, and wheel-thrown pottery with pedestal bases and cordon decoration that had distinct 'zones' of patterning. Fibulae (brooches) and Italic-type bronzes are also known, and the 'Aylesford- Swarling culture' continued beyond the Roman Conquest.

Celtic people were members of distinct tribes, whose names and way of life were written down by classical authors who encountered them. For example, Pytheas the Greek, a trader and merchant who crossed the Channel during the later Iron Age, often credited as the man who discovered Britain, wrote about his journey in the fourth century BC (above). The famous Iceni tribe ruled by Prasutagus, and later by his wife Boudicca, inhabited East Anglia in an area roughly the size of Norfolk and controlled much of the Fenland in the later Iron Age (Figure 73). To their east was the Coreiltauvi who inhabited an area in the East Midlands spanning Lincolnshire, Leicestershire, Nottinghamshire, Derbyshire, Rutland and Northamptonshire and to their south were the territories of the Catuvellauni, occupying Bedfordshire, Hertfordshire and South Cambridgeshire, and the Trinovantes whose territory lay in Essex and Suffolk. The Isle and the people who lived there stood somewhat apart from these larger territories, retaining an individual island identity that marked the people as different. Ely appears to lie just outside the sphere of Iceni control, lying to the west of their main territory and just south of their later expansion into the central Fenland islands around March and 'north of the Aylesford-Swarling border and the limits of the Late Iron Age Romanised gaulish influence' (Evans *et al.* 2007, p.41). As such the inhabitants of the Isle of Ely displayed a unique character reflecting their homogeneity.

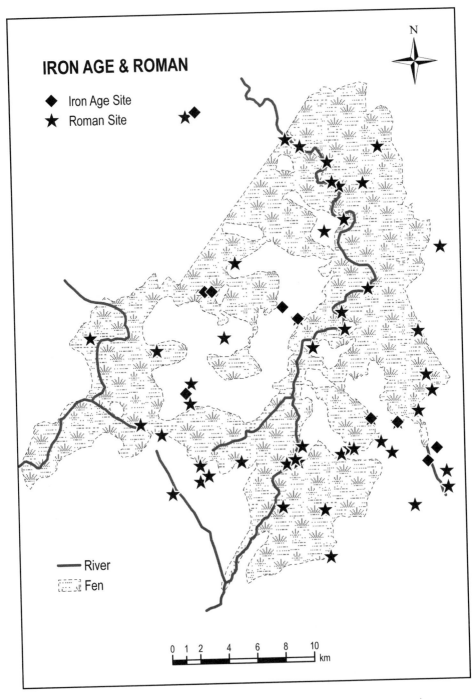

Fig 72. Location map showing the distribution of major Iron Age and Roman sites mentioned in the text in and around the Isle of Ely. Map data © OpenStreetMap contributors, CC BY-SA.

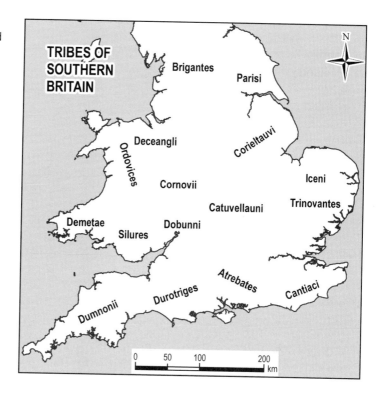

Fig 73. Map of eastern England showing the names and extents of the local tribes during the later Iron Age. Map data © OpenStreetMap contributors, CC BY-SA after Cunliffe 2005, p.87, Fig 6.9.

The Iron Age is famous for its large enclosed hilltop enclosures or 'hillforts', such as Maiden Castle in Dorset, but it would be a myth to assume that all of these were inhabited all of the time. The period saw a great diversity in settlement types within Britain ranging from isolated, single farmsteads, to large nucleated agglomerated settlements with a substantial level of occupation (Carroll and Lang 2008, p.95). Houses were circular buildings, not surprisingly, called roundhouses, made usually from timber with wattle-and-daub walls and thatched conical roofs. We know this from evidence of the postholes which once held the huge timbers (viewed in plan as circular patches of darker earth) that are found in excavations. Experimental archaeology, at places such as Flag Fen, near Peterborough, help to show how these marks are made in the soil and by reconstructing these houses, archaeologists can understand the processes used to construct them, and equally how they weather and rot thus leaving the marks in the ground for the archaeologists to discover (Figure 74). This technique has proved that an extra curvilinear mark in the soil to the outside of the postholes was a drainage gully, caused by the rain running off the roof and onto the soil creating a depression.

Increasingly Iron Age settlements became enclosed within ditches and banks. In the early period this began with palisade enclosures, that is, a fence or wall

Fig 74. Photograph of a reconstructed Iron Age roundhouse at Flag Fen, near Peterborough. Source: the authors.

made from tree trunks set close together. This was followed by hillforts with single defences of a bank and ditch termed 'univallate'. By the mid Iron Age, many had either been abandoned or had their defences rebuilt (Carroll and Lang 2008, p.99). These hillforts, such as the one at Wardy Hill, Coveney (Figure 75), had more than one bank and ditch, and were known as 'bivallate' or 'multivallate' but, by the Late Iron Age, most had been abandoned. The term 'hillfort' implies a defensive fortified settlement, but archaeological evidence shows that they were in fact used for a variety of functions, such as for cattle enclosures, refuges, meeting places, religious centres as well as permanent settlement. The most impressive example of this in the Fens is at Stonea Camp, March.

On the Isle mixed farming was undertaken during the Iron Age with sheep being the dominant species followed by cattle, which were used for pulling ploughs and their hides, meat and dairy products. Pigs were also reared for their meat. The main crops were spelt and emmer wheat and hulled barley, along with flax, oats, beans and peas.

Generally there is little evidence for human burials or other funerary practices for large parts of Britain in the Iron Age. This is because in most parts of Iron Age Britain people were excarnated (left out in the open to decay), and sometimes some of the defleshed bones left behind were buried around the settlements as part of other rituals. More rarely, the complete skeletons of a small number of people are found placed in pits, postholes or in ditches. A rare warrior burial consisting of a male adult accompanied by a spear and two dogs was excavated at Soham (Hall 1996, microfiche).

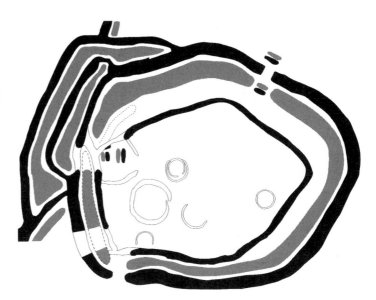

Fig 75. The site plan of Wardy Hill hillfort, Coveney. The plan shows the sequence of ditches (black) and banks (grey) that form the defences of the site, together with the circular ditches that surrounded the internal roundhouses. Source: after Evans and Hodder 2006b, fig 43.

The Roman Period in Britain lasted less than 400 from their invasion in AD 43 until they left in AD 410 to defend Rome from barbarian attacks, but the legacy that they left behind has lasted for sixteen centuries. Credited with the first programme of systematic fen drainage, as can be seen from the various canals that criss-cross the Fens, the Romans brought with them a completely new way of life to the people of Britain. It is possible that these canals were more likely connected to transport than as fen drainage. The Romans built an impressive network of roads across England which are noted for their straight lines. The roads that crossed the Fens took maximum advantage of the higher ground above the fen, which they crossed at the narrowest suitable places (Wilkes and Elrington 1978, p.19), perhaps utilising the foundations of earlier trackways. From Cambridge, the road, known as Akeman Street, ran towards Stretham and then straight across the east end of Grunty Fen towards Ely, heading towards Littleport and then Southery in Norfolk. Parts of the modern road follow the ancient line and parts of the Roman road appear to cross the Car Dyke and interrupt the channel, implying that this dyke may have been out of use by the time the Roman road was built (Wilkes and Elrington, 1978, p.19). The Car Dyke stretches 140km across the western edge of the Fens and William Stukeley in the eighteenth century was the first to postulate that this ditch was once used for transport. A number of excavations since the 1990s strengthen this theory: a Roman boat and cargo of Horningsea pottery was found at Waterbeach, and coal from the Midlands found at sites between Cambridge and the Wash. The Foss Dyke in Lincolnshire, which was a known transport route during the Roman Period, was perhaps connected to the Car Dyke.

Roman towns were laid out on a regular grid pattern within which were houses, outbuildings, wells, courtyards, ovens, and pits. Most buildings were timber framed with wattle-and-daub walls, with a smaller number of stone and concrete structures. The absence of these regular features on the Isle suggests continuity of settlements between the Late Iron Age and the Roman Period.

THE EARLY IRON AGE OCCUPATION ON THE ISLE

Since Hill wrote in the late 1990s (Hill 2000) that the Early Iron Age (*c*.800 BC-300 BC) on the Isle of Ely is poorly understood, but that there was obvious continuity between the Late Bronze Age and Early Iron Age in terms of pottery, settlement and aspects of domestic life; new excavations have deepened our understanding of the period. The end of the use and ritual deposition of bronze swords and other objects and an increase in the use of decorated pottery thus marked the beginning of the Iron Age (Figure 76). There have been many individual finds of pottery dating to the early Iron Age but with very few settlements excavated on a large scale it is difficult to determine exactly what the way of life would have been like (Hill 2000, p.19). The evidence available, from excavations at places such as at Fordham and more recently at West Fen Road, Ely, point towards a pattern of Late Bronze Age/Early Iron Age groups of individual, unenclosed farmsteads within field systems, which were unevenly spaced across Cambridgeshire. Many sites were used seasonally with little evidence of permanent settlement, perhaps to herd livestock, to collect raw materials, or carry out rituals. This period saw the earliest evidence in Britain for salt making at places such as at Old Croft River, Littleport, and this activity could well have been undertaken on a seasonal basis (Hill 2000, p.19).

The dominant type of farming in the area was mixed (above) as evidenced by 'Celtic fields', which are the traces of prehistoric agricultural field systems, and by floral and faunal analyses at sites revealing the cultivation of hulled barley, emmer and spelt wheat, and an emphasis on rearing sheep and cattle (Evans *et al.* 2007). Excavations have also revealed, at West Fen Road, the presence of loom weights, showing that weaving was becoming a common activity.

Typically the Early Iron Age in Britain saw the emergence of large enclosed sites or hillforts, but there is no conclusive evidence that there were any dating to this period on the Isle with places such as Wardy Hill, Coveney, coming into being in the Middle Iron Age. This suggests that the Isle resisted the cultural changes associated with the Early Iron Age. Indeed no formal burials are known from the Isle dating to this early period. Instead, as can been seen at Haddenham, parts of bodies would occasionally be ritually placed around

Fig 76. An Iron Age decorated pot found at Wardy Hill during the excavation of the hillfort. Source: after Evans 2003, fig 80.

settlements, along with animal sacrifices, pots and other objects, practices that continued to the Roman Conquest.

THE LATE IRON AGE AND ROMANO-BRITISH OCCUPATION

Unlike the Early Iron Age, the understanding of which is still in its infancy, the later Iron Age occupation on the Isle is well known through excavation at sites such as Haddenham, Wardy Hill and recent excavations in Ely itself. The later Iron Age (c.300 BC–AD 43) is traditionally divided into the Middle and Late Iron Age. From around 300 BC there is evidence of an increased number of sites, including large enclosures or hillforts, along with an increased number of finds, and a greater number of metal objects and coins being found in the landscape. Evidence for an increase in the population is seen through permanent settlement spreading into the Fens where occupation had not been seen before.

There are two broad patterns of settlement that can be seen in the later half of the Iron Age on the Isle: single, enclosed farmsteads; and loose spreads of unenclosed villages and other structures within extensive ditched field systems. Larger villages are found in river valleys and on some fen islands with relatively large groups of houses commonly situated inside complex systems of fields and trackways, as at West Fen Road (Mortimer *et al.* 2005). Contrasting with this are enclosed single farms which, as has been noted elsewhere (Hill 2000), appear to be the feature of the new settlements, as at Haddenham, which will be discussed later. Here farming depended on mixed agriculture with most settlements becoming self-sufficient with food, pottery, wood and iron working, although there is evidence to suggest settlements began to concentrate on cattle, sheep and grain and evidence for the exchange of materials and objects is more common.

After the invasion, during Hadrian's reign (AD 117–138), followed a time of expansion and material prosperity. This is reflected in an increase in both the density and extent of settlement on the Isle, along with associated droves and waterways, which reached a peak during the second half of the century, perhaps as a result of the Fenlands belonging to an imperial estate (Wilkes and Elrington 1978, p.3). A number of villa estates known from around the Isle – for example, at Isleham and Stretham, indicate that not all of the Fens were under imperial rule. Much of their income came from animal husbandry, utilising the rich and extensive pastureland along the river valleys, with summer grazing on the Fens, and arable farming where they could utilise the impressive transport system to export bulk commodities (Malim 2005, p.191).

Freshwater flooding greatly affected the pattern of settlement in the Fens and fen margins (Wilkes and Elrington 1978, p.33) during this period with Roman settlements on fen edges displaying gaps in the pottery sequence, evidence that occupation was interrupted between c.AD 230–c.270, while settlements occupied throughout the third century lie further from the edge of the peat. Flooding at the fen margin is the most likely cause of abandonment of settlements in the late fourth century.

NATURE OF THE LATER IRON AGE AND ROMAN SETTLEMENT

Our review of the settlement evidence begins with perhaps the most striking of the sites Wardy Hill, Coveney. This consisted of a large enclosure approximately 8,000m^2 in area situated on a spur of Ampthill Clay jutting into the peat fen. Rising only 6–10m above sea level, it commanded the northern approach to the Coveney basin. Its strategic location was chosen as the site of a defended Iron Age enclosure, arguably a fort positioned to command a causeway crossing the Cove (Evans 2003). The interior revealed a series of defences that radiated off from the western landward aspect of the double-circuit of the main enclosure. These then joined up with an early dyke-like system, possibly dating to the Early Iron Age. Evans (2003) notes that the position of the site implies that it controlled access to a causeway running across the marsh between Coveney and Ely. To support this theory a major later Iron Age settlement has been discovered on the supposed far shore of the causeway at West Fen Road, Ely, and will be discussed later. Excavations showed that the interior of Wardy Hill was clearly settled with evidence of two successive large roundhouses each with additional structures (Figure 75). Metalworking was undertaken here and, on the whole, the evidence would suggest a seat of power strategically situated to control the marsh-landscape access (Evans 2003). There is another potential Iron Age site at the fen edge near Willingham (Evans 2000, p.23). No excavations have taken place at Belsar's Hill, which commands the Aldreth causeway to Ely, but pottery from this period has recently been recovered from its eroded ramparts, which strengthens the theory that they were positioned to defend the causeways.

The landscape around Wardy Hill was extremely open with few trees. Pollen analysis revealed that emmer wheat, oats, spelt, barley and bread wheat were all found on site. Sheep, cattle and pig bones were also present, and the dominance of sheep is typical on Iron Age sites. It has been suggested that between twelve and fifteen family groups could have been supported here based on an estimated flock of 600 sheep, those numbers utilising the 65ha of winter grazing and 50ha of summertime pasture provided by the fen-edge meadow within the 300m radius along the north and eastern side of the site. That would mean that the Wardy Hill environs could have supported a population of approximately twenty-one to forty-three people, equivalent of two or three times the average population of 'typical' domestic compounds of the period (Evans 2003, p.144).

In the 1920s a Roman cavalry helmet was discovered in the Witcham Gravel pits about 3km from Coveney, along the causeway (Figure 77). The helmet, which can now be seen in the British Museum (a replica of which is at Ely Museum), dates to the first century AD. Its discovery indicates that there was some form of military presence on the Isle, and fieldwork carried out on the former Witchford Aerodrome revealed late Roman ditches that may attest to this, perhaps to monitor the imperial estate or as a means to control the society after the Boudican rebellion. The helmet's survival may be attributable to the cult practices during the Iron Age, which will be discussed below.

Approximately 8km from Coveney is an interesting and complex structure at Snow's Hill Farm, Haddenham. Excavation revealed a roughly square ditched enclosure, dated to the later Iron Age, which was built on top of an Early Bronze Age round barrow. Inside the structure, known as HAD III, large numbers of deliberately deposited artefacts were found by archaeologists in the ditches leading to an interpretation of the site as a two-phased Romano-British shrine (Figure 78; Evans and Hodder 2006b). Within the square enclosure archaeologists revealed evidence for the construction and rebuilding of seven roundhouses within the last two centuries of the first millennium BC and the first century AD. A roundhouse 9m in diameter was built directly over an earlier building and it was possible to see some of the internal structures. It is from such evidence that reconstructions such as that at Flag Fen can be

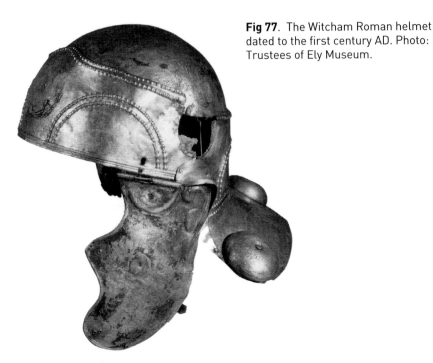

Fig 77. The Witcham Roman helmet dated to the first century AD. Photo: Trustees of Ely Museum.

made. The discovery of quern stones associated with the houses points towards this being a site of permanent settlement. Evidence from the excavations show that the people living here were relatively prosperous, rearing sheep and practising arable cultivation on the Delphs, where ardmarks have been found on the ground surface. Farming of cereal crops was supplemented with food taken from the wild, which could be obtained within a 1-5km radius of the enclosure, including birds' eggs collected in the spring, beaver (for their pelts) trapped in the autumn and winter, and eating wild birds such as pelican, hunted spring to early autumn (Evans and Hodder 2006b, p.276).

Evans and Hodder (2006b) note that butchery, plucking and skinning of the animals took place at the site and because the carcasses of the beaver and larger birds stayed on site, it is assumed that their pelts and feathers were exported. Evidence to support the theory comes from elsewhere, for example in Aylesford-Swarling where bear paws and the traces of pelts have been found in burials (Hill *et al.* 1999). Up to fifty percent of the pots found on the site were non-local, potentially imported containing food or drink, having been traded in exchange for the pelts. In addition, most of the personal ornaments were also imported and these included jet, shale beads and bracelets, an iron dagger and a billhook (Evans and Hodder 2006b, p.277).

Roughly 8km away from Haddenham lies Watson's Lane, Little Thetford. This site lies on the Kimmeridge and Boulder Clays, on a narrow peninsula of high ground *c*.6m OD that extends into the floodplain of the River Great Ouse south-east of Ely. Excavations revealed that it was densely occupied in the later Iron Age and Roman Period although no definite Romano-British buildings were found (Lucas and Hinman 1996, Lucas 1998, Evans *et al.* 2007). Portions of eight later Iron Age round buildings were excavated along with later Roman components including a tile kiln and cemetery (Figure 79). The lack of first-century AD pottery with most pottery found dating to the second and third centuries AD suggested an Iron Age tradition continuing for fifty years into the Roman Period (Evans *et al.* 2007, p.70). A number of enclosures relating to industrial activity were discovered along with finds of slag, which indicated copper alloy was worked on site. The tile kiln debris, including unusual tile types: structural *lydions, pedales* and *sequipedales* and roof tile *tegulate* and *imbrices*, indicated the work of a skilled craftsman who served high-status clients elsewhere (Evans *et al.* 2007, p.71). Another interesting find were paw impressions from a dog in some of the tiles (Figure 80). In the fourth century AD, the site changed in character with a reduction in the deposition of pottery and the kiln being abandoned. A square enclosure dating to this period could

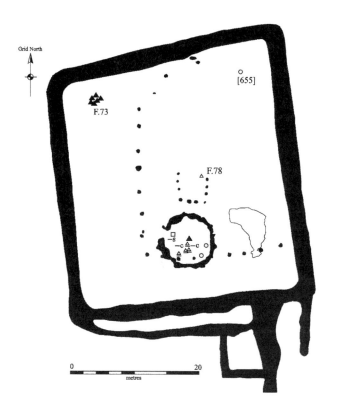

Sheep

▲ Skeleton
△ Head
⌂ Head and Hooves
−s Hooves

Pig

■ Skeleton
□ Head

Cattle

○ Head
⊝ Head and Hooves
−c Hooves

Fig 78. The ditched enclosure HAD III built over an Early Bronze Age barrow at Haddenham. The structure was interpreted as a Romano-British shrine based on its shape and the large number of votive objects found by archaeologists. Source: after Evans and Hodder 2006b.

have been a shrine, but the only material evidence here was fourth-century pottery. Three inhumation burials were discovered of two adult males and a female: none were buried with grave goods and one male had been decapitated with his head placed between his legs (Evans *et al.* 2007, p.71).

Located on the fen edge 1.5km from the cathedral at 2–4m above sea level is Hurst Lane near Little Downham, which was another major settlement (Evans and Knight 2000). Excavations of 2.85ha revealed thirty-five later Iron Age roundhouses within and around compounds, overlain by an early Roman field or paddock system making it one of the 'most dense Iron Age sites in the region' (Evans *et al.* 2007, p.41). The site origins lay in the Middle Iron Age with some third- or even fourth-century BC components. It began as an open settlement with a series of interconnecting ditched compounds, with those

Fig 79. The Roman tile kiln excavated at Watson's Lane, Little Thetford. Photo: Trustees of Ely Museum.

Fig 80. One of the tiles from the tile kiln at Watson's Lane, Little Thetford was found with the impression of a dog's paw in it. The tile can be seen in Ely Museum. Photo: Trustees of Ely Museum.

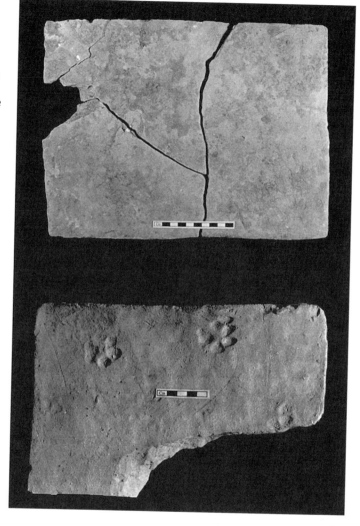

of the main southern cluster conjoining a large horse-shoe-plan enclosure, similar to that of Wardy Hill. Dating to the first and early second century AD, the site's subsequent usage in the Romano-British Period saw the laying out of a rectilinear field system with a network of smaller paddocks within its south-east part, showing clear evidence of Iron Age/Roman continuity. The alignments of a number of the latter boundaries were directly determined by the paddock system of the earlier phase, and Iron Age roundhouse occupation actually seems to have continued until early Flavian times following the discovery of a first-century AD fibula (brooch) (Evans 2003, p.248). A first-century BC Iron Age coin, known as a Class II potin, was important as it was one of the few instances when a coin of this type has been found in a settlement context (Evans 2003, p.248).

Human remains were discovered from twelve contexts at Hurst Lane. Seven were without firm attribution, but three could be dated to the Iron Age and two to the Roman Period. One crouched adult and two infant inhumations were discovered from the unphased sample and one calvarium (dome of the skull) dating to the Iron Age was found, which showed signs of serious trauma. A blow to the back of the head probably split the skull, and there were additional cuts that crossed the fracture line. A further two partial skulls were recovered, and all three displayed an unusual, highly polished surface, one both internally and externally (Evans *et al.* 2007, p.66). This deliberate manipulation of the skulls will be discussed in depth below.

Excavations in Ely itself as a result of building work have revealed evidence for further levels of settlement not previously thought to have existed on the Isle. Much of the city lies on top of any potential prehistoric sites, but traces of Iron Age occupation have been exposed in the city in the area of the cathedral and market (Hunter 1992a and b; Evans *et al.* 2007) as well as further out at West Fen Road, Prickwillow Road and Trinity Lands, which all point to major Iron Age settlements that continued into Roman times.

The West Fen Road excavations revealed a multi-period site, which during the later Iron Age was a substantial settlement of around thirty roundhouses that continued well into the Medieval Period, constituting the single largest excavation of Iron Age roundhouses from the Fens until excavations at Hurst Lane (Gibson 1996; Malim 2005, p.88). The Anglo-Saxon occupation of this site will be discussed below in Chapter 6. The site is located 0.5km south-east of Hurst Lane and 1km from the cathedral on the north-west margin of the Isle of Ely proper, 6m above sea level on the Kimmeridge Clay. Beginning as open settlement, the intercutting of features shows several phases of activity with the origins in the Early Iron Age, although pottery evidence suggests occupation was likely to be in the second and first centuries BC rather than earlier (Figure 81). It has been suggested that the site's location was determined by the route of a causeway heading either north to Downham, or west to Coveney (Mortimer 2000, Regan 2001a, Mudd and Webster 2011). Since Wardy Hill, Coveney, may have been chosen as a site to defend one end of this causeway, the site at West Fen Road may have been chosen to defend this shore, continuing in existence into the Roman Period and beyond (Figure 82).

In the later Iron Age roundhouses were within concentric pairs of enclosures. The 150 pottery vessels recovered suggest occupation by ten families, or perhaps just two or three families at a time over a period of fifty years (Mudd and Webster 2011, p.65). The bulk of the pottery excavated from ditches suggesting that it was domestic, thrown in as part of routine disposal rather than having any ritual connotations (Mudd and Webster 2011, p.64). Pottery was limited in form and predominantly plain and handmade. More intriguing was the discovery of an Iron Age horse burial (Figure 83). Evidence of furnace or lining slags indicated that iron smelting was undertaken on or near the

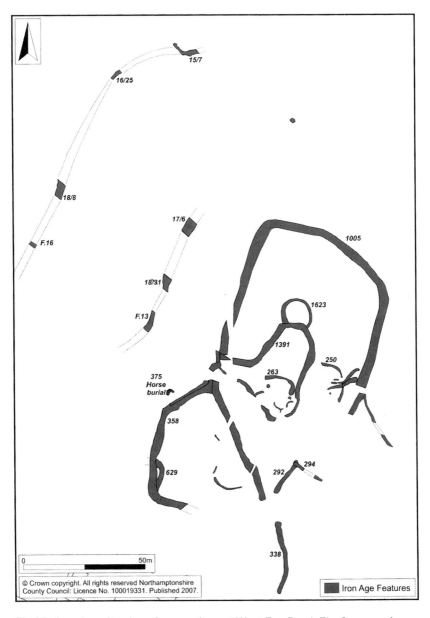

Fig 81. Iron Age site plan of excavations at West Fen Road, Ely. Source: after Mudd and Webster, 2011, fig 2.3.

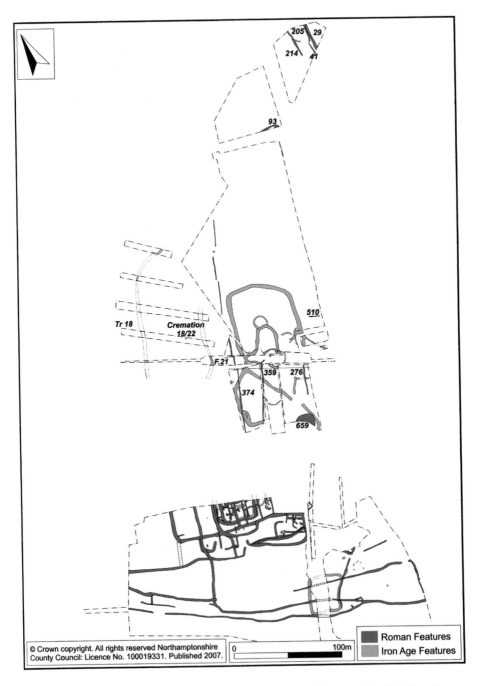

0   100m

Roman Features
Iron Age Features

Fig 82. Roman features excavated at West Fen Road, Ely. Source: after Mudd and Webster, 2011, fig 3.1.

site, but no furnaces or hearths were discovered. Flora and faunal analysis showed that there was a lot of open, damp pasture and many drainage ditches, pools or ponds which supported large numbers of amphibians. Emmer, spelt, bread-type wheat and hulled barley were grown on the local damp soils and also cattle, sheep/goats, pigs and horses were reared. Unlike at Haddenham, the resources of the local natural environment were not exploited and there was no evidence of fish bones, otter or beaver (Mudd and Webster 2011, p.106). This combined with the fact that the pottery was limited in its range and forms, when there was an increasing variety in the ceramic vessels needed to accommodate the adoption of a more sophisticated Roman way of cooking, all suggests that this community were insular and with limited access to trade and imported wares.

Trinity Lands lies only 400m south of the West Fen Road site and was the location of another later Iron Age and Early Roman site over 1ha in size (Masser and Evans 1999). The proximity of Trinity Lands to West Fen Road suggests that both belonged to a single large settlement. Two potential roundhouses were discovered along with evidence for a ditched paddock system. Judging from the pottery discovered, the site was not particularly distinguished. The Roman pottery dated to the first century AD, the period of the immediate aftermath of the Conquest (Evans *et al.* 2007, p.69), and there was a limited range and form of pieces which comprised locally produced vessels. Whilst sheep, goats and cattle were found in relatively equal measures in the Iron Age levels, by the Roman Period cattle had become the principle domesticate. In addition

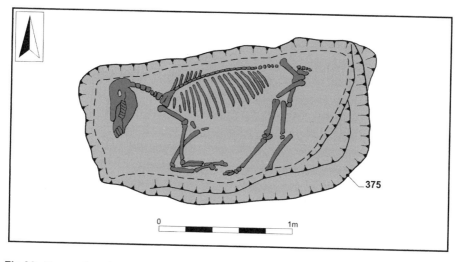

Fig 83. Excavation plan of an Iron Age horse burial excavated at West Fen Road, Ely. Source: after Mudd and Webster 2011, fig 2.17.

pig, dog and bird bones were identified from the Iron Age contexts, but were completely absent from the Roman. A highly polished fragment of human skull dating to the Iron Age was also noted from this site.

Excavations at Prickwillow Road north-east of the city and 1km from the cathedral revealed part of a rural settlement, with evidence of one house gully within a larger sub-circular enclosure. Evidence pointed towards this settlement being intermittently occupied from the fifth to the third century BC and from this context two inhumations were discovered along with the partial remains of a skull. From the third century AD onwards, the site was continuously occupied into the late fourth century. Roman paddocks and a cemetery containing five cremations and fifteen inhumations all dating to the third and fourth centuries AD were excavated. Artefacts of Roman date are also known from Prickwillow where a bronze skillet (saucepan) dated to the second century AD was found. The skillet is interesting as it has on it the maker's name, Boduogenus (Figure 84).

Less than 3km south-east of Ely lies the village of Stuntney. The name is thought to derive from Anglo-Saxon words meaning 'the steep island' and it has been connected to Ely via a causeway since Bronze Age times. Evidence for Roman docks were discovered here in the 1950s and a short distance away, on Thorney Hill, a Roman coffin was discovered in 1981 when a farmer's plough struck and broke the coffin lid (Taylor 1984, p.15). Inside was the skeleton of an adult male, approximately 1.75m (5ft 9in) tall (Figure 85). The muscle attachments to his right collar bone were bigger than those on the left

Fig 84. Bronze skillet of the second century AD found at Prickwillow. Source: Wilkes and Elrington 1978, p.78, pl. XIIc.

Fig 85. The excavation of a Roman coffin at Thorney Hill in 1981. The coffin was found when a farmer's plough struck the coffin breaking the lid. Inside was the skeleton of a man approximately 1.75 m (5ft 9in) tall. Photo: Trustees of Ely Museum.

suggesting that he was right handed. The coffin was aligned east-west and had been buried on a local high point, which sloped down to an ancient tributary of the River Ouse. It contained no grave goods, apart from two cattle tarsal bones. The coffin resembles modern coffins and was unusual for the Roman Period, when most were simple rectangular boxes. Of the twenty further examples known from Cambridgeshire, only two are similar to the one found at Stuntney (Taylor 1984). The coffin was made of Barnack stone, quarried in Peterborough, 92km away, and the Romans were the first to utilise this stone, famous for its use in Ely and Peterborough cathedrals. It continued to be quarried well into medieval times.

To date no complete Roman villas have been excavated in Cambridgeshire (Wilkes and Elrington 1978, p.43), but a small number of incomplete examples are known from around the Isle, identified through the many limestone tesserae from destroyed mosaics, which are often the sole trace of once high-status buildings. A mosaic of red and grey tesserae is known from the villa at The Temple, Isleham, along with debris of painted plaster and roof and box tiles. Biggin Farm, Fordham, revealed second- to fourth-century pottery along with wall plaster and roof and flue tiles which appeared to indicate a villa, albeit small and well designed (Wilkes and Elrington 1978, p.44). It may be that the tile kiln in Little Thetford was supplying the tiles for these villas.

RITUAL AND BELIEF ON THE ISLE

It has long been known from Classical writers, such as Herodotus, in the fifth century BC, and Strabo, Diodorus and Livy from the first centuries BC/AD that it was a battle custom to remove the head of a vanquished foe and to return from the battlefield with that head suspended from the horse's bridle. The head would then be nailed upon the entrance to their house as a badge of glory. In some instances the head would be embalmed with cedar oil and displayed to strangers, or turned into a vessel from which the victors could drink (Green 2001, p.95). Traditionally, scholars have postulated the importance of head hunting and the importance of the severed head amongst Celtic customs in relation to superstition and fertility (Laing, 1981; Powell, 1958), while Ralph (2007) has suggested there was no such religious or spiritual motivation for taking the heads: it was simply a by-product of warfare, 'a secular activity connected with social display and insulting one's enemies' (Ralph 2007, p.305). It would be easy to think that these written documents were merely propaganda to show how uncivilised the Celtic people were. However, certainly in parts of France there is strong evidence that supports these Classical writings. At Entremont there is a relief carving of a mounted warrior with a severed head dangling from the bridle and this is similar to a fragment of painted pottery found in the Auvergne that also depicts a warrior on horseback with a head suspended from its bridle (Green 2001, p.97). Likewise, there are examples of Iron Age coins, which depict a mounted warrior displaying the severed head of his vanquished foe (Figure 86); very similar is a Roman tombstone discovered in Lancaster in 2005, uniquely depicting a Roman cavalryman on horseback brandishing the head of a cowering Briton in his sword hand (Bull 2008).

At Gournay-Sur-Aronde, France, the enclosure ditch contained 3,000 animal bones along with 2,000 broken weapons while human remains of skull fragments, teeth and vertebrae were found almost exclusively in a ditch south of the entrance. Examination of the cervical vertebrae has revealed that decapitation was undertaken by a series of blows struck from different directions using both a knife and a heavier instrument and the crania were removed after death (Ralph 2007, p.306). In the Lower Rhone Valley, a number of skeletal and iconographic images made reference to the warrior and the severed head. Crania were discovered there embedded with iron nails, and shrines dating to the mid-second to mid-first century BC were found containing life-sized stone sculptures of male warriors, many holding heads (Ralph 2007, p.306). Some Iron Age coins from Breton and Burgundy are depicted with a warrior or priest brandishing a severed head or a group of severed heads joined together with chain or cord (Green 2001, p.101).

Closer to home, at All Cannings Cross, Wiltshire, the dispersed remains of thirty-two skull fragments in a midden deposit suggests evidence for head hunting, while at Danebury disused corn-pits contained the heads of people and horses. Eight of the pits contained complete or partial skulls of six men, one woman and a child. A skull fragment from a hillfort in Caithness, Scotland, was discovered with three drill holes suggesting that it had been suspended. The entrance to certain hillforts in Yorkshire and Worcestershire were festooned with severed heads, which had subsequently fallen into the ditch below (Green 2001, p.104).

The archaeological record from the Isle fits with this story of pagan practices. Excavations at Stonea Camp, March, have revealed a series of human skulls found in its ditches; excavations at West Fen Road, Ely, revealed three fragments of human skull from the enclosure ditches; and eight craniums are known from the Ashwell site to the south of West Fen Road (Evans *et al.* 2007, p.73, Mortimer *et al.* 2005, p.20). Hurst Lane, Wardy Hill, Trinity Lands and Prickwillow Road all bore evidence to imply a special meaning was placed onto the skull. Interestingly Hurst Lane revealed one instance of a traumatic injury and three fragments of cranium with a polished appearance that suggest manipulation of the remains after death. Evans *et al.* (2007) suggest that this evidence should be interpreted as being the result of excarnation, with the 'prevalence of skull elements of interest, possibly reflecting a cult peculiar to the Ely region' (Evans *et al.* 2007, p.72). This focus on the head is reinforced by evidence from sites elsewhere in Britain. Three Roman parade helmets were found in a pit at the Roman military site of Newstead, Scotland, close to which was another pit containing a skull along with the skulls of horses and cattle. It has been suggested that this demonstrates some form of head-cult (Green 2001, p.104). If this is correct the excavation of the Witcham Roman cavalry helmet is significant being found in a gravel pit just a short distance from Wardy Hill (above). It would suggest that the Isle had adopted these widespread practices and adapted them for their own use, establishing a cult centre on the Isle in the Iron Age well before the arrival of Christianity. Indeed the fact that the Isle was an established cult centre may be one of the reasons that it made it attractive to Etheldreda as a holy place suitable for her monastery, founded in the seventh century AD.

The archaeological evidence for Roman religion on the Isle represents veneration of many deities including a mixture of the Classical gods of the Capitoline Triad (Jupiter, Juno and Minerva) along with Celtic deities and even occurrences of the Imperial cult (Figure 87, Taylor 2000, p.18). Liminality was an important characteristic of Roman and prehistoric sacred sites and it is therefore not surprising that temples and shrines can be found in parts of the Fens and on the fen edge. In many cases these sites are multi-period, strengthening the view of continuity from one period to the next.

Fig 87. Carved stone head of a female Roman deity. Photo: Trustees of Ely Museum.

There is evidence from all around the Isle of religious activity, from large temples in towns, such as at Stonea, to small shines on hilltops, such as at Haddenham. A feature of pagan, Roman and Christian religions, is a close association with water. Votive offerings placed into rivers are commonly found by farmers and metal detectorists, such as at Sutton where a bronze statuette of Hercules was found in the nineteenth century (Heichelheim 1937, p.73), all suggesting small-scale sacrifice in areas of religious association (Taylor 2000, p.35).

Temples and shrines would have been like geographical honeypots: the focal point for the local community, and a place of pilgrimage for people from further afield, which would have had a significant economic impact on the surrounding communities, where over time they could acquire great wealth and landholdings (Malim 2006, p.193). Excavations reveal that typically in plan, the temples were square or rectangular, with a veranda surrounding a *cella* (an internal room) where votive gifts or sacrificial offerings would be made, and the whole was contained within a larger compound (Taylor 2000, p.35). Often the Roman foundations date to the second century AD and many seem to represent a continuation of earlier traditions (Malim 2005, p.194).

The Roman shrine at Upper Delphs, Haddenham (above) dates to the second century AD. The site was an earthwork until 1953 and the rectangular enclosures were visible as banks with ditches on the outside. Excavations revealed that there were two phases of the shrine. Originally the shrine was octagonal with masonry foundations. It was surrounded by a rectangular ditch, located on top of a Bronze Age barrow, the only definitive example known of a formal Roman shrine on top of a Bronze Age barrow (Beech 2006, p.409). It was remodeled as a square timber shrine some time in the third century and was abandoned as a result of flooding in the later fourth century. The entrance to the shrine was positioned north-east as a track flanked by ditches and in the floor of the octagon there were many placed depositions of sheep mandibles and hooves (Wilkes and Elrington 1978).

At some sites, Beech notes that there is the potential to associate certain animal remains to a particular cult (Beech 2006, p.388). This seems to be the case on the Isle as at Haddenham there were several complete sheep sacrifices,

Fig 88. A bronze votive model of a ram found
at Barway by Phillip Randall while metal
detecting. Source: the authors.

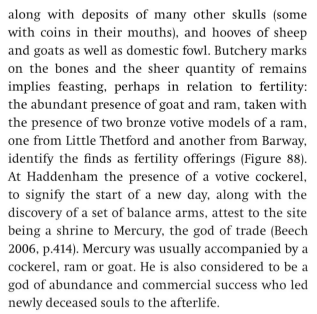

along with deposits of many other skulls (some
with coins in their mouths), and hooves of sheep
and goats as well as domestic fowl. Butchery marks
on the bones and the sheer quantity of remains
implies feasting, perhaps in relation to fertility:
the abundant presence of goat and ram, taken with
the presence of two bronze votive models of a ram,
one from Little Thetford and another from Barway,
identify the finds as fertility offerings (Figure 88).
At Haddenham the presence of a votive cockerel,
to signify the start of a new day, along with the
discovery of a set of balance arms, attest to the site
being a shrine to Mercury, the god of trade (Beech
2006, p.414). Mercury was usually accompanied by a
cockerel, ram or goat. He is also considered to be a
god of abundance and commercial success who led
newly deceased souls to the afterlife.

A metal baton found at Haddenham, and near identical ones found as part
of the Willingham hoard, which depicted the bust of Antonius Pius atop a
mace of Hercules, suggest the presence of the imperial religion on the Isle
(Beech 2006, p.417). If this was the case, it would mean that the Roman Fens
were managed as an imperial estate. Religion was used by the Empire as a
tool to control the population, and at certain 'times in the ritual calendar
the hoard's cult objects and its attendant priests (parading their batons of
office) may have migrated between the festivities of neighbouring shrines'
(Beech 2006, p.417). The local populace would be enthralled and Beech cleverly
suggests that 'under the (sculpted) gaze of the emperor the future was foretold,
and through the control of the calendar, "time" was managed and ritualized'
(Beech 2006, p.417). This activity didn't just happen randomly; it took place
within the backdrop of local meaning.

Generally votive deposits fall into three categories. First, ordinary items
such as coins, brooches (Colour plate 9) and rings; secondly curiosities, such
as Neolithic axes (Taylor 2000, p.18); and thirdly items made specially as votive
artefacts. These included miniatures (commonly axes), feather-shaped plaques
of bronze, silver or gold, certain forms of brooches, 'horse and rider' forms,
and along with many small bronze figurines, attest the presence of shrines on

the Isle. The statuette of Hercules found in Sutton represents the young divine hero standing naked, with the skin of the Nemean lion as a head-dress. His upraised right hand holds his club, while the left holds his cloak. The same hero appears in miniature statuette from Ely, this time older and bearded, standing naked with the lion skin draped over his left forearm. His club rests in his left hand against the upper arm with the right stretched out downwards (Figure 89). Two statuettes of Venus are also known from Ely: one depicts the goddess as a tall and thin young woman naked and executed in a very provincial style. Her anatomical features, especially her face, are represented superficially. Her breasts are small and her left hand covers her pubic region whilst her right hangs down by her side slightly forward. The band binding the front of the hair is represented with simple incised decoration. Another miniature statuette from Ely represents a walking god wearing a double-folded mantle with shoulder-length hair. The left hand carries a torch which rests on the shoulder whilst in the right the god carries a flagon by the side (Wilkes and Elrington 1978, p.82). Some of these figurines, including a votive axe and altar, can be seen in Ely Museum and represent the wealth of Romano-British religion being practised on the Isle.

As shown above, the Isle of Ely's importance as a cult centre began in the Iron Age, but towards the end of the Roman Period this cult focus moved in a different direction. In AD 313 Christianity was legitimised within the Empire

and with the demise of the imperial system in Britain, Church leadership began to take over from the Roman civil administration (Malim 2005, p.221). It may have been a combination of this and other factors such as flooding that resulted in the end of use for the shrine at Haddenham.

A number of fourth-century AD Christian objects have been found on and around the Isle: a pewter bowl with Chi-Rho from Ely; a pewter jug from Quanea; lead baptismal vats and pewter plates from two locations in Willingham, the sites of important Romano-Celtic temples; and a Christian hoard dating to the fourth century discovered in Sutton

Fig 89. Bronze statuette of Hercules standing naked with a lion skin draped over his arm. Photo: Trustees of Ely Museum.

Fig 90. Pewter tazza from Sutton with Christian symbols. Photo: Wilkes and Elrington 1978, pp.83 and 86, pl. XII A and B.

in 1898. This contained six large platters, a bowl and a pewter tazza in the shape of an eight-pointed star (Figure 90). The flange was decorated with Chi-Rho symbols flanked by the Greek letters alpha and omega, two peahens, a peacock, an owl and mermaids. Beneath the flange was an inscription: SUP...T...EPICL Q 'Supectili epi (scopi) clerique', which may translate as, *a furnishing or utensil belonging to the Bishop and clergy*. Clarke (1931) notes that it has had many diverse translations but, if correct, this is the first known reference in Roman Britain to a Bishop and his clerical staff (Frend 2000, p.45) and the symbols could pertain to regeneration and baptism. If so, all the vessels in the hoard may have had liturgical functions and the tazza may have been used as a portable font (Wilkes and Elrington 1978, p.86).

Other pewter items found on the extinct river course of the Lark in Isleham included two jugs, three bowls, two tazze, one dish, a pedestalled bowl, and many indented beakers. It has been suggested that these may have been a cargo either lost or thrown overboard (Wilkes and Elrington 1978, p.83) and it is possible that these were lost en route to a Christian centre on the Isle. The locations of Christian centres in Roman Britain are uncertain but we know that Restitius, the fourth-century Bishop of London, along with the Bishop of Lincoln and York all attended the Council of Arles in modern France (Roman Gaul) in AD 314 and there is a coin from the Arles mint in Ely Museum of slightly later date suggesting continued contact with this region, perhaps religious in nature.

Malim (2005) suggests that many centres of early Anglo-Saxon monasticism are also places of importance in late Roman Christianity. He notes that the co-location of minsters with seats of royal or aristocratic power indicates continuity in the basic division of landholding carried through from the end of the Roman rule until the sixth century, and establishes potential links between the 'emerging Anglo-Saxon elite and their Romano-British ancestors' (Malim 2005, p.240). Archaeological evidence on or around the Isle supports this theory of transition: a Romano-Celtic altar was found buried in a pit at a villa at Great Wilbraham; a baptismal vat was excavated at Earith Road, Willingham, in addition to the important hoard from Sutton (above). These locations are all places on the Isle with evidence for early Anglo-Saxon occupation, which points to a *longue durée* of religious belief and practice from its Romano-Celtic origins into early medieval Christian worship (Malim 2005, p.223).

DISCUSSION

Prior to 1990, little systematic excavation had been undertaken on the Isle and the assumption was that sites were not found regularly spaced, which would be expected if they represented territorial centres. Instead, it appeared that they were strategically sited to command routes through the landscape, their origins then related to changes in the socio-political environment of the later Iron Age in the region (Evans 2000). The place names themselves suggested their function, for example Wardy Hill, *Wardeye*, an 'island where there is a look-out' (Reaney 1943, pp.230–31). While that does make sense, through the Fenland Survey and more systematic excavation, it is now found that at least on the eastern half of the Isle, the Iron Age and Romano-British settlement can be found roughly every 500m to 1,500m (Evans *et al.* 2007, p.74). An interesting observation is that it is apparent that all the enclosures on the Isle seem to date to the Middle or later Iron Age in contrast to the earlier Iron Age origins of the classic hillforts (Evans 2000, Hill 2000).

The economic basis of later Iron Age society was primarily derived from agricultural produce, in particular sheep and cattle, but the cultivation of cereal crops was also a significant and important activity. Celtic beer was highly valued in the Roman world, and the arable land of East Anglia would have produced grain not only for bread but also for making beer. Granaries and storage pits are abundant features on Iron Age settlement sites, as are droves and enclosures for coralling stock (Malim 2006, p.40). By the Roman Period, certainly parts of the Fens were used as an imperial estate and evidence to support this comes from Horningsea Ware found on Hadrian's Wall (Malim 2005, p.179). Horningsea Ware was a coarse-ware pottery made in the Cam valley and used for storage. Its discovery at Hadrian's Wall suggests it was used to contain and transport grain from the Fens to the garrisons stationed in the

North of England, perhaps via the Car Dyke and other Fenland waterways and by the network of roads.

In saying that, the number of villa estates discovered on the Isle would suggest that these were not part of the imperial estate, but were *private* farms, with a relationship akin to the medieval manor and village (Wilkes and Elrington, 1978, p.56). Some of these were clearly of considerable importance and hoards of pewter, silver, and gold have all been recovered from their hiding places by farmers and metal detectorists. Most important of these is an impressive coin hoard from Barway containing 471 coins found by Philip Randall in 1958 (plate 10). The coins, which are now in the British and Fitzwilliam Museums, date the deposition of the Barway hoard to *c*.AD 180, and it is suggested that the disruption associated with the late second century was the driving force behind the burial of the hoard.

During the later Iron Age much of western and central Fenland came under the control of a tribal group based in Norfolk, the Iceni. They had nine forts across East Anglia, mostly in Norfolk and Suffolk, but they also had one in Cambridgeshire, at Stonea Camp. Tacitus described them as having three sub-groups and the westernmost group occupied this area around Stonea. It was this group who rebelled in AD 47 before the famous Boudican revolt of AD 60–61. Distribution of their coinage is one way in which the extent of their territory has been mapped, but the Iceni tribe is also visible through the fact that they did not engage in the same kind of trade with the Continent that their southerly neighbours did, which is evident by the lack of luxury Roman imports across their whole territory (Malim 2006, p.40). Boudicca's rebellion was apparently marked nearby by the burial for safekeeping of 872 silver coins, the largest hoard of Iceni coins ever discovered (Malim 2006, p.93; Potter 2000, p.25). Despite the affiliation with the Iceni and close proximity to Stonea, there does not appear to be any archaeological evidence for military revenge in the form of conflagration on the Isle. However, the re-organisation of some sites may indicate increased suppression over the unruly Britons (Evans *et al.* 2007, p.72). In fact, the geographical location of the Isle, outside of the Iceni locale, and also the sphere of influence of the Aylsford-Swarling culture, results in the interesting social make-up of the Isle, whereby more Iron Age culture survives into the first century AD on the Isle than in the surrounding Cambridgeshire areas particularly as compared to Stonea in March.

CHAPTER 6

ANGLO-SAXON PERIOD: SAINTS AND SINNERS

In this Isle, this handmaid of Christ (Saint Etheldreda) desired to have a monastery, because as we said before, she came of the nation and blood of the East English.

Bede, AD 731.

INTRODUCTION

The Anglo-Saxon Period lasted 650 years, beginning when the Romans left in about AD 410, and ending in 1066 when the Normans invaded. During this period life in Ely, as in the rest of England, saw numerous changes, including the introduction of distinctively Anglo-Saxon jewellery and weaponry of which many local examples still exist (Chester-Kadwell 2012).

Traditionally the Anglo-Saxon Period is divided into the early, middle and late Saxon phases. The early Saxon phase, *c.*AD 410–650, begins with the end of Roman rule in the early fifth century, when the last Roman legions were recalled, at which point Britain fragmented into a number of small groups each competing for control of a local area. At this time the Isle of Ely fell under the control of the Gyrwe chiefdom. From *c.*AD 450 cemeteries with distinctive 'Anglo-Saxon' grave goods are found, and in AD 597 St Augustine brought Christianity, again, to England.

The middle Saxon phase spanned from *c.*AD 650 to *c.*AD 850. By the seventh century a number of larger kingdoms had emerged, which formed the basis for the medieval kingdoms of England. The major kingdoms were Northumbria, Mercia, Kent, Wessex and East Anglia, which included the Isle of Ely (Figure 91). During this period St Etheldreda founded Ely monastery near Cratendune, in AD 673, and we see the emergence of trading settlements and coinage. By around AD 730 the practice of burial with elaborate grave-goods came to an end. We normally think of this as being due to Christianisation, but this is

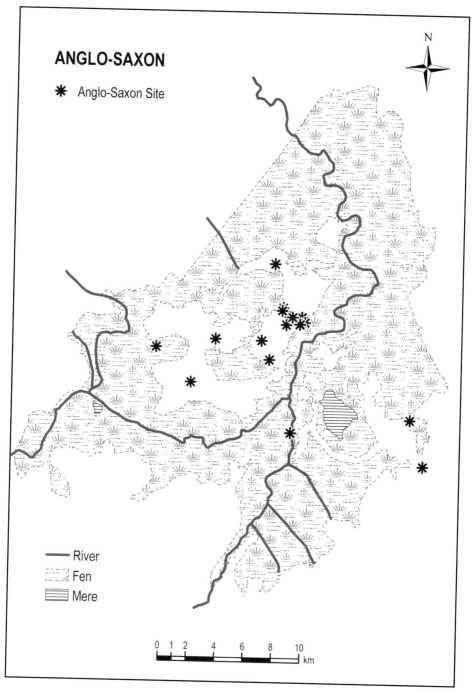

Fig 91. Map of major Anglo-Saxon sites mentioned in the text. Map data ©
OpenStreetMap contributors, CC BY-SA.

in fact some considerable time after Christian conversion and considerably earlier than burial in church yards, which we think of as distinctly Christian but which does not appear until the tenth century. By the eighth century the Midlands kingdom of Mercia, under King Offa, appeared about to form the core of a consolidated England, until it fell victim to eighth- and ninth-century Viking invasions, which included, in AD 793, the Viking attack on Lindisfarne.

Finally, the late Saxon phase was from c.AD 850 to c.AD 1066. During the first half of this period what we now think of England was divided into two, with Alfred, king of Wessex, and his descendents ruling the southern half of England, and the Danes ruling the northern half under the Danelaw. This division came to an end when, during the tenth century, the kingdom of Wessex conquered the whole of England, and Æthelstan was crowned king of all England in AD 932. It was at about this date that we see the beginning of burials in churchyards.

THE EARLY ANGLO-SAXON PERIOD: CRATENDUNE, ELY MONASTERY AND BURIAL

The most important question for the early Anglo-Saxon Period is the identification of the sites of Cratendune and of the original monastery in Ely. Historical records reveal that Etheldreda (or Æthelthryth) established a monastery on a site a mile away from an existing settlement at Cratendune in AD 673 (Book 1 of Liber Eliensis, Blake 1962). Archaeological research suggests that the best candidate for the location of Cratendune is the area south of Ely, near Bedwell Hay Farm. The Fenland Survey (Hall 1996) found both Roman and Anglo-Saxon pottery sherds there, which indicates possible continuity of settlement between the Roman and Anglo-Saxon Periods. The site covers 2ha and lies on the top of a low sand-capped hill, and the topography fits well with the dun, 'hill', element of the name Cratendune. Close by early Anglo-Saxon burials were found at Witchford Aerodrome in 1947 (Meaney 1964, p.64). The cemetery contained thirty skeletons buried with grave goods, which included iron and bronze buckles, an amber bead necklace (discussed below), two saucer brooches, a large square-headed brooch, an annular brooch, two iron spearheads and a sword, a wheel-shaped brooch and 'several' glass melon beads, a knife and a bronze girdle hanger, all dated to the sixth century (Fowler 1948, pp.70–6). The sword with tang 86cm long has a pattern-welded central band which can clearly be seen in the photograph (Figure 92, Maryon 1948, pp.73–6 and plate XVIII). The burials may represent a cemetery attached to Cratendune.

A crystal, gold, garnet and amethyst pendant was ploughed out nearby in 1952 (Figure 93, Lethbridge 1953, pp.1–3). It is decorated with a gold cross and herringbone pattern set with garnets and has marked similarities to objects from the princely Anglo-Saxon burial ground at Sutton Hoo, Suffolk. The pendant with its crystal jewel, its cross and its amethyst-coloured central setting (a protection against intoxication) is a religious charm of considerable potency and value. It would be attractive to think that it had once been associated with the powerful royal family who founded Ely although there is no direct evidence for this (*contra* Lethbridge 1953, p.3).

History records that Etheldreda's monastery, a house for both monks and nuns, was located about a mile from Cratendune in Ely. The early Anglo-Saxon settlement record from Ely is rather thin. However, the most likely location of St Etheldreda's monastery is the site of the St John's Hospital, which lies

Fig 92. Iron sword from Ely Fields Farm cemetery. Source: Maryon 1948, pl. XVIII.

Fig 94. Eighth-century stone sculpture from St John's Hospital, Ely. Source: the authors.

c.2.5km from Bedwell Hay Farm at the highest point in the city. A stone sculpture at St John's Hospital has been identified as part of an eighth-century frieze (Figure 94) and may have originally formed part of the first stone church (Cobbett 1934, Henderson 1997).

A small number of possibly early Anglo-Saxon pottery sherds were found at 2 West End (Kenney 1999) and there is some suggestion that there may have been a small early Anglo-Saxon settlement, limited to the roadside, along West Fen Road (Mudd 2000), but the best evidence for early Anglo-Saxon occupation in Ely comes from burials. To the north of the city centre, at least four furnished sixth-century burials were recorded during the construction of the New Barns housing estate in 1959 (Bushnell and Cra'ster 1959; Wilson and Hurst 1960, p.134). The site is unusual because it coincides with the cropmarks of three sides of a rectilinear enclosure, which may have defined the cemetery. Grave goods included a gilt bronze square-headed brooch, a small-long brooch, two iron shield bosses, an iron socketed spearhead and an iron sword 85cm in length, all dating from the sixth century and discussed below (Chester-Kadwell 2012). Excavations south of Witchford Road in 2003 revealed the remains of a cemetery that had unfortunately been badly damaged by ploughing (Steve Parry in Lucy *et al.* 2009, p.134).

Better evidence comes from an excavated cemetery at Westfield Farm, which comprised at least fifteen burials (Figure 95, Lucy *et al.* 2009). The central, primary, burial may originally have been covered by a barrow, and was that of a ten or twelve year old who had been buried with rich grave goods including a wooden casket containing a matched pair of glass palm cups and a bone comb. Around the neck of the skeleton was a necklace; a silver pin lay across the chest, and from a belt was an iron girdle-group and an iron knife. The necklace consisted of silver, gold and gold-and-garnet pendants, and included a cross-shaped gold pendant. Palm cups have been reported from minster cemeteries at Peterborough, Faversham and Minster-in-Thanet, perhaps suggesting that such vessels were thought appropriate for burials with ecclesiastical associations (Lucy *et al.* 2009, pp.88–9). The remaining burials were arranged around the central burial. Most notable of these was Grave 2, the burial of a young woman aged fifteen to seventeen years accompanied by a cylindrical bronze workbox, a Roman bronze brooch, an antler spindle whorl, and 10 amethyst beads, the largest collection found in a single grave in the East of England (Lucy *et al.* 2009, p.125).

Isotopic analyses of the burials are particularly intriguing as they suggest that the majority of those buried here came from outside the local area, and that at least four of them came from outside Britain, two possibly from North Africa (Dekker and O'Connell in Lucy *et al.* 2009, p.119). Dekker and O'Connell were cautious about accepting these surprising results at face

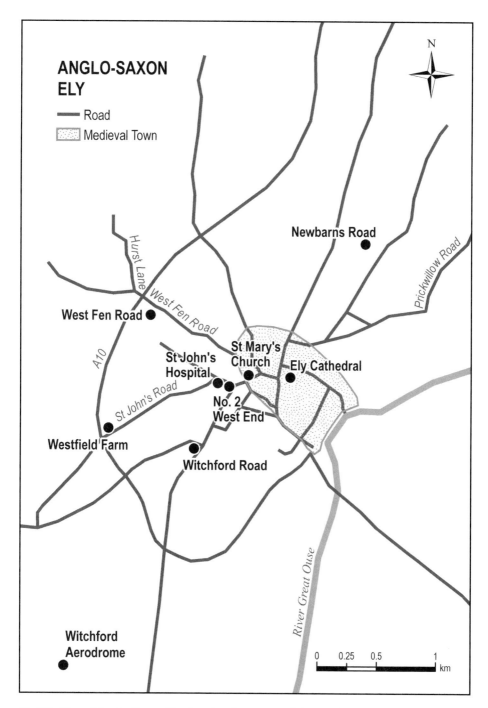

Fig 95. Map of Anglo-Saxon Ely showing the extent of the medieval town and the location of the sites mentioned in the text. Map data © OpenStreetMap contributors, CC BY-SA.

value but they may reflect a genuine pattern of diverse childhood origin for the population buried here. Aristocratic and ecclesiastical connections in the later seventh century were far reaching, extending across Europe and beyond, and early documentary sources depict people constantly on the move, between kingdoms, countries and continents (Yorke 2005). For example, Bede reports that Abbot Hadrian, a North African, went to Canterbury from Italy via the Frankish kingdom in AD 664 (Bede IV, I). Moreover, two of Etheldreda's own sisters became abbesses of the Frankish nunnery of Faremoutiers in Brie, to the west of Paris (Yorke 2005, pp.24–5).

It seems highly likely that the burials excavated at Westfield Farm represent people associated with the religious community in later seventh-century Ely (Lucy *et al.* 2009). This is known to have been a mixed-sex community with a nucleus of nuns residing under a royal abbess, with Continental contacts with Frankish religious communities near Paris, as well as strong links with the Kentish, Northumbrian and East Anglian royal houses. The burial wealth displayed in Graves 1 and 2 suggests aristocratic connections with the monastic institution, a suggestion reinforced by the Ely casket, intricately carved from ivory (Figure 96). Excavations at similar sites elsewhere in England, for example Hartlepool, suggest that Anglo-Saxon religious establishments were diverse in nature, extensive, and often possessed more than one area for burial; indeed, historical and archaeological sources for Whitby suggest that seventh- to ninth-century occupation, presumably monastic, spread right across the headland (Carr *et al.* 1988; Daniels 1999; Blair 2005, p.198). The natural topography of hills and islands may, indeed, have been one of the ways in which some monastic precincts were defined (Blair 2005, p.196). It could conceivably be the case that the monastic precinct at Ely occupied the hilltop, with an extensive settled area, perhaps encompassing the site of the present cathedral, and multiple cemetery areas for both lay and ecclesiastical members of the community. The Westfield Farm cemetery may represent one such cemetery.

Elsewhere on the Isle an Anglo-Saxon inhumation cemetery was discovered at Little Downham in 1934. Three skeletons, one with a brooch, were found, but Fowler reported that others had been found in *c.*1885 (Phillips 1939). At Soham burials were discovered within the modern cemetery, and finds included at least six brooches, several beads, pottery sherds and spearheads (Fox 1923, p.263; Meaney 1964, p.69). Another cemetery was excavated containing twenty-three inhumations and two cremations at Soham (Lethbridge 1933; Meaney 1964, pp.69–70). All the burials were laid within a circle suggesting they had been placed around a barrow. There were very few grave goods, among them a small-long brooch, a cruciform brooch, a finger-ring and an iron adze. One burial had a whetstone and another was covered with charcoal. Dates of mid-sixth to seventh century were assigned to two of the graves.

Fig 96. The Ely casket, intricately carved from ivory. Source: the authors.

THE MIDDLE AND LATE ANGLO-SAXON PERIOD: SETTLEMENT

The principal settlement on the Isle since the middle Anglo-Saxon Period has been Ely. It is first recorded in *c*.AD 750 by Bede as elige, when it was a regional name, denoted by *ge* 'people land', to which was added the suffix *eg*, 'island'. Excavations either side of West Fen Road have revealed an extensive middle Anglo-Saxon settlement, dated by the presence of Ipswich ware and a single coin dated to *c*.AD 730–40 (Mortimer *et al*. 2005, p.144). The settlement consisted of a series of twelve rectangular enclosures or plots defined by shallow ditches (Figure 97; Mortimer *et al*. 2005, p.144; Mudd and Webster 2011, p.124).

Each individual plot was small, typically measuring *c*.20–30m in width, and was probably occupied by an individual household, with some owning or sharing more than one plot. Within the plots were buildings, identified from postholes and gullies. Most were *c*.8m long and 3–5m wide, and it is difficult to

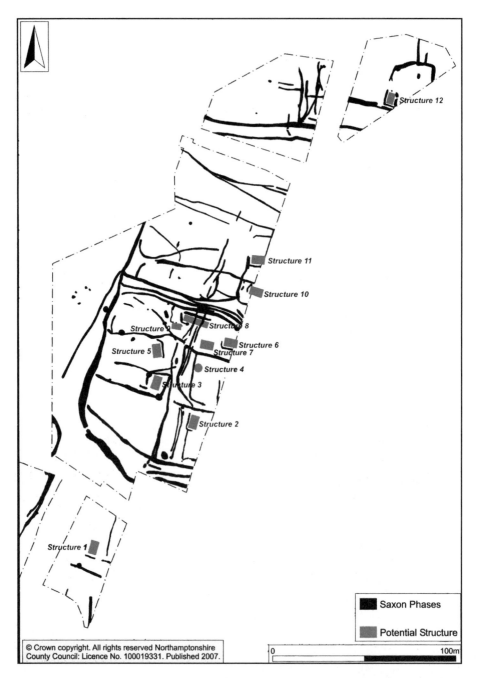

Fig 97. Location map showing the position of middle Anglo-Saxon boundary ditches, possible houses and a well. Source: after Mortimer et al. 2005, and Mudd and Webster 2011.

determine whether they were houses or agricultural buildings, assuming that the Anglo-Saxons made such a clear cut distinction themselves. One structure may have been a hall and comprised five postholes in one direction and four, set at right angles, in another (Mudd and Webster 2011, p.126). The overall size of this building, 9m by 4m, would be typical for a building of this type as shown by the reconstruction from West Stow Anglo-Saxon Village in Suffolk (Figure 98). A well c.2.5m deep was found within one of the plots suggesting it was for use by the occupiers of the plot, and not those to the north or south (Mudd and Webster 2011, p.129). Overall the settlement follows a relatively orderly layout of ditched enclosures and trackways, which is usual for the period, and provides evidence for this being a planned settlement dated to c.AD 725 and built along the existing, possibly Roman, West Fen Road (Mudd and Webster 2011, p.126).

Analysis of the remains from the site show that barley was the dominant crop, perhaps used for fodder, with free-threshing wheat also present in large quantities, presumably for human consumption. There were only small quantities of oats and rye. The evidence points to a strong pastoral component to the economy, dominated by sheep rearing, although arable agriculture was practiced especially south of West Fen Road. Querns show that wheat was

Fig 98. Reconstruction of an Anglo-Saxon hall at West Stow Anglo-Saxon Village, Suffolk. Source: the authors.

being ground to make flour on site. Sheep were the most common domestic animal although young cattle were also present. Craft activities included many of the stages of woollen textile manufacture, indicated by spindle whorls and loom-weights. Weaving was a key domestic activity and the community would have made their own fabrics. Iron smelting and metalworking were also taking place on the site. Pottery was limited to Ipswich ware, and there were no Continental imports. In contrast middle Anglo-Saxon imported North French Blackware pottery was found at excavations of the Lady Chapel at Ely Cathedral (Regan 2001b). The apparent scarcity of imports at West Fen Road is therefore a consequence of the site's status rather than its physical isolation from wider trade networks (Mudd and Webster 2011, p.131).

The settlement north and south of West Fen Road was most likely sited on part of the monastic estate, and was created from scratch in c.AD 725 (Mortimer et al. 2005, p.147). The site saw continuous occupation from the middle Anglo-Saxon to the late Anglo-Saxon Period and beyond, often within the same ditched property boundaries. The settlement, characterised by a small number of buildings set within large ditched enclosures, seems to be typical of many Saxon towns (Gardiner and Greatorex 1997, pp.168–70). The archaeological evidence points to a very stable, but gradually evolving, settlement, which probably provided food and other services to the monastic site. The finds suggest that the occupants did not enjoy a high-status lifestyle; a lack of imported pottery and high-value metalwork, and an almost total absence of coinage all indicate that the settlement was somewhat removed from the ecclesiastical power centre to the east (Mortimer et al. 2005, p.ix).

As well as the extensive remains at West Fen Road, middle Anglo-Saxon features and sherds of Ipswich ware have been found at Chief's Street, West End and St Mary's Lodge in Ely (Kenney 1999; 2002; Robinson 2000). To the east, in a field called The Paddock, late Anglo-Saxon boundary ditches filled with rubbish were discovered. The ditches represent the boundaries of urban properties, once part of Ely before the monastery expanded over it (Holton-Krayenbuhl 1988). Further features and sherds of pottery have been found within the cathedral precincts at the Lady Chapel, as already mentioned, and at Walsingham House (Regan 2001; Hunter 1992), and outside them nearer the river at Broad Street (Cessford et al. 2006). As the presence of features and sherds of Ipswich ware can be taken as indicators of settlement, the evidence suggests an extensive area of settlement, although not necessarily one intensively occupied, stretching for at least 1.75km west from the current city centre in the eighth and ninth centuries (Mortimer et al. 2005, p.147).

Outside Ely the evidence is less, often limited to a small number of pottery sherds. For example at Haddenham, middle and late Anglo-Saxon pottery sherds came from an excavation at the site of Linton Hall, and at Wicken

(Hall 1996, Site 6) a single possible early Anglo-Saxon sherd was found. Also at Wicken a large site has yielded many finds including lead plugs and fishnet weights, a bronze ring, a strip of bronze with two rivet holes and zoomorphic decoration (Hall 1996, Site 4). At Soham an Anglo-Saxon spearhead and a late Viking spear were found when dredging the Cam near Dimmock's Cote (O'Reilly 1928). From the form of the placename this site would be expected to be a Saxon settlement, controlling the fording point of the Cam.

Three Anglo-Saxon sites are known at Waterbeach. One lies on a slight rise of gravel and is represented by sherds of hard, black gritted hand-made pottery, and a fine piece of metalwork, probably from a casket, made of gilt bronze with zoomorphic decoration associated with a sunken-featured building, probably a house or outbuilding.

The second site consists of a smaller area of dark-stained soil with a lot of bone and some hard black sherds of pottery. Finally, the third site, at Waterbeach Lodge, consists of a sunken-featured building on a berm on the edge of Car Dyke (Lethbridge 1927). There were no post holes or hearths but 'short lengths' of wood with a small diameter suggesting a construction of wattle. The floor was covered by a black fill in which there was the skeleton of a dog and many plain gritty hand-made pottery sherds. Four decorated sherds were found similar to types used as cinerary urns. Other finds were five opaque glass beads, a bronze needle, two bone needles, a disc of bronze with silver on one side, probably deriving from a square-headed brooch, and three spindle whorls.

AN OVERVIEW OF ANGLO-SAXON OBJECTS FROM THE ISLE OF ELY

Mary Chester-Kadwell

The distinctive material culture of the Anglo-Saxon Period is typically represented by the weapons, jewellery and cremation urns buried with the dead in cemeteries. The designs of many of these artefacts originate in northern Germany and southern Scandinavia. Together with evidence from written sources such as Bede's *An Ecclesiastical History of the English People*, the presence of typical Anglo-Saxon objects in England suggests there was an influx of settlers from Germanic areas of mainland Europe in the fifth and sixth centuries AD. Most Anglo-Saxon metalwork found by chance ('stray finds') or during archaeological excavations are grave goods, but some would have been accidentally lost during daily activity. Nowadays many objects are found by metal detectorists in the ploughed fields of England and Wales, and reported to the Portable Antiquities Scheme.

This overview of Anglo-Saxon objects from Ely is arranged broadly chronologically from the fifth to the ninth centuries AD, and all the artefacts can be found on display in Ely Museum. Often the design of the artefacts is specific to East Anglia or Cambridgeshire, so while their stylistic origins may lie in the traditions of Germany, Scandinavia or the late Roman provinces, English craftsmen quickly developed types of objects and styles of decoration of their own.

The early Anglo-Saxon Period is characterised by grave goods found in cemeteries, and one example in Ely is the cemetery at High Barns (above). The cemetery was disturbed during building work for the housing estate in 1959, and the grave goods most likely came from at least four adult graves, dating to the early or mid-sixth century, c.AD 500–575 (Chester-Kadwell 2012, p.2). Seven objects were recovered from High Barns, including jewellery and weaponry.

Great square-headed brooches were the most expensive items of dress jewellery produced in Anglo-Saxon England (Hines 1997). They were worn by women of wealth and high social status to fasten a cloak or as a decorative piece in the centre of the chest. It is likely that this type of brooch was worn with the square head pointing downwards, but museums typically display them with the square head upwards, following archaeological convention. Since they were almost always worn singularly, each brooch discovered most likely represents a single adult female grave. Production of square-headed brooches developed during the seven decades from c.AD 500–570 so all examples can be dated to the sixth century (Hines 1997). Changes in the elaborate designs over time demonstrate inter-regional influences within England and long-distance cultural contact between England, Scandinavia and other places on the Continent. Only 200 or so examples have ever been found, so great square-headed brooches remain relatively rare artefacts.

Colour plate 11 shows one of two local examples of great square-headed brooches. It dates to the period c.AD 550–570, and was made of bronze (copper alloy) and then gilded and silvered. The brooch is mostly complete, but the square head-plate is missing. The main decoration is formed in 'chip-carving' style consisting of the eyes, heads and bodies of animals and birds, combined with simple lines, dots and rings. This style, called Style I, dominated Anglo-Saxon metalwork for 150 years, and derived from provincial late Roman techniques and styles (Webster and Backhouse 1991, p.47). The foot is a stylised and immensely elaborated form of horse head, where the eyes are represented by the two round knobs and the nostrils by the curls in the form of birds. The horse was a prestigious animal in Anglo-Saxon society.

This brooch is an unusual hybrid form known only from Cambridgeshire. A similar brooch was found at the Little Wilbraham Anglo-Saxon cemetery, east of Cambridge (Hines 1997, Fig.80a). The head-plate and bow derive from the 'square-headed brooch' tradition of manufacture, while the middle section and foot derive from the 'florid cruciform brooch' tradition. This demonstrates craftsmen in the area were innovating, creating new forms of art by combining traditional forms.

A second almost complete great square-headed brooch (c.AD 530–560) was buried at the High Barns cemetery (Figure 99). It is also made of bronze and the front surface has been tinned and gilded. The head-plate has two squares of openwork and is missing some of its corners. The chip-carving-style decoration includes S-shaped curls around the head-plate, a popular motif in this period, and on the foot there is the head of a man. This brooch is the type specimen of its kind from the definitive scholarly work on great square-headed brooches (Hines 1997, pp.183–85, Fig.93a). Hines describes it as a hybrid of a transitional form between two typological groups (IX and XV) and another group form (XVI). As such, it can be dated to the transition between Phases 2 and 3, around the mid-sixth century. This brooch was made by a craftsman of modest skill, but it is an important artefact for Ely due to its experimental design.

In contrast to the great square-headed brooches, small-long brooches may have been cheaper copies of, or substitutes for, the larger cruciform and square-headed types (Lucy 2000, p.31). Locally one was found in the High Barns cemetery (Figure 100) dated c.AD 450–650. This example is made of bronze and is missing only the iron pin on the reverse, which would have been used to fasten it. The brooch is fine, but worn, and plainly decorated, belonging to Leeds' square-head (plain) type (Leeds 1945: Fig.18d). Small-long brooches are common in this area because they are a type local to the mid-Anglian (eastern) region of England. They are of home-grown design and manufacture with no similar forms on the Continent (Leeds 1945, p.5). Typically they were worn in pairs at the shoulders to fasten the cloth of the traditional peplos-style woman's dress. Sometimes they were sewn onto the garment, or the pin was bent round to permanently fasten it. In this way they may have been considered essential fittings, like a zip is today, rather than as purely decorative jewellery. Small-long brooches were often lost and they are amongst the most common Anglo-Saxon finds found by metal detecting (Chester-Kadwell 2009, Fig.6.12).

The sword was the single most prestigious weapon of the Anglo-Saxon Period, considered a worthy gift between men of high rank (Figure 92, Hawkes 1989). The sword was the weapon of an aristocrat in life, and the weapon of the hero in poetry. There were probably three different ways a sword could have been worn in the Anglo-Saxon Period: fixed directly onto a belt, fixed onto a sword belt that hung from the main belt, or fixed to a strap called a 'baldric' over the shoulder. Swords were double-edged and designed to be used one-handed as slashing weapons (Bone 1989, p.63–4). They could cause a great deal of damage, easily cutting through an unfortunate warrior's arm, leg or head.

Fig 100. Small-long brooch from High Barns cemetery, Ely. Photo: Steven Stanley Jugg.

Swords were often made using the technique of pattern welding, where a number of twisted iron or steel rods were merged and beaten together in complex layers by the craftsman at his forge. A shallow, rounded groove on either face (the 'fuller') would have made the sword lighter without reducing its strength. The 'hilt' (handle) may have been richly decorated with brass, copper, silver, or gold inlay or plating, over a wood-and-leather grip. Swords were finished with detachable fittings including a metal 'pommel' at the end of the hilt, a 'scabbard' with a metal 'chape' at its apex, and a variety of leather straps with metal strap ends, hooks, clasps or rivets. One of the most attractive of these is the sword pyramid (see below and Chester-Kadwell 2012, p.34–5).

Around half of all Anglo-Saxon adult males were buried with weapons, of which fewer than one in ten burials had a sword (Härke 1989). They would have been very expensive objects, so they were often curated and passed down the generations with the various fittings replaced over the years. The presence of a sword in a grave suggests the deceased was wealthy and probably a healthy adult male warrior (Bone 1989, p.69; Härke 1992).

The iron sword blade found at High Barns dates to *c*.AD 450–650 and comprises a complete blade with tang surviving, but missing any trace of the hilt. The good degree of iron preservation is relatively unusual since many recovered Anglo-Saxon swords are more fragmentary than this example. It is possible to see the shape of the long, broad blade that tapers slightly towards a rather rounded point. This is the form typical throughout the early Medieval Period. Since most sword blades were similarly shaped it is difficult to date them without the hilt, yet since hilts were made with organic materials they rarely survive. The hilts of later Anglo-Saxon swords, however, included a lower guard of iron, welded one with the blade. Since this example is without a metal guard it must be an earlier example.

While the sword was the weapon of prestige, the spear was the weapon of the masses. Without elaborate decoration, the spear is amongst the most common of finds in Anglo-Saxon cemeteries (Härke 1989). In fact, people were buried with spears more than almost anything else, and about half of all weapon burials consist of a lone spear. Spears are found with boys and men of both high and low status, where they were often the only accompanying item. High-status women have also been found buried with spears. Probably most types of spear would have been used to jab opponents, rather than being thrown like javelins. Spears were made in two parts: the spearhead of iron (the part that most often survives to be found) and the wooden shaft. A spearhead is made of a blade and a socket into which the shaft was inserted. Sometimes a 'ferrule' also survives: this is a wrap of iron formed around the shaft to discourage splitting of the wood.

Spearhead (1) is dated to between *c*.AD 450 and AD 650 and comes from the High Barns cemetery. Although corroded the small leaf-shape blade and short socket can be seen, and the total length is 19cm (Figure 101a).

Spearhead (2) is dated to between *c*.AD 500 and AD 600 and has a leaf-shaped blade and a long socket compared to the blade, with a solid shank (Figure 101b). It is possibly a type D2 (Swanton 1974), which would date it to the sixth century, possibly the early seventh century.

Shields were used to protect the warrior's body from the blows of his opponent, although some of the very earliest ones had points and may have been used offensively (Dickinson and Härke 1992, p.54). In the Anglo-Saxon Period shields were almost invariably round and made of wooden boards covered in leather. The shield boss in the centre of the shield was an iron dome riveted to the boards, covering the open hole in the centre where the handle was attached. It protected the warrior's hand and helped to deflect weapons away from the shield. Shield bosses were rarely elaborated but the shield face

Figure 101. Top: Spearhead 1 from High Barns cemetery, Ely. Bottom: Spearhead 2 dated to the sixth, or possibly early seventh, century. Photos: Steven Stanley Jugg.

is sometimes found with iron studs, or even decorative appliqués of animals made from bronze.

Shields are quite common in graves, where often only the shield boss survives. From the shield boss alone it is quite difficult to tell the size of the shield face, though some are found with iron rim binders that give away the diameter of the perished wood boards. About a quarter of weapons burials consist of a shield-and-spear combination, the second most popular combination after the single spear. Burial with just a shield is the third most common weapon burial option (Härke 1989). For weapon burials in general, there is frequently a discrepancy between the weapons used in the burial rite and those used in real life. Often the sets or combination of weapons included would not necessarily have been practical. This suggests that weapons included in graves refer to the idea of the warrior, rather than representing the warrior fully prepared for battle after death.

Shield bosses (1 and 2) date to between *c*.AD 450 and AD 600 and come from the High Barns cemetery (Figure 102), where they were found with the sword (above). Made of iron it is possible to determine a complete profile of the 'apex', 'dome', 'waist' and 'phlange' of one of the bosses (1). The shape of this shield boss suggests it is a Group 1.1 type, dating to the late fifth or sixth centuries (Dickinson and Härke 1992).

Cremation was the dominant form of burial in the early Anglo-Saxon Period in the East of England. During burning, the body and associated goods were destroyed. Cremation urns are pottery vessels used to hold the ashes and burnt and unburnt grave-goods of one or more people, and sometimes animals (Figure 103). The weight of bones recovered from most cremation urns suggests only a partial collection of the remains was commonly removed from

Fig 102. Shield bosses 1 and 2 from High Barns cemetery, Ely. Photo: Steven Stanley Jugg.

Fig 103. A typical Anglo-Saxon urn in which the cremated body was buried. Photo: Steven Stanley Jugg.

the funeral pyre for storage in the urn (McKinley 1994, pp.11, 72). A lack of pyre debris suggests they were carefully chosen and perhaps even washed. One particular difference between the grave-goods included with cremations in comparison to inhumations (burials) is the popularity of 'toilet sets' made up of tweezers, shears, blades, combs and/or 'ear-scoops', suspended from a ring (Lucy 2000, p.108).

Cremation urns were handmade from tempered local clay using a coil-winding or pinching technique, then dried, decorated, and fired under bonfires. About eighty percent of early cremation urns were decorated using a mixture of techniques and motifs. Some of the most popular were lines made by the incision of a sharp point; rings, dots, crosses, S-shapes and swastikas made using bone or antler stamps; and bosses made from lumps of clay added on. Some of the stamps can be interpreted as religious in nature, such as the rune T for the god Tiw, while the meaning of others is more difficult to understand. It is likely that all the decoration on funerary urns had some significance in terms of identity, either of the group or the individual.

Potters in the Anglo-Saxon Period appear to have been itinerant since pots with similar stamps sometimes appear in different cemeteries. Later potters may have become semi-specialised and stayed in one village. Many households probably made their own basic pottery with only the really elaborate pots being made by specialists.

Beads are the most numerous of Anglo-Saxon grave-goods. Amber and glass were the most common materials with which beads were made, but sometimes they were made of quartz, chalk, flint, amethyst, bone, antler or metal. Amber is still found today washed up on the Anglian coast from deposits in the Baltic and amber beads were most likely made locally from this material. The style of many East Anglian glass beads show that they were also locally made, whilst other types were imported from Scandinavia, the Continent and even Turkey.

Beads were often worn as a necklace between a pair of brooches, or kept inside a purse as small talismans or to ward off the 'evil eye' (Colour plate 12). They were worn usually but not exclusively by women. Bead fashions changed over time: during the sixth century translucent blue beads went out of fashion in favour of yellow, green and red opaque ones (Brugmann 2004). By the seventh and eighth centuries amethyst beads were very much in vogue. The great variation in style, number and arrangement of beads suggests there was a significant aspect of personal taste in the way they were chosen and worn. However, older women tended to wear beads of better quality so they may also have symbolised womanhood and the development of womanly status in the household.

A rarer type of personal ornament is the finger-ring. The gold finger-ring in Ely Museum (Colour plate 13) has two mirrored lines of horseshoe-shaped stamps, slightly offset, and a diameter of 16mm. The finger-ring dates to the sixth century and would have been the property of a high-status individual. The relatively small size of the ring suggests it was probably that of an adult woman, but it is possible it was worn by a man. Since the finger-ring was found 'stray' and not as part of a set of grave-goods it is difficult to be more specific about its original owner.

Sleeve-clasps (also called 'wrist-clasps') were used to fasten the opening in the cuffs of long-sleeved garments (Figure 104). Sleeve-clasps came in two parts, one side (the 'hook-piece') having a projecting hook, and the other side (the 'catch-piece') having a pierced hole through which the hook would fasten. In England sleeve-clasps were worn almost exclusively by women, and are usually found in graves in pairs, one for each sleeve.

The use of clasps was originally a southern Scandinavian fashion where they were used to fasten sleeves, trousers and other parts of clothing too (Hines 1993). During the last quarter of the fifth century people from south and western Norway migrated, bringing with them the idea of the sleeve-clasp. Arriving originally in Humberside, the sleeve-clasp design spread to northern East Anglia, the east Midlands, Lincolnshire and Yorkshire during the sixth century. Cambridgeshire seems to have been the centre of this regional costume.

Fig 104. A reconstruction of an Anglo-Saxon woman wearing sleeve-clasps, beads and brooches. Photo: the authors.

Almost all English sleeve-clasps were made in England, not imported, and craftsmen created their own designs. Sleeve-clasps were made by casting bronze or silver, and finishing the cast pieces in a number of ways. A knife or file would be used to shave off casting marks, and perforations would be made for rivets and sewing holes. More unusually sleeve-clasps might be gilded, silvered, tinned or inlaid with niello – a soft black metal sulphide.

The sleeve-clasp found in Soham (*c*.AD 500–600) is one side of a gilt silver sleeve-clasp (the hook-piece) with just over half surviving (Figure 105). It is finely decorated with highly stylised curved bird heads (one missing), which are bordered by tiny stamped triangles inlaid with niello. The bird head has similarities to the ones on the foot of the great square-headed brooch from High Barns cemetery, Ely (above). The front of the hook is decorated with the popular S-shaped motif, reserved on an enamel field. Enamelled sleeve-clasps

Fig 105. A gilt silver sleeve-clasp from Soham. The surviving part of the clasp is decorated with stylised bird heads (one missing). Photo: Steven Stanley Jugg.

Fig 106. Sword pyramid from Weston Colville, south of the Isle. The silver pyramid is decorated with inlaid niello set into chip-carved triangles. Photo: Steven Stanley Jugg.

are found only in East Anglia. This example is a Hines' Form C1 sleeve-clasp (Hines 1993).

Sword pyramids formed part of the fittings of a sword, and typically a pair would have been used to decorate straps holding the scabbard to the belt (Figure 106, Bruce-Mitford 1978). They were prestige items in late sixth- and early seventh-century high-status male graves, and by the second half of the seventh century they are often found fulfilling a secondary function in lower status female graves too. Sword pyramids, which often came set with garnets, were heavily influenced by Continental metalwork and may have been imported.

Two sword pyramids have been found by metal detecting in Weston Colville, just to the south of the Isle, and date *c.*AD 580–680. The first was found in 2007, is 12mm square, made of silver, with inset chip-carved triangles, gilded and inlaid with niello. Originally it would have had a setting in the top, probably a garnet, which was very fashionable in the late sixth and early seventh centuries. Objects of a similar date from the ship burial at Sutton Hoo in Suffolk, and those in the Staffordshire hoard, have a comparable fabrication in gold with garnet inlay.

A similar, almost identical, sword pyramid was found in the same area in 2010. It is highly likely that they come from the same sword, and therefore the same burial of a late sixth-century or seventh-century person, probably a man. They are similar to other examples from Flixton, North Yorkshire.

From the late seventh century AD, the Anglo-Saxon economy included coastal and inland trading settlements. Ipswich is East Anglia's largest known coastal trading post, but the nearest inland trading settlement to Ely is at West Walton, near Wisbech, where above-average quantities of eighth-century metalwork have been recorded. From the middle of the Anglo-Saxon Period Wisbech was one of the richest manors belonging to Ely Abbey, so a connection with West Walton seems likely (Pestell 2003, p.124).

Coincident with the rise of focussed trading sites was the re-introduction (late 660–c.AD 680) of silver coinage, when coins came to be used as the currency of commerce. Silver pennies (commonly called 'sceattas') weighed about 1.3g of good silver until the early eighth century when a reduction in the supply of silver meant they started to be made baser and lighter. Pennies continued in use until c.AD 760 (Williams 2008).

Different types of silver pennies can be attributed to specific Anglo-Saxon kingdoms, even regions or towns. By contrast, some types seem to have circulated much more widely and were minted on the Continent. 'Porcupine' types (Series E) occur in both England and Frisia (what is now Belgium through

Fig 107. Silver 'porcupine' penny, named because the hair on the bust resembles the spikes of a porcupine's quills. Photo: Steven Stanley Jugg.

to the Danish border), but the majority were minted in Frisia, with some poor English imitations (Grierson and Blackburn 1986, p.153). Single silver pennies found today, often by metal detectorists, were accidentally lost during the course of everyday life, rather than buried with the dead.

A silver penny found by metal detecting near Wicken is of the 'porcupine' type (Series E) and sub-type variety G2, type 4 (Figure 107, Grierson and Blackburn 1986). The coin was minted in Frisia in c.AD 700-705. One side (the obverse) is derived from a crude version of the Roman bust, degenerated into an abstract design that looks more like a stylised animal. This is referred to as a 'porcupine' because the hair looks like spikes. The other side (reverse) has a typical design of a square beaded standard containing a central annulet with pellet bordered by two lines on each side, a design also said to be of Roman origin.

Hooked tags (or 'hooked-clasps') were multi-purpose articles, common in the ninth century AD (Figure 108). Unlike hooked-clasps from other periods, hooked tags are often delicate and would have been used to fasten only relatively light clothing fabrics or perhaps objects such as purses, bags, pouches (Webster and Backhouse, 1991). At this time, socks or stockings were made of fabric or leather bands wrapped around the legs, worn by both men and women. A hooked tag may have been sewn to the loose end of such a wrap, and the sharp hook poked into a small metal eye sewn into the other side of the fabric (Read 2008) to prevent the stocking unwinding. By the ninth century AD graves were no longer provisioned with grave-goods, so hooked tags are found only where they have been lost accidentally during everyday activities.

The hooked tag found at Chippenham, east of Fordham, is an attractive example. It dates to the period c.AD 800–900 and is made of silver with niello inlay. The tag has a complete hook, but is missing one corner where there would have been a second pierced lug for attachment. The hooked tag is

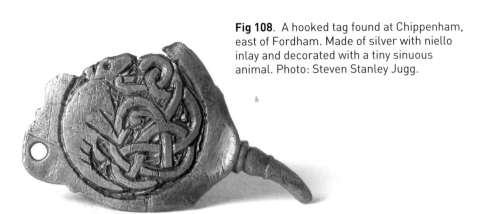

Fig 108. A hooked tag found at Chippenham, east of Fordham. Made of silver with niello inlay and decorated with a tiny sinuous animal. Photo: Steven Stanley Jugg.

decorated by a tiny animal of 'Trewhiddle style', its sinuous tail interlacing with itself in a complex knot. Trewhiddle style decoration is typical of ninth-century metalwork and had its origins in the south and east of England, but became universally popular, enjoying lively regional variations (Webster and Backhouse 1991, p.220). The main features of Trewhiddle style are small exuberant animals reserved in silver against a niello background; interlace and simple plant and geometric motifs; and division into self-contained fields. The Chippenham example has one single circular field, undivided, containing an animal. It is forward-looking and unspeckled, with a prominent eye and eyebrow, square snout, semi-foliate ear, and nicks in the contours of its body, typical of the third Trewhiddle decorative group (Green 1980). Most of the niello is now missing but some specks remain.

CONCLUSION

It was in the early Medieval Period that a distinctly island identity can be observed in the material culture, particularly that of the City of Ely itself. Distinctive classes of objects, for example the handled beakers of the Early Bronze Age, and fine metalwork of the Wilburton Period of the Late Bronze Age, discussed in previous chapters, hint at a distinctly island identity but it is only in the Anglo-Saxon Period that this emerges fully. Much of the wealth excavated in burials relates to the ecclesiastical associations of the settlement, which continue into the High Middle Ages and beyond (discussed in the following chapter).

CHAPTER 7

NORMAN CONQUEST AND BEYOND

Now Ely is an agreeable island, large and thickly inhabited, rich in land that is fertile and fit for pasture, impenetrably surrounded on all sides by meres and fens, accessible only in one place where a very narrow track affords the scantiest of entries to the island and a castle, wondrously set long since, right in the middle of the opening of the track in the water, makes one impregnable castle of the whole island.

Gesta Stephani, Trans. Potter, 1976.

INTRODUCTION

The domination of the Isle of Ely by the cathedral and City of Ely can be dated to the Medieval and post-Medieval Periods, AD 1066–1600. The name Ely, *elige*, is recorded by Bede in the eighth century AD meaning 'eel-district' and referring to a religious community first founded by St Etheldreda in *c*.AD 673, and subsequently refounded by King Edgar as a Benedictine institution *c*.AD 970. The abbey church became a cathedral in 1108, resulting in the expansion of the town. Although Ely has grown rapidly since the 1990s the present plan of the city reflects the layout of the medieval settlement (Figure 109). The geographical location of Ely, on high ground surmounted by the massive cathedral building, allows the city to dominate the Isle and Fens for many miles around. It was this location that, as we have seen in the previous chapters, allowed it from the earliest times to serve as a place of refuge. Ely was key in the resistance against the Norman invasion being the last refuge of Hereward the Wake and his supporters. William the Conqueror's first two attempts to cross the causeway at Aldreth ended in disaster, but after he threatened to confiscate the monastery's lands the monks surrendered the Isle. William responded with heavy fines for the Church and with the garrisoning of forty Norman knights at the monastery's expense (Rex 2004).

Fig 109. Aerial photograph of Ely. In the foreground to the left is Witchford aerodrome, the site of an Anglo-Saxon cemetery, and to its right below the arable fields, the probable site of Cratendune. In the middle distance is the city of Ely itself. The traditional boundary of the river Great Ouse lies to the right of the city, but to the left the city has expanded in recent years up to the A10, which now marks the city limit. Source: the authors.

The Isle of Ely was also important during the baronial and monarchical tribulations of the twelfth and thirteenth centuries. Of key importance to its position as a refuge was the control of the causeways which gave access to the Isle, particularly those at Stuntney and Aldreth, which gained importance in the Bronze Age, and which during the medieval and later periods came under the control of the monastery.

Discussions of the origins of Ely have tended to focus on successive religious institutions known from documentary sources (*Domesday* 1086; Speed 1610; Moore 1685) particularly Book I of *Liber Eliensis* compiled between 1131 and 1174 by a monk of Ely (Blake 1962, pp.1–62) and the survey of 1417 (BL Harley 329, fos10–24v). These have been supplemented in recent years by a number of large-scale excavations. Taken together these sources of evidence allow us to understand the settlement pattern of the medieval city and its relationship to the world beyond (Figure 110).

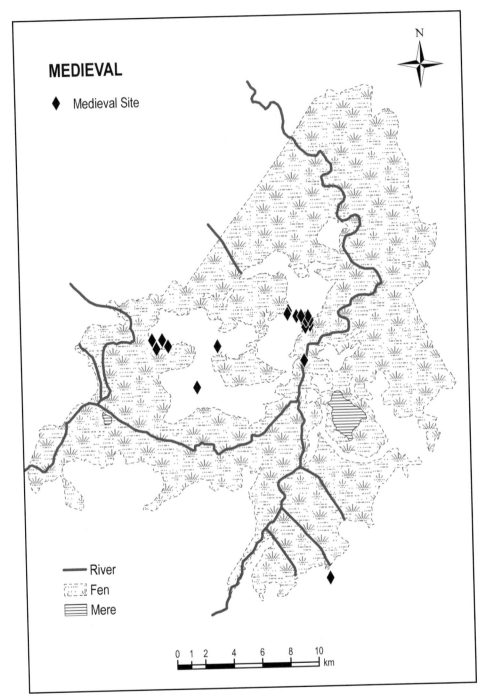

Fig 110. Distribution map of major medieval sites mentioned in the text. Map data ©
OpenStreetMap contributors, CC BY-SA.

THE MEDIEVAL AND LATER SETTLEMENT

Material and documentary evidence, in particular the survey of 1417 (see Holton-Krayenbuhl 2011), suggests that the topography of medieval Ely was established by *c.*1200 when occupation concentrated north and east of the monastic precinct, orientated towards the river (Figure 111). From the 1417 survey it is clear that the modern layout of the city follows closely the medieval street plan, although the names of some of the streets may have changed. For example, Brodelane is now Broad Street, Schendeforthlane is Nutholt Lane, and Catteslane is Chapel Street. Within the city there were two sources of religious authority, the Bishop and the monastery (Cessford and Dickens 2007). The Bishop's palace complex stood on the highest land on the island, west of the cloister and his home farm south of Barton square. The monastic enclosure stood on the east-facing slope, as did the vineyards, overlooking the river Great Ouse. Running south-east from the Market Square, adjacent to the cathedral, down to the river runs Forehill, which evolved as the main thoroughfare between hilltop and river, with dense settlement from the twelfth century (Alexander 2003). This was a largely mercantile area with, for example, evidence for specialist leatherworking, creating relatively high status and wealth. Broad Street, running parallel to the river, was a busy area of mercantile activity, whilst the river, fronted with wharves was a bustling trading area (Cessford, Alexander and Dickens 2006), provided the main means of linking Ely with Cambridge, King's Lynn and the world beyond, creating a focus for activity in the city. North of this busy area on the outskirts of the city, centred on Potters Lane, was a manufacturing area where potting and tanning activities took place away from the main centre of population (Owen 1993, 11). Further out still, but this time to the north, lay the early-medieval agricultural settlement of West Fen Road, discussed in the previous chapter (Mortimer *et al.* 2005). There a large settlement, possibly established as a food producing site for the nearby religious community, was geared towards crop and animal husbandry (Mortimer *et al.* 2005). Beginning in the twelfth century, and increasing during the thirteenth and fourteenth centuries, was a process of agricultural intensification, with increasing amounts of land at West Fen Road being given over to plough or pasture. Settlement consolidated throughout this period so that by the end there were just three farms set within large blocks of land of roughly equal size (Mortimer *et al.* 2005, p.148). This settlement pattern continued into the late twentieth century when the area was redeveloped as a housing estate.

There were two vineyards and numerous small orchards dotted about the city giving medieval Ely a rural appearance. Most households kept livestock, such as pigs and poultry, in their gardens where they would also have grown

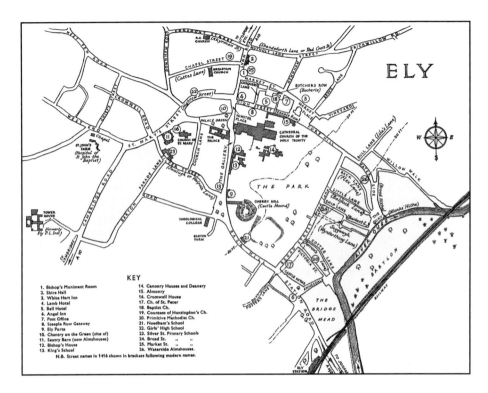

Fig 111. Street map showing the location of the main excavations in Ely: West Fen Road, Broad Street, Forehill, Lady Chapel, Ely Cathedral, Bishop's Palace, Potters Lane. Source: Pugh 1953, p.29.

their own fruit and vegetables. Within the city horses were the beast of burden not only for transport but also as means of power in the three horse mills situated in Broad Street. A fourteenth-century record details how to counter the churning of the roads created by horses and carts using rushes that were strewn across the road near Schegwyk (Holton-Krayenbuhl 1984, p.8).

In the later twelfth century the monastic community consisted of around seventy monks and their servants, declining to about forty-five monks in the later fourteenth century. When in residence the Bishop and his household was large, but his duties led him to spend long periods away from Ely. The secular community included carpenters, shipwrights, butchers, bakers and ale-brewers, dyers and tailors, many of whom were dependent on the Church for their livelihood. To this general population should be added specialist craftsmen who swelled the population during the course of major building works, such as the construction of the cathedral's Lady Chapel, Octagon and Lantern. Temporary residents also included pilgrims to St Etheldreda's shrine, visitors to the monastery and merchants. Communications with the outside world allowed foodstuffs and building materials to be brought to the monastery from its various outlying manor farms on a regular basis. From this it is clear that the isolation of the island monastery and its hinterland was only partial.

The Ouse, which was subject to flooding when rain, tides and winds were high, flowed along the foot of Stuntney Hill toward Quanea, until the first half of the twelfth century when the river was diverted 2.5km into a cut made from Caldwell Fen to Ely, and then north east along the Middle Fen Bank (Hall and Coles 1994). Equally important in the success of Ely was the cutting of the Ten Mile River sometime before 1250, taking water from the eastern Ouse-Cam from a position close to Littleport and emptying it into the Norfolk river system that met the sea at King's Lynn. These changes allowed King's Lynn port to expand and develop extensive trading links with the markets of North West Europe (Spoerry 2005; 2008). In the thirteenth century corn, ale, salt and wool were among the chief exports, while wine, fish, timber, wax and furs were all imported. In Ely the exchange of goods took place at three annual fairs, chief of which was that of the feast of St Etheldreda held in June. Records from the mid-thirteenth century record that among the goods on sale were furs and silken cloth, and that the merchants selling them came from as far away as Sweden and Germany, as well as from elsewhere in England.

The earliest standing buildings in Ely date from the second half of the twelfth century. They comprise the Norman cathedral and a number of conventual buildings including the prior's hall and infirmary (Holton-Krayenbuhl 1997, pp.122–23).

THE HOSPITALS OF ST JOHN THE BAPTIST AND ST MARY MAGDALENE

The Hospital of St John the Baptist has already been mentioned in the previous chapter as the most likely site of St Etheldreda's monastery. The current St John's Farm includes three buildings dated to the early thirteenth century and originally belonging to two separate hospitals, that of St John the Baptist and that of St Mary Magdalene. The two hospitals were later amalgamated by Bishop Northwold in 1240 under the name of the Hospital of St John the Baptist. Two of the surviving buildings on West End lie close to each other, and the third lies about 120m to the west along St John's Road. This last structure, which faces onto the present day road, was the chapel of St John, measures 16m by 7.3m, and is dated to the very early thirteenth century (Figure 112). The chapel of St Mary and another building nearby belonged to the Hospital of St Mary. The surviving building was the nave of the chapel; it is rectangular and measures 12.5m by 7.6m, although the doorway, windows and stepped

Fig 112. Photo of
St John's Chapel, Ely.
Source: the authors.

Fig 113. Photo of St
Mary's Chapel, Ely.
Source: the authors.

gables date from the sixteenth century when it was converted into a house (Figure 113). Nearby is another stone building measuring 6m by 5.8m whose original function is unknown.

THE MONASTERY AND CATHEDRAL

Ely is famous for its cathedral, a building that dominates the city and the surrounding fenland. A minster was begun after AD 673 but had to be reconstructed after Danish raids in AD 870. The following abbey was refounded by King Edgar, and rebuilt in AD 970, but following the appointment of Abbot Simeon in 1081, building began on a new church in 1083 instead of altering the Anglo-Saxon church (Figure 114). By 1093, when Abbot Simeon died, the east end was complete and the construction of the transepts had begun (Figure 115). In 1106 the relics of St Etheldreda and her sisters were transferred to the building in time for the creation of the Diocese of Ely in 1109 when the church became a cathedral, and the Abbot, a Bishop. The oldest part of the brick-built Bishop's Palace, the tower closest to the cathedral, was built by Bishop Alcock (1486–1500) and connected to the cathedral via a private covered way. The present building is largely the work of Bishop Laney (1667–75) who demolished much of the Alcock building, save for the surviving tower. The Bishops also had a much-loved palace at Little Downham where five medieval Bishops died. The surviving brick building at Tower Farm dates to c.1500.

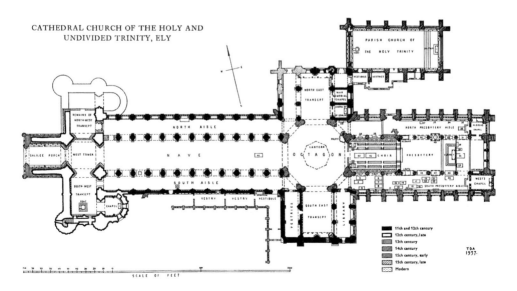

Fig 114. Plan of the Cathedral showing the construction phases. Source: Pugh 1953, p.53.

Building	Date	Bishop/Architect
Nave	1110 to 1130	Bishop Hervey le Breton
West front and transepts	c.1180 to c.1200	Bishop Ridel
Galilee Porch	Begun c.1210	Bishop Eustace
	Finished c.1250	Bishop Hugh de Northwold
Spire	c.1230	Bishop Eustace
Presbytery	1234 to 1252	Bishop Hugh de Northwold
Lady Chapel	1321 to 1353	Bishops Hotham, Montacute & de Lisle
Octagon & Lantern	1322 to 1342	Bishops Hotham & Montacute
Lantern on West Tower	Late fourteenth century	Bishop Fordham

Fig. 115. The building sequence of Ely Cathedral with the names of the Bishop/Architect responsible for the work. Source: the authors.

The remains of the Norman cloister, rebuilt in the fifteenth century, can be seen from what is now a staff car park and links the cathedral with the monastic complex. The monastery was founded to follow the rule of St Benedict and the monks committed themselves to a life of prayer and study. The Abbot was the head of the monastery until 1109 when the Abbots became Bishops, after which the Prior was head of the monastery. The Prior lived in the complex of buildings, which included the Prior's Hall and Prior's House, and he ran the monastery in conjunction with a team of managers, each with their own specific responsibilities, and often their own buildings, some of which survive (Figure 116). The Prior's Hall was destroyed, and all that remains are the late thirteenth-century porches of the entrances, one on the north for the monks and one on the south for the laity. Attached to the hall was the knight's lodging, the sleeping chamber of the Prior's squires and knights, who dined in the great hall. The Prior's House has an early twelfth-century vaulted undercroft, but the hall itself was rebuilt by Prior Crauden in the early fourteenth century. The house has its own first-floor chapel built by Crauden between 1321 and 1341 (Figure 117), and was connected by a bridge to the Queen's Hall, built by Crauden for the reception of Queen Philippa in 1330 (Figure 118).

Religious services were organised by the Precentor, assisted by the Succentor, who led the singing and looked after the books. The buildings and their contents were the responsibility of the Sacrist, whose offices and workshops were located along what is now the High Street, and was then named Stepil Row (see below). The Cellarer collected the taxes and tolls that paid for the

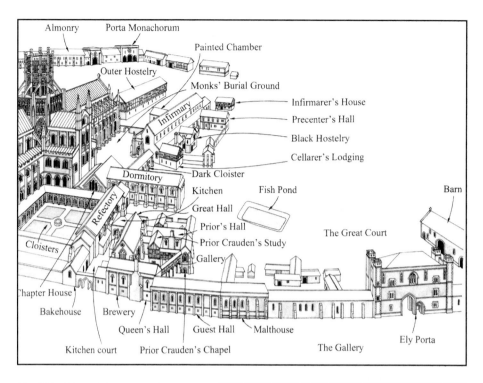

Fig 116. Plan of the monastic buildings of Ely. Plan: Jason Gibbons after Gardiner 1997.

Fig 117. Photograph of Prior Crauden's Chapel. Photo: the authors.

establishment. The Sub-Cellarer, Kitchener and Fraterer were located in buildings adjacent to the Prior's Hall, and were concerned with the everyday routine of providing and cooking food, and seeing to general cleanliness. The remains of the Prior's kitchen consists of two of its three fireplaces. The Frater was built in the thirteenth century and today only the lower part of the south wall remains with evidence of the staircase up to the lectern.

The Chamberlain supplied the clothes and was housed on the edge of the monastic buildings on Oyster Lane, back-to-back with the Infirmary. The Master of the Infirmary cared for sick and old monks in the Infirmary, which was, ominously, separated from the cathedral by the Monks' Cemetery. The Infirmary was entered via the undercroft of the now demolished dorter, and

Fig 119. Part of the surviving Infirmary, which now forms Infirmary Lane and amongst other things houses the Choir School. Note the original arches which have been bricked in to form the walls of the buildings. Originally the lane would have been roofed over to form the main body of the Infirmary. Photo: the authors.

then through a long vaulted passage built in the thirteenth century and called the 'Dark Cloister', the south wall of which can still be seen. Infirmary Lane marks the location of the Norman Infirmary, the lane itself originally being the roofed nave of the Infirmary, and its surviving walls now forming the walls of the Second, Third, Fifth and Sixth Canonries and a Minor Canon's House. Examination of these walls reveals the blocked arcades of the hall dated to 1175 (Figure 119).

The Almoner looked after the poor and orphans from buildings now occupied by the Almonry restaurant on the High Street opposite the Market Square. The building is intact and the lower story has vaulting dating to the end of the twelfth century. The blocked lancet windows in the east wall suggest that the almonry chapel, dedicated to St Martin, was at that end (Figure 120). The Almonry included a school for the boys who took part in Lady Chapel services. Adjacent to the Almonry was a gateway, now lost, called the *Porta Monachorum*.

The Hosteller was responsible for hospitality to travellers who would have stayed in extensive buildings, since demolished, to the rear of the cathedral and Lady Chapel, the foundations of which may be traced on the turf in a dry

Fig 120. Blocked lancet window in the Almonry. Photo: the authors.

summer. It was a self-contained establishment with its own chapel, and was used chiefly by the commercial classes, standing as it did fairly near the river, which in the Middle Ages carried a good deal of traffic between Cambridge and Lynn. A wall running from the south-east angle of the church, which existed until the present pathway was made round the east end of the cathedral about 1854, was probably connected with the ostium versus cimeterium monachorum, a gate near the outer hostelry dividing the more public part of the monastery from the monks' own quarters.

Novice monks would have been taught by a Master, and other Masters taught boys in the school, where it is said that King Edward the Confessor was a pupil in c.1010. The school still exists as the King's School Ely. The modern-day school occupies many of the surviving monastic buildings, including Ely Porta, the barn and the West Range. The latter were built in the twelfth century to serve as granaries and storehouses for the monks. Ely Porta was built between 1397 and 1405, the exterior of which has hardly changed since. At ground level the Porters' lodge lay on the south side and the north formed a prison. The upper floors of the Porta were originally used as manorial offices, and are now the school library. The barn, which now serves as the school refectory, dates to 1375, and retains many original features, including traces of an external staircase.

Elsewhere on the Isle the remains of an important Abbey can be seen at Denny, Waterbeach. Denny, or *deneia*, meaning 'Danes' island'. The remains of the Abbey, including walls dated to the Norman, fourteenth, fifteenth and eighteenth centuries, and the barn to the north, originally the refectory, has a medieval tiled floor. The Abbey was founded before 1159, and was under the care of Ely for eleven years until it was transferred to the Knights Templar, who used it as an infirmary. When the Knights were suppressed in 1309 the nuns of St Clare moved to the buildings where they stayed until 1539 when the buildings passed to Pembroke College, Cambridge (Christie and Coad 1980; see also Salzman 1948, pp.259-62, pp.295-303; Knowles and Hadcock 1971, pp.266-67).

THE CASTLES

Situated in Cherry Hill Park are the remains of a Norman motte-and-bailey castle, the surviving mound of which is now known as Cherry Hill (Figure 121). The precise history of the castle is surprisingly vague. It is presumed that the castle was built by William the Conqueror after his army defeated Hereward the Wake, whose last stronghold had been the monastery at Ely. Possible archaeological evidence for resistance to the Norman invasion includes a tenth/eleventh-century spearhead with inlaid silver decoration found in the river near Ely (Lethbridge and O'Reilly 1928); another spearhead also of tenth-eleventh-century date was found 'near Ely' (Salzman 1938, p.324) and parts of two swords, a spearhead and a shield boss with human skulls have been dredged out of the river near the mouth of the Car Dyke (Salzman 1938, p.309).

Upon William the Conqueror's son's death, civil war (1135-54) broke out between Stephen, who was William the Conqueror's grandson, and Matilda, sole surviving heir of William's son, Henry I. Stephen usurped Matilda, who was away in France, and seized the throne on Henry's death with the support of the barons. As a result he was a weak king dependent on the support of powerful robber barons who built their own unlicensed castles from which they terrorised the local people. At this time Bishop Nigel (1133-69) built 'a strong fort of lime and stone' within the precincts of Ely, which may refer to a second castle a few hundred metres away by the river after which Castelbrigge and Castlehythe were named. The presence of two castles causes confusion when reading ancient documents as it is often far from clear to which castle they refer.

The period of the civil war is known as the Anarchy (1135-53) due to the turmoil it created throughout England, and the castle at Castlehythe, and

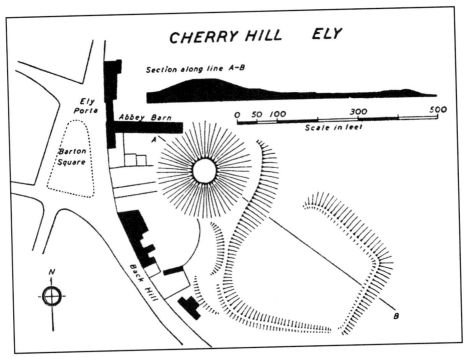

Fig 121. Plan of Ely castle showing the surviving earthworks. Source: Salzman 1948, p.29.

a third at Aldreth, would have protected the Isle from possible attack via the causeways at Stuntney and Aldreth, whilst that at Cherry Hill, from its prominent position on the higher ground, protected the monastery and town. Conflict must have reached Ely on several occasions as documents record that Bishop Nigel's fort 'being often destroyed' he built another one 'of timber and walled in the round hill, called the keep', which may refer to the refortification of Cherry Hill. Following the Anarchy the castles may have fallen out of use. Indeed Revd. James Bentham, an early historian of Ely, says that there was a windmill on the mound in 1229 (Bentham 1771), and a house is said to have stood 'where the old castle stood' at Castelhythe in 1251. Later references to castles suggest that one, and possibly both, were refortified during the Second Barons' War (1264–68) during which time Ely was captured by Prince Edward (later Edward I) in 1268. It may be that around this time the castle at Castehythe was demolished. The castle on Cherry Hill may have survived somewhat longer as there is a reference to 6s being spent on repairs to 'the castle' in 1586–87. However, by 1610 John Speed's map (colour plate 14) shows another windmill on what was then called 'Mount Hill' a name later changed, around 1649, to 'Mill Hill', whilst the name 'Cherry Hill' was in use by 1821, by which time the windmill had been demolished.

SECULAR BUILDINGS

There are several other medieval buildings in the city apart from the surviving monastic complex. Steeple (or Stepil) Gate, on the High Street, is one of the oldest, the present building having been built during the Tudor Period and first documented in the 1417 survey of the city (Figure 123). The site has, however, been occupied for much longer, being known as *Turris S. Petri* or St Peter's Tower in the twelfth century when it housed a church bell. The present building is timber-framed and served as the gateway to the burial ground of the parish church of the Holy Cross, both of which were in what

Fig 123. Photo of Steeple Gate, Ely. Photo: the authors.

are now the lawned grounds of Ely Cathedral behind Steeple Gate. The timber gateway dates to the Tudor Period, *c.*1500, but the carved oak lintels which span the gateway may be a hundred years older, and were perhaps taken from St Peter's Tower when it was demolished in 1354. The lintels are decorated with carvings including those of a green man (Figure 124a) and the heraldic device of three gold crowns on a red shield of the Bishops of Ely (Figure 124b). On the first floor at the rear is a fifteenth-century wooden oriel window.

Using ecclesiastical records it is possible to trace the occupiers of the building because it was owned by the Sacrist of the monastery to whom the tenants paid rent. Although we lack a full record we do have details of the occupiers from 1417 to the 1970s (Figure 125, Holmes 1980, pp.1–2).

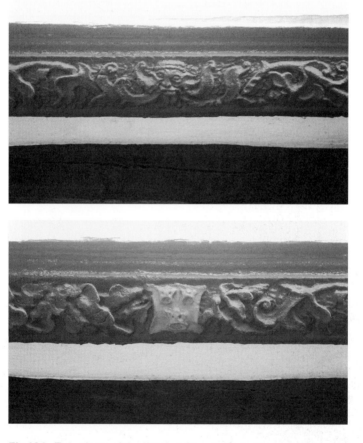

Fig 124. Top: photo of the lintel at Steeple Gate showing the carving of the green man. Bottom: photo of the Bishop's shield of three crowns on a red background carved into the lintel at Steeple Gate. Photos: the authors.

Date	Occupier	Occupation
1417	John Roos	
1476	Robert Coy	Tailor
?–1616	John Applea Snr	Blacksmith
1616–1637	John Applea jnr	Blacksmith
1637–1672	William Sawyer	
1672–?	Will Wenham	
?–1810	Sara Johnson	
1810–1812	Ephraim Harle	
1812–c.1885	William Giscard	Clock maker
c.1885–1927	Harriet Briggs	Pork butcher
1927–1949	Lilian Snell	Florist
1949–1978	Thomas Butler Harrison	Pharmacist
1978	John Samuel Ambrose	

Fig. 125. Occupiers of Steeple Gate from 1417 to 1978. Source: the authors after Holmes 1980.

Fig 126. Cromwell's stables, Ely. Photo: the authors.

Beneath the gate is an arched cellar, possibly built as a small chapel in the fourteenth century (Holmes 1980, p.4). This period saw the Sacrist, Alan de Walsingham, undertake large-scale building works including the construction of the Lady Chapel, Octagon and Lantern. To facilitate this he extended his own buildings along what is now the High Street, then called Stepil Row. These buildings were used to house the craftsmen engaged in the building work and extended as far as the Sacrist's Gate, taking in the Goldsmith's Tower. For example, in 1325 he took possession of four cottages to the west of the Goldsmith's Tower. The history of these cottages can be traced back to 1109 when the properties belonged to the Prior and were used to support the Sacrist's office by providing candles for the altars of the monastic church. In the twelfth century the buildings passed into the hands of the Bishop, only to be reclaimed by the Sacrist sometime between 1189 and 1197. Small-scale excavations in the area revealed evidence for stained glass working – possibly the remains left by craftsmen employed by Alan de Walsingham to work on the cathedral and Lady Chapel (Colour plate 15, Holton-Krayenbuhl *et al.* 1989, pp.56–7, Fig.7).

Elsewhere there are sixteenth-century buildings in Cromwell Road, where the stone-built stables of Oliver Cromwell, now converted into residential

Fig 127. Timber-framed cottages at Nos 7–11 Silver Street, Ely. Photo: the authors.

Fig 128. Early sixteenth-century stone built cottages at Nos 3–5 Silver Street, Ely. Photo: the authors.

accommodation, can still be found (Figure 126). The detached timber-framed house at 20 Church Lane dates to the same period, *c*.1550. Along Silver Street are a row of timber-framed cottages (Figure 127), which originally formed a single dwelling, dated to *c*.1400. The central cottage has fourteenth-century vine-scroll ornament on the ground floor. The adjacent stone-built house, now split into two, dates to the early sixteenth century (Figure 128). The property still retains a stone three-part window in the upper story, and at the rear a four-part one, partly cut through to form a doorway. Inside there is an original stone newel staircase, and a seventeenth-century chimney. Medieval wall paintings were discovered in the bedroom, which include a dove with the words 'Deale Justlye' (Preston in Hall 1996, p.30).

From the various documentary surveys it has been suggested that in 1086 Ely was 'purely rural', in 1251 it was 'largely rural, though with marked urban beginnings' and in 1416 it had assumed much of its modern form, but 'with the early possibilities of normal municipal development unfulfilled' (Hampson and Atkinson 1953, p.34). This view is supported by the excavations at Forehill, where it was argued that the thirteenth century was a period of development

Fig 129. Bat House, No. 47 Forehill, Ely, dates to 1490. Top left: Externally, part of the timber frame can be seen to the side. Top right: The interior retains the original roof joists. Left: detail of roof. Photos: the authors.

with a network of streets and settlement in several areas and that by the end of the fourteenth century it was a fully formed small town (Alexander 2003, p.173). All that remains are the timber-framed properties of Bat House, at 47 Forehill, dated to 1490 (Figure 129a, b and c), and further up the hill the much altered mid-sixteenth-century timber-framed houses at number 31 and 22 Forehill, the latter now part of the Royal Standard public house (Figure 130). On the ground floor a three-part window with moulded wooden mullions remains at the rear, and the front room has original chamfered beams and plain joists. Closer to the river at Waterside, on a late-seventeenth-century house, can be seen a fire insurance plaque belonging to the Sun Fire Office (see back cover). These marks were used in the eighteenth and nineteenth centuries to indicate to the fire brigade that the building was insured; if not, the owner would be billed should the brigade have to extinguish a fire.

A similar picture emerges from the archaeological investigations between Broad Street and the river. At the time of the *Domesday Book* the area was not occupied at all, with activity beginning between the second half of the twelfth and the early thirteenth century. Occupation was relatively dense and buildings were encountered everywhere that archaeological excavation occurred, suggesting mercantile activity. Occupation on Broad Street was less intensive than on Forehill, where individual property plots were built upon at different times, rather than simultaneously (Alexander 2003). Along Broad Street, in the twelfth century, planned development took place when the street frontage was divided into individual plots from one of which a sword cross and coins were found suggesting a high degree of wealth (Figure 131). Behind the Broad Street frontage was a less intensively used area extending 60m to the river. A warehouse and fishponds plus evidence for the cultivation of hemp, animal grazing and butchery suggests that the land was used for the production and storage of agricultural products for use elsewhere within

Fig 130. The Royal Standard at No. 22 Forehill, Ely, parts of which date to the mid-sixteenth-century. Photo: the authors.

Fig 131. Reconstruction drawing of a twelfth-century property excavated on Broad Street, Ely, based on the archaeological site plan. The building consisted of living accommodation at the front with a large warehouse at the rear. Illustration: Jason Gibbons.

Ely. Along the river itself were a number of hythes or wharves. Development continued throughout the Medieval Period and by the fourteenth and fifteenth centuries the density of occupation along Forehill and Broad Street allows the area to be characterised as urban.

The Bishop and the monastery were the two main landlords and their holdings were unevenly distributed. For example, along Broad Street the monastery owned sixty tenements and the Bishop, twenty-one, but most of the area around West Fen Road had been awarded to the Bishop. The West Fen Road area was from the start a secular rural settlement contemporary with the monastic centre for which Ely was famous; it seems possible that the settlement was even founded in order to provide food and services to the monastery (Mortimer *et al.* 2005). It was certainly part of the monastic estate. Archaeological evidence shows wheat was being grown and that cattle and increasingly sheep were husbanded, reflecting the growing importance of the wool trade in the Medieval Period. As farming intensified in the West Fen Road area the population of what had been a thriving rural settlement was relocated to the area along Forehill and Broad Street. There is archaeological evidence of a major reorganisation of the Bishop's holdings in the twelfth and thirteenth centuries, with intensification of settlement between the new cathedral and the Ouse, corresponding to the decline in activity at West Fen Road where the focus was on producing surplus crops (Ballantyne 2004), and later wool, for export. The area between Broad Street and the River Ouse can be seen as an intermediate area between agricultural production sites in the rural hinterland – such as West Fen Road – and the noxious industries centred on Potters Lane, and the consumption sites of urban Ely focused on the religious establishments of the Bishop and Abbey.

The presence of a well-organised consumer centre at Ely, with its wide-ranging trade connections and good river network, increased the importance of the riverside area. There were several wharves by the river, and the area between Broad Street and the river was settled by merchants and craftsmen. Merchants' houses, which combined warehouse, counting house and accommodation under one roof, were built. The Three Blackbirds on Broad Street is the only surviving merchant's house in this area (Figure 132). It was built towards the end of the thirteenth century and considerably altered in the first half of the fourteenth century. The discovery of millstones imported from Germany in the earliest floor level of the house testifies to the wide-ranging trading contacts that existed at the time, while the 1417 survey of Ely shows that The Three Blackbirds was owned by the Prior and occupied at that time by Thomas Hervy.

Partial excavation of The Three Blackbirds (Pugh 1953, pp.30–2, Hotlon-Krayenbuhl 1984) has added to our knowledge of this building. The roof of the open hall is of particular interest and may date to as early as c.1280. The pine rafters used to form the roof may be re-used scaffold poles, possibly ones used in the construction of the Cathedral Octagon (Rackham in Holton-Krayenbuhl 1984, p.13). The original thirteenth-century building plan was centred around the open hall, which has survived in its roof structure along with a wooden door frame with Caernarvon arch typical of the period (Rackham in Holton-Krayenbuhl 1984, p.13). There was also an undercroft, used for storage, and inner room (counting house), with a chamber above them open at roof height to the open hall. Excavations of the floor revealed a stone hearth and fragments of late-thirteenth-century pottery, together with domestic animal bone, oyster and mussel shells (Rackham in Holton-Krayenbuhl 1984, p.27).

The sophistication of the hall shows that the thirteenth-century builder of The Three Blackbirds was a wealthy man. The location of the building near the river suggests that the owner was a merchant. The hall served as a communal room, with its hearth made from millstones used for cooking and heating. The small

Fig 132. Photograph of the Three Blackbirds, Broad Street, Ely, the last surviving merchant's house in Ely. Photo: the authors.

fragments of animal bone represent food debris trodden into the floor. There was some evidence of small-scale copper-alloy (bronze) smelting, an activity commonly found in medieval buildings. The millstones that made up the hearth were imported from Germany, via King's Lynn, perhaps suggesting that the owner was himself a mill owner (Rackham in Holton-Krayenbuhl 1984, p.35).

In the fourteenth century the outer walls were rebuilt in brick. Surviving from this period are a pair of niches dating to the early fourteenth century and used as cupboards (Figure 133). This building provided living accommodation in the open hall. To the east of the hall were the commercial rooms, the undercroft for storage and the inner room or counting house with a staircase from near the north door leading to the upper chamber. This may have been used for storage, perhaps as lodgings, or as a trading room, although the room appears unheated. Excavations of the floor again revealed animal bone and oyster and mussel shells, this time together with fish bones. The floor had been repeatedly re-laid on a regular basis and was fashioned from beaten clay mixed with ox-blood. In the fifteenth or sixteenth century a chimney stack was inserted into the hall. Excavation revealed that the floors of this period were pink in colour and made of crushed tile and mortar. Within the fill were fragments of bird, cow and horse bone, as well as mussel and oyster shell and contemporary pottery. There was also a silver penny of Edward III (1327–1377).

The façade facing onto Broad Street dates to the nineteenth century and relates to the then-function of the building as a public house, and floors of this period consisted of early-nineteenth-century brick.

RELATIONSHIP OF CHURCH AND TOWNSPEOPLE

The influence of the Church was temporal as well as spiritual, being the owners of much of the Isle from medieval times until the middle of the nineteenth century. The consequences of this were that, for those living in and around Ely, life was rigidly controlled, but there were also benefits. In times of great hardship the citizens of Ely could call upon financial assistance from the Almoner, which at the height of the Church's powers could be considerable. The Church also created work in construction and maintenance of its buildings, the town and its roads, and in the repair and maintenance of the fen drains.

The documentary records are biased in favour of the Church, because of their extensive landholdings and careful custodianship of official records in the Church muniments chests (Figure 134), and often ignore the lives of the ordinary people. For example, we know from documents that the Black Death hit Ely, c.1350, and that there were fifty-three monks before the plague and only twenty-eight after (Stewart 1868, p.207), but there is no mention of its effects on the townspeople even though this must presumably have been equally devastating.

We sometimes have a hint of the lives of ordinary people through their interaction with the monastery. One of the more surprising of these documents is the satirical poem 'Flen flyss' which includes the first recorded publication of the F-word. Composed around 1500 the poem takes aim at the friars for their earthly desires – '*Non sunt in celi quia fuccant uuiuys of heli*', which translates as:

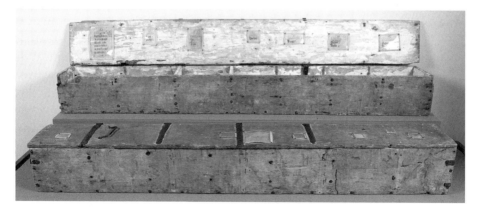

Fig 134. Two muniments chests used to hold official documents, now in Ely Museum. Photo: Steven Stanley Jugg.

'they [the monks] are not in heaven because they fuck the wives of Ely'. The poem opens a window on the earthly temptations and less than holy lives of the monks at this time. Archaeology is better placed to address the hidden relationship between the Church and townspeople, often revealing more than reviews of historical documents.

Taking the faunal remains recovered through archaeological excavation it is possible to look more closely at differences and similarities between the different zones of occupation in Ely (Figure 135). Over the period from the twelfth to the fifteenth century the pattern of exploitation remains similar making it possible to deal with this time span as a single unit. Generally, the evidence from the area between Broad Street and the river shows that butchery of animals was taking place for consumption elsewhere. Sheep/goat and cattle dominate the assemblage in more or less equal numbers, whilst pig is a minor element. The archaeological pattern is similar at West Fen Road and it is probable that it was from this and similar settlements on the Isle of Ely that the animals being butchered originated. Confirmation that the area backing onto the river was a butchery is provided by more detailed analysis of the bones from the site. The majority of animals were killed at prime butchering age: cattle were three to four years old, sheep/goat two to three and pigs one to two years of age. The dominant parts of the skeleton present were associated with primary and secondary butchery with very little kitchen or meal waste present. There were also very few bones of wild animals such as fallow deer and hare, suggesting that hunting was insignificant. This contrasts to other sites in Ely where there was a greater quantity and range including roe deer and rabbit (Dickens and Whittaker in prep; Higbee in Alexander 2003, p.170). At Forehill the faunal assemblage represents remains of animals exploited for food. The skeletal element suggests that dressed carcasses or joints were purchased and that some carcass preparation was carried out on site. Among the wild fowl was a crane, a particularly expensive bird. The broad and rich meat base is indicative of increasing socio-economic status, which corresponds with other evidence showing that from the fifteenth century Forehill was occupied, or owned by, a mix of traders and professionals as well as some minor gentry. The richness of the diet suggests that their social and economic status was comparable to other high-status residences. Comparison with an assemblage from the Bishop's kitchen (Higbee 1999) is interesting. In the later phases there was a diversity of wildfowl including lapwing, swan, wood pigeon, snipe, golden plover, woodcock, grey heron, red grouse, godwit and Whooper swan. In earlier phases pig played a greater role, an indicator of high status.

Overall, it appears that cattle, sheep and pigs were brought to the area between Broad Street and the river for slaughter and butchery but that consumption occurred elsewhere, probably in the religious communities

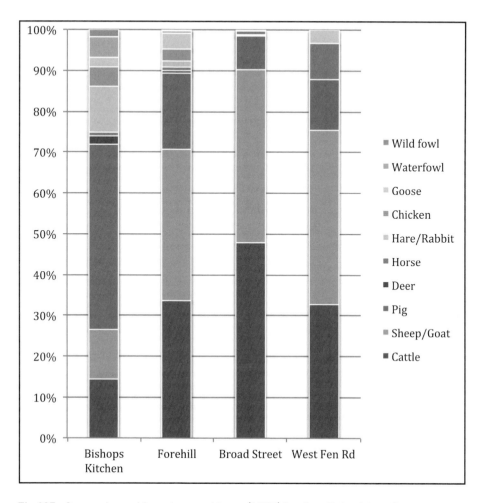

Fig 135. Comparison of faunal assemblages (NISP) fourteenth to sixteenth century. Percentage source: Barrowclough 2010.

of Ely. Excavations at the Lady Chapel of the cathedral show that prepared carcasses were imported ready for further butchery into individual joints (Regan 2001b) and at the Abbey beef and mutton were arriving as dressed cuts although pig, lamb and rabbit were arriving as whole carcasses (Dickens and Whittaker in prep.). At Forehill (Higbee in Alexander 2003) beef and mutton were probably arriving largely as dressed carcasses or joints, so there was a secular market as well. This pattern may explain the lack of rabbit and the low quantities of lamb and pig in the Broad Street area. Killing these species but exporting them as whole carcasses would leave no trace. There is little evidence for consumption of wild species at Broad Street, in contrast to Forehill and more especially the Abbey and Bishop's Palace. Generally whilst higher in status than the agricultural site at West Fen Road, and the production site at Potters Lane, Broad Street seems to be lower in status than both Forehill and the religious communities of the Abbey and Cathedral. In particular, Broad Street produced little or no evidence for high-status foods such as various types of fish, bird and deer or fruits such as fig and grape. This is supported by the ceramic evidence.

Within Ely, sites at Broad Street, Forehill and the religious precinct all contain a similar range of imported pottery. The site at West Fen Road has quite a different pattern, with much more local production and fewer imports (Figure 136). Within this general pattern Broad Street has a lower percentage of fine ware than Forehill and the Abbey and Bishop's Palace, but higher than West Fen Road (Figure 137). Broad Street has a high percentage of intermediate wares when compared to Forehill and greater than West Fen Road and the Abbey. Overall, the impression is that occupation at Broad Street was of lower status than Forehill and the Abbey and Bishop's Palace, but higher than West Fen Road. In addition to confirming the spatial patterning of relative status, analysis of the distribution of different types of pottery sheds light on attitudes to the outside world.

The medieval pottery industry in Ely differed from that of others in East Anglia in being urban. The urban nature of production can be traced to the influence of the Church which first provided a local market for the products and also directed the cutting of new rivers which made the 'export' of Ely ware beyond

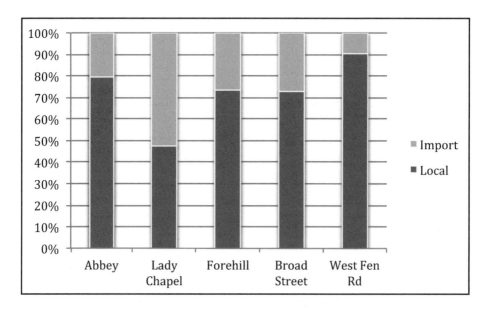

Fig 136. Local versus imported pottery wares: Percentage source: Barrowclough 2010.

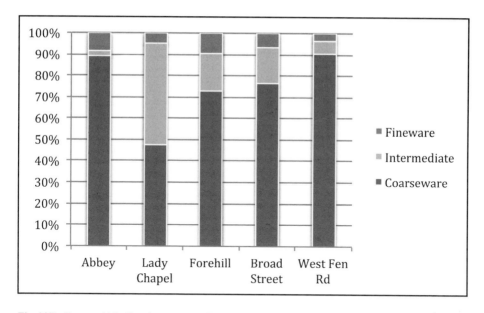

Fig 137. Types of Medieval pottery at Ely sites: Percentage source: Barrowclough 2010.

the boundary of the fen island possible. Medieval Ely ware was the main type of pottery in use on the island between the twelfth and early sixteenth centuries. The date is consistent with the reference to *potterslane* in 1280, when the industry was presumably well established. The industry was very conservative and there were few changes in either fabric or forms over nearly four hundred years to the fifteenth century. The only changes were in decoration. Thumbing, especially applied in strips, is early, mostly thirteenth century, and on bowls, decoration is mainly a fifteenth-century feature. The pottery from the twelfth to fifteenth centuries can therefore be treated as a single group.

Ely's pottery industry had a long life, even though the pottery is not of the best quality in comparison to that available in other parts of eastern England (Colour plate 16). This longevity was owed to the political and economic dominance of the religious establishments in Ely, which owned much of the Fenland and southern Cambridgeshire and was able to control what products went to its estates. The dominance of medieval Ely wares on the island therefore represent a 'parochial cluster' and are not what might be expected for a busy market town (Jones 1993, p.132). As the Church also controlled the river Ouse, the chief southern Fenland waterway, it also had influence on what went to Cambridge from the north. Hence the distribution of Ely wares is greater than might be expected from the quality of the material (Figures 138 and 139). Pottery produced on the Isle of Ely generally did not travel far from the fen, and was probably transported exclusively within waterborne communication networks

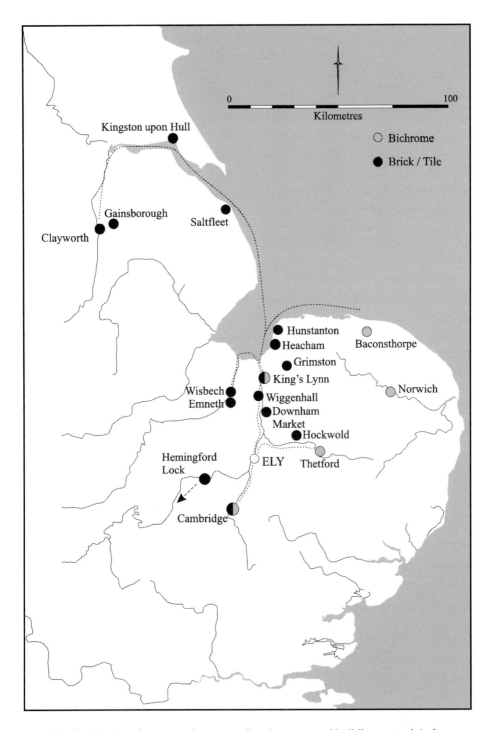

Fig 138. Distribution of exports of post-medieval pottery and building materials from Ely. Source: after Cessford et al. 2006, p.94 fig 65.

(Spoerry 2008). It is found on all Fenland sites and at Cambridge and elsewhere in the south. North of Ely, it occurs at King's Lynn; Ely wares have been noted in southern Lincolnshire and west Norfolk. Although we cannot be certain, evidence from other religious establishments such as Colne (Healey *et al.* 1998, p.57) suggests that the manufacture of pottery in Ely was predominantly for the Bishop's Palace, although the urban location also meant that there was a significant secular market for its wares.

Whilst Ely ware dominates the local assemblage there were significant imports of pottery, mostly fine wares, from Grimston, Norfolk; Lyveden, Northamptonshire; Toynton, Lincolnshire and various sites in Essex plus a little material from Yorkshire and Surrey and a few French imports. Most of the material travelled via King's Lynn; exceptions are the Lyveden ware, and fine Essex redwares that travelled overland to Cambridge and then via the river Cam (Figure 140).

The evidence of the fine wares found in Ely can be linked with the data from Cambridge and King's Lynn to form a larger picture. Imports to Ely arrived via King's Lynn in the main; its importance as a port is illustrated by the occurrence of fine quality decorated jugs from Scarborough and northern Europe (Clarke and Carter 1977, pp.112–18, 225–32). It is possible that fine red wares from Essex arrived at Lynn by sea via Colchester. From the regional pattern of recovery it can be shown that the route was landward to Cambridge and then by the Fenland waterways to Lynn. This is proved from the large quantities of Essex red wares that occur in Cambridge (thirty-six percent at

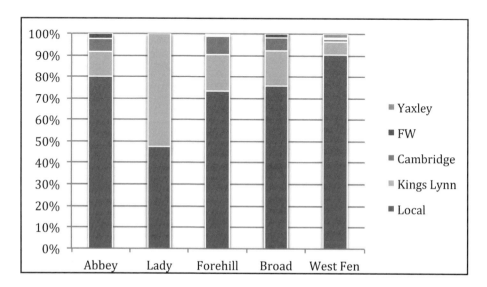

Fig 139. Source of wares from sites in Ely: Percentage source: Barrowclough 2010.

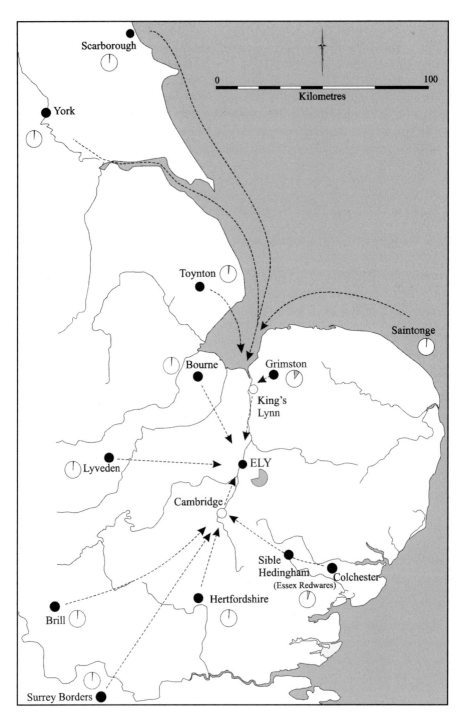

Fig 140. Sources of thirteenth- to fifteenth-century pottery found at Broad Street. Source: after Cessford et al. 2006, p.93 fig 64.

Bene't Court, Edwards and Hall 1997, p.156), with a smaller amount at Forehill in Ely (6 per cent) and yet smaller quantities at Lynn (1 percent, Hall 2001). The differences are striking: had the trade route been by sea and then via the Fenland to Cambridge, then the amounts of sherds recovered would be the other way round, Lynn and Ely keeping more of the fine wares before the residue reached Cambridge. The reverse effect can be seen with the fine quality Scarborough wares. At Lynn they amount to 4 percent, falling to 0.7 percent at Ely, with none so far identified at Cambridge.

CONCLUSION

Much of what we call Ely today can be traced to the Medieval Period. As we have seen the street pattern that we follow is remarkably similar to that of the Medieval Period, and even some of the houses are the same. Shifting our discussion to the world immediately beyond the Isle we find that Ely was the dominant religious centre beyond the Isle ranging over the southern fens, most of which it owned.

Although descriptions of the Fens often focus on their role as a barrier inhospitable to outsiders, typical of which are the accounts of Hereward the Wake and his followers, there is a more passive aspect to them as a valuable resource of food, fuel and grazing. Access to, and control over, the Fens was controlled by manorial officers. Overseen by the officers, peat was dug extensively for turves, but only by the inhabitants of the manor who were prohibited from selling them to neighbouring villages. Sedge was likewise freely available to villagers, who used it for thatching, but again they were prohibited from selling it to outsiders.

If the construction of Ely Cathedral was the most significant change in the cultural landscape of the Isle during the Medieval Period, then the most significant change in the physical landscape was the action taken to control the River Ouse. The river originally ran from Earith, west of the Isle of Ely, to Benwick, where it joined the River Nene, before continuing to Wisbech via March. On March island an artificial channel, 12km long, was cut through a narrow neck of land forming a connection to the Old Croft River at Upwell. In the early Middle Ages water from the River Ouse was able to flow from Earith, south of the Isle of Ely, where it joined the River Cam. The eastern Ouse-Cam river had a sinuous course flowing between the Ely islands of Stuntney and Quanea, but in the twelfth century a diversion was made to Ely where quays, called hithes, were built at Ely before 1210 so as to fascilitate the transport of building stone for the construction of the cathedral and its associated buildings. Examples of these hithes were found by the river, under what is now Jubilee Gardens, off Broad Street. The river once continued to Wisbech, and thence the Wash, but another straight length of the Ouse, the Ten Mile River, probably also made in the twelfth century, diverted all the south-eastern Fenland waters to King's Lynn via Downham Market.

Ely had been an important trading site since before the Norman Conquest, because of its significance as a religious centre, and formed part of a trading network along with Cambridge, Huntingdon and Peterborough. A market was held each week to sell livestock, field and garden produce. At Ely, like the other larger markets, specific areas were allocated to particular commodities. For example, butchers had semi-permanent stalls in an area which became known as the 'botcherie', and butter was sold in the 'butter market'. The word hill was commonly used in this region for the open spaces in which markets were held, hence Forehill being the site of Ely's market, although in Ely the market is literally at the top of a hill.

Whilst markets were held on a regular weekly basis, fairs were only held annually, marking the saint day of St Etheldreda. Most successful medieval markets like Ely's, and also those in Cambridge and Peterborough, had good water and road communications, a factor that was even more important in the success of a fair. The manipulation of the River Ouse was key to the success of Ely as it permitted the free movement of goods across the Fens and from beyond that supplied the fair at Ely, as it also did those at Wisbech, St Ives, Peterborough and Cambridge. Just how important waterborne communication was is highlighted by the effect of the seventeenth-century fen drainage schemes that improved links to several smaller settlements allowing, for example, Haddenham to obtain a market and fair charter in 1612 and Stretham one in 1634, thus lessening to some extent the mercantile monopoly of Ely. Items sold at the fair in Ely consisted in the main of non-perishable materials and products that could be stored and stockpiled by the producer, and bought annually by the consumer. These included building materials such as: timber, cloth (especially luxury imports such as silk), spices, wine and also livestock.

In addition to the commercial imperative of the fair there were also social and religious aspects to it. Ely's fair, as with those at Peterborough and St Ives, offered an element of pilgrimage allowing the devout to visit the shrine of St Etheldreda, but was also associated with entertainment and recreation. There is no modern equivalent annual event which combines shopping with religious worship and also recreation, although each of these activities seems familiar to a modern reader. For those who know Ely well, it is not hard to imagine how we might combine the festivities of the annual fair with that of a busy market day and a religious festival, conjuring a vivid image of bustling streets filled with music, the calls of hawkers and exotic smells of spices and food.

CHAPTER 8

CONCLUSION

How shall we come into Ely? As archaeologists, as pilgrims spiritually inclined and chanting a sursum corda *as we go, or shall we be gross and earthly, scenting lamb and green peas, spring duckling and asparagus from afar...*

Charles Harper, 1902.

INTRODUCTION

We began this book with a discussion of theories of time, explaining how it is often seen as progressing in a linear way, as an arrow in flight, following Zeno (Chapter 1). This view, we argued, was over simplistic, failing to address on the one hand why it is that for long periods of time things often appear remarkably stable, and yet at a later date may suddenly change. A way to conceptualise time better is to adopt the *Annales* model, which has the ability to combine long-term change and also short-term cyclical events (Figure 141).

We have adopted this approach to offer new insights into the historical development of the Isle of Ely. In this chapter we will now consider how individuals and societies, places, events and trends in the medium and long

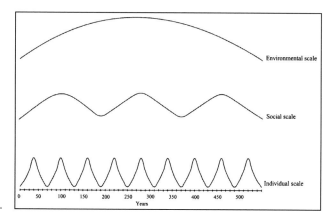

Fig 141. Schematic representation of different rates of change for different processes. Source: Lucas 2005, p.18.

term come together to make the Isle's specific pasts. We must say 'pasts' rather than 'past' as there can be no definitive past; interpretations of historic events are necessarily subjective, and the narrative that we construct here is but one of several equally valid histories.

A DIACHRONIC STUDY OF THE ISLE OF ELY

The longest time scale that we consider, that of geological processes changing over the *longue durée*, was considered in Chapter 2. We, like our forefathers, are currently experiencing one of the regular warm Interglacial Periods, the

Fig 142. Nine models of hominid ancestors. Top row, from left to right: *Australopithecus anamensis, Kenyanthropus platyops, Australopithecus afarensis.* Middle row, from left to right: *Australopithecus africanus, Homo rudolfensis, Homo hablis.* Bottom row, from left to right: *Paranthropus boisei, Homo heidelbergensis, Homo neanderthalensis.* Source: Sebastian Niedlich.

Flandrian, that began *c.*12,000 years ago. At some point, and it is hard to predict exactly when, this warm period will end, and we will enter the next Glacial cold phase. Sea levels will fall as much, if not all, of Britain becomes uninhabitable. By the time the glaciation ends and we enter into the next warm phase, many thousands of years in the future, Britain will be reoccupied, possibly by a further evolved species of human, just as we replaced our earliest ancestors, or perhaps if our species has become extinct, by some other species of animal altogether (Figure 142). Should they care to investigate the archaeology of the Isle it is likely that only the faintest traces of our occupation will survive, with much of what we have striven to build over the last millennia having been scoured away by the bull-dozing effect of the glaciers.

Within the Flandrian (Figure 12) we are currently living through the Modern Period of history (AD 1800 onwards), a period marked by great technological advances, which began with the Industrial Revolution and currently sees no sign of ending. Indeed, if anything the rate and frequency of technological changes have increased since the advent of microprocessors, which have changed the way we work and socialise. Current developments in genetic engineering, which are led by companies based around Cambridge, are likely to have an equally significant impact on medicine and agriculture, promising to change our life expectations and those of our children. The *moyenne durée* of medium-term history forms the focus of Chapters 3 to 7, each taking a different period for consideration. At this scale we are able to consider the nature of islandness itself, and when we do it rapidly becomes clear just how fluid a concept this is in the context of the Isle of Ely. The extent to which the Isle has been isolated by water and fen has varied considerably through time as is shown in Figure 143. What is important is the way that the inhabitants, and the outside world, view the Isle. In this way islandness is as much, if not more, a mental construct as a physical reality.

One of the most remarkable features of the evidence presented in these chapters is the continuity across the different historic periods. The causeways at Aldreth and Stuntney have been in constant, daily, use since at least the Bronze Age, with that between Stuntney and Ely remaining one of the major arterial routes into and out of Ely and the Isle. Although much resurfaced, the actual route would be familiar to any of our forebears who would have no difficulty in navigating the route onto the Isle. Similarly, once in Ely they would find the street pattern of the city remarkably familiar. Broad Street, Backhill and Forehill, the Market Square and monastic/cathedral precincts have changed very little in the last 900 years. Excavations at West Fen Road, Ely, illustrate this very well (Figure 144). A large settlement was established, most likely by the Church, in the mid Anglo-Saxon Period to provide supplies for the monastery. The site seems to have been located with reference to an

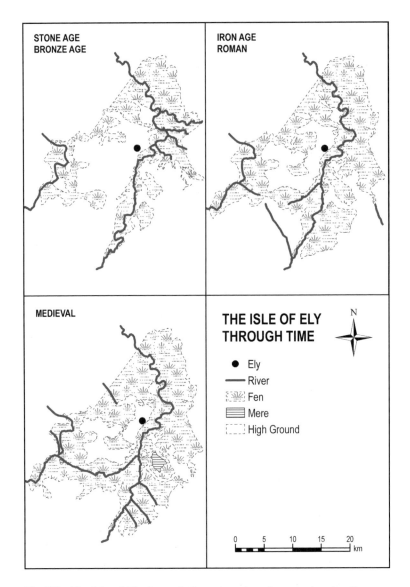

Fig 143. The Isle of Ely through time. A series of maps showing the extent to which the Isle has been separated by water and fen from the Bronze Age through to the medieval period. Map data © OpenStreetMap contributors, CC BY-SA.

existing routeway of possible Iron Age or Roman date linking Ely to Coveney via a causeway. Activities on the site were agricultural consisting of crop production and animal husbandry, which increased in the later Anglo-Saxon Period, probably as a result of the growth of the monastery and increased population. Following the Norman Conquest there is a suggestion from the archaeological analysis of food waste that increased taxes led the inhabitants of the settlement to seek out wild foods from the Fens. The settlement was reorganised, again probably by the Church, with much of the population being relocated to the Broad Street area in the twelfth and thirteenth centuries. This allowed for the consolidation of the small Anglo-Saxon plots into larger farms and the consequent intensification of agriculture.

Individual buildings have come and gone, and the cathedral undergone extension and modification, but in truth surprisingly little has changed. What might be more noticeable to a returning visitor is the suburban expansion that has occurred in the last three decades, but that would be equally true of an emigrant returning after thirty years abroad as to someone returning after three centuries, such has been the rate of development in the recent past. We will leave it for history to record as to whether it has been prudent to develop the city so much in such a short space of time.

At the level of the individual, short-term *evenements*, each generation has faced its own challenges and witnessed triumph and tragedy. The Isle has faced the dramatic battles and skirmishes of Anglo-Saxon, Viking and Norman invaders, played host to kings and queens and has also been the temporary home of Oliver Cromwell. Important as they are the fact remains that, for the large part, life carries on much today as it did in the past. The rites of passage of the human life-cycle – birth, marriage, parenthood, old age and finally death – continue to be universals in the lives of the people who live on the Isle, and at an individual level figure much more in importance than the great events of the day.

UNDERSTANDING SOCIAL REPRODUCTION ON THE ISLE OF ELY

One of our aims has been to make sense of the patterns in the landscape as they changed through time. Since this question can only be answered after a review of all the separate periods, which was the subject matter of the previous chapters, dealt with from the point of view of relations between objects, sites and monuments, the landscape and people, it is only now that we can turn to this question. It may well be the most difficult question for us to answer as we are dealing with attitudes towards objects and places that are often alien to us.

In Chapter 1 the notion of a particular island identity was introduced. It is now time to revisit that notion in the context of the identity of the Isle's inhabitants, and to propose a new, diachronic, model for this small island society.

In the preceding chapters we saw that a feature of the archaeological record, as elsewhere in Britain and beyond, was the burial of individuals in funerary monuments and the deposition of metalwork in natural places. It was through those acts that the identity of places in the landscape was constructed. The evidence from the Bronze Age hoards is particularly informative in this regard, with the siting of hoards on causeways and major routes to and from the island, reinforcing the separation between the Isle and the world beyond. We also saw that the particular form of burials, and the particular metalwork types selected for deposition had a distinctly local flavour. Burial barrows were often constructed on higher ground overlooking the island coast, as in Ely and

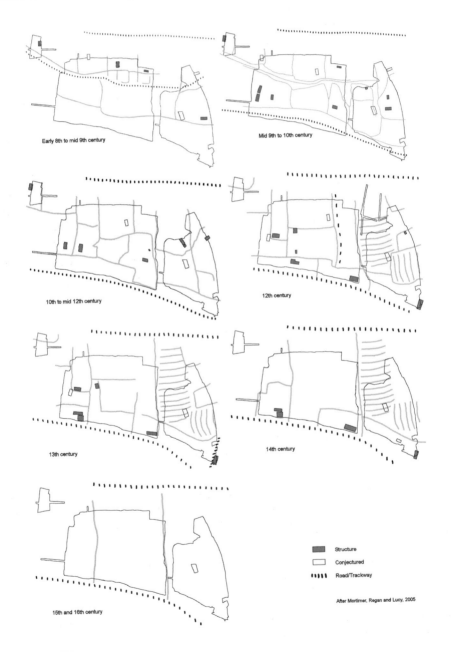

Early 8th to mid 9th century

Mid 9th to 10th century

10th to mid 12th century

12th century

13th century

14th century

15th and 16th century

Structure

Conjectured

Road/Trackway

After Mortimer, Regan and Lucy, 2005

at Sutton, where burials were also constructed on small islets. The Isle seems to have been a regionally important focus for Bronze Age, and also Anglo-Saxon, metalwork innovations, which saw the development of the nationally significant later Bronze Age Wilburton style of metalwork and the creation of new types of object in the flesh-hook from Little Thetford. During the Anglo-Saxon Period it was of course the home to the wealthy religious community founded by St Etheldreda, and the richly furnished burials of the period include a great square-headed brooch of a type native to Ely (Hines 1997). It was in the selection and performance of those acts of burial that the participants defined themselves, through practices, as an island community with its own identity. This is how the small-scale later prehistoric community reproduced itself as a community with a distinct island identity whilst at the same time being recognisable as part of the wider Bronze Age or Anglo-Saxon worlds.

A number of archaeological studies (see papers in Canuto and Yaeger 2000) have demonstrated that an individual can be, simultaneously, a member of different communities: a household, an age group spanning several households, a burial community, and a sacrificial community. This is because a community is a symbolic construction: it is about differentiating between 'us' and 'them'. Membership is based on practices, knowledge and symbols, by which a group distinguishes itself from others (Yaeger and Canuto 2000, pp.1-15). In a study of later prehistoric society in North West England, Barrowclough (2007) showed how different practices, carried out in the landscape, were related to the construction of communities. Similarly, in the case of the Isle of Ely, the siting of particular practices in the landscape can be linked to the construction and maintenance of communal identities.

Burials of the Early Bronze Age are one example. In life individual households were dispersed across the island. In death individuals were brought together

Fig 144. Opposite: Continuity and change on West Fen Road. From top left to right. **1**. Mid-Saxon, early eighth to mid ninth century, the establishment of the settlement showing a number of enclosures between and to the south of two parallel roads. **2**. Late Saxon, mid-ninth to tenth century, the expansion of the settlement with a larger number of smaller enclosures coming into being as the population increased. **3**. Late Saxon, tenth to mid-twelfth century, continuation of agricultural activity with very little significant change. **4**. Twelfth century, consolidation of some of the smaller plots and the beginning of ridge-and-furrow agriculture. **5**. Thirteenth century, continuation of the consolidation and reorganisation of the settlement that had begun in the twelfth century. **6**. Fourteenth century, by this time the consolidation had been completed and three substantial farms had been created along the routeway to the south, with smaller buildings functioning as ancillary structures to the farms. The northern part of the site had all become agricultural land. **7**. Fifteenth and sixteenth century, the continuation of the three farms which were still in existence up to the twentieth century when the land was purchased for the construction of suburban housing. Source: after Mortimer et al. 2005.

in funerary monuments, which perhaps represented the household, at least symbolically, of the dead. These monuments tend to cluster in groups, for example in Ely and at Sutton (Chapter 4), bringing together several households, in a community of the dead. By burying the dead of several households within the same barrow cemetery, a sense of community was expressed that did not come to the fore in other aspects of culture. Funerary monuments are therefore a symbolic resource, through which people defined themselves as an island community.

In the Middle and Late Bronze Age a different type of community was constructed, a sacrificial community centred on bronze deposition in natural places. In this case, as we saw in Chapter 4, special practices of deposition were performed in particular, often wet, places in the landscape. The focus of depositing large amounts of metalwork in one place, hoarding, often on or adjacent to causeways linking the island to the outside world, resulted in the construction and maintenance of community affiliation.

Although there are stark differences between burial and sacrificial communities, particularly in the material forms chosen to display their affiliation, there are also important similarities. In particular, the types of places selected as significant locations emphasise the boundary between dry and wet land, and between the island and the world beyond. Both periods also, whilst expressing wider, national, cultural traits, articulate these in a distinctive manner. This gives the assemblages of objects a local island identity, implying the existence of a community, not just of people who co-existed, but also of shared ideology. This is rendered visible to us in the selection and adoption of particular local forms of metalwork, the Wilburton Style, and the choice of some innovative metalwork types, the flesh-hook. Island identity was therefore constructed in opposition to supra-regional Bronze Age identities.

Once established in the Late Neolithic and Early Bronze Age we can trace through the archaeological remains how this island identity was maintained, with each generation continually reworking the landscape to reflect its island identity. Thus, in the Iron Age we see the construction of Wardy Hill hillfort (Chapter 5), located both strategically and symbolically at one of the causewayed entrances to the Isle, linking Ely to Coveney, where an earlier generation had deposited a hoard of bronze shields. The entrance to the Aldreth causeway was controlled by Belsar's Hill hillfort. To date no hillfort has been found on the Stuntney causeway, which was in the Medieval Period controlled by a castle at Castlehythe, but we consider that a site either in Stuntney or Ely would be a likely candidate for such an Iron Age structure (probably laying beneath modern development). The Iron Age also saw the emergence of the insular cult of the head, furthering the symbolic and physical separation between the island and the world beyond. A division reinforced, for example, by the construction of Iron

Age and Romano-British shrines on an Early Bronze Age barrow at Haddenham, maintaining a *longue durée* of ritual and ceremony on the island edge of Ely. This continued in the later Anglo-Saxon and Medieval Periods, generally across the Isle, famous as a monastic and ecclesiastical centre.

UNDERSTANDING ISLAND IDENTITY

The difference between insular and non-local identity mattered on the Isle and had implications for the way in which objects were treated. Islandness was important, and as one of the 'ties that bind', was inextricably linked to the diachronic reproduction of society. The reality of a community firmly rooted in a specific environment, and the ensuing sense of belonging, seems to have been at odds with another reality, that of participating in long-distance, supra-regional, exchange networks. These were not just about acquiring access to non-local materials, but also about sharing cultural knowledge of the supra-regionally acknowledged categories that give periods their distinctive character such as 'Stone', 'Bronze' or 'Iron' Age (Figure 145).

In the previous chapters we saw that although the island contains some raw materials, clay and a variety of food stuffs, which were exploited, the inhabitants of Ely often chose to import from elsewhere. In Chapters 3 and 4 we saw that this was true from the late Neolithic onwards when flint was imported from mines in Norfolk for the manufacture of Beaker style flint daggers. In Chapter 7 we saw that medieval pottery was also imported from Essex and even Scarborough, although in small numbers, even though there was an insular industry located around the waterside of Ely. Thus, the necessity to participate in exchange networks spanning vast distances must have been an essential characteristic of the *longue durée* of communities on the Isle.

This point has consequences for the way the Isle's inhabitants perceived themselves as part of the wider world. Helms (1988, p.22) showed that all social groups recognise spatial and cosmological frames, within which they occupy the central position. However such frames were conceptualised, they are essentially about the identity of the group as constructed in opposition to the world beyond. We know that the island's inhabitants systematically derived vital items via long-distance contact networks, so it can be assumed that there must always have been a tension between two different kinds of social reality:

1. The reality of the island community rooted in a sense of belonging to a specific locality. This is the reality of daily life and feelings of belonging. It is also about feeling attached to the area in which one lives: the specific environment, the buildings, the monuments and its idiosyncratic local history (Gerritsen 2001). For the island society that we

are studying this local identity must have been the most important and pervasive social reality (Chapman 1998, p.110).

2.   There is also a reality that is detached from locality. This is the reality of the 'importing' society, in which one's own group is perceived as being part of a wider social network (Barth 1992, p.29). Here people saw themselves as necessarily linked to a more encompassing social world, acknowledging that the cycles by which a social unit reproduces itself draws upon resources derived from a wider geographical and social world (see Barrett 1998, p.19).

These two realities need to co-exist. For an island group to reproduce itself, the world beyond that group is vital, if only for the exchange of breeding stock and of crucial non-local materials. At the same time, the outside world is potentially ambiguous and dangerous. A sense of belonging to a wider social world denotes the dependency of the local group on others for the

Fig 145. Martial identity was an important component of an idealised male identity in both the Bronze and Iron Ages. In Theodor de Bry's engraving 'The Trvve Picture of One Picte' (based on a watercolour by John White) two decapitated heads are seen, emphasising the warrior's prowess. Source: Hariot 1588.

reproduction of the island group. It emphasises dependency on factors beyond one's own control. Crucial is the realisation that what effectively links both realities is the imported object or material. Helms shows how foreign things for that reason alone tend to be seen as imbued with meaning. They are the objectification of the reach of the island group upon resources beyond their existence as determined locally (Helms 1993, p.99).

THE SIGNIFICANCE OF NON-LOCAL IDENTITY

Non-local materials were of importance from the Late Neolithic and Early Bronze Age onwards. For example, even when a local industry existed such as metalworking in the later Bronze Age, or pottery manufacture in the Medieval Period, metalwork and ceramics continued to be imported. Bradley has shown that one of the characteristic features of the European Bronze Age was the enormous distances travelled by some types of artefacts, and the same can be said about those of the Iron Age, Roman, Anglo-Saxon and Medieval Periods. He makes the argument that it must have been the foreignness of the object which mattered. There must have been a cultural preference for non-local material (Bradley 1990, 131–35). Such a preference has wider implications than just the objects themselves. By adopting supra-regional artefacts, membership was claimed of distant non-local communities. Following Isbell (2000, 243–66), we may perhaps speak of membership of 'imagined' communities.

The point is that within the Isle there was a concern with concepts of identity in which the links with the world beyond were emphasised. As Barrett (1998, p.23) puts it: 'In such cases the biographical histories of objects and of the body itself may have converged in such a way as to ensure that the body's identity was expressed in terms of distances travelled and of absent origins'. The significance of adopting such non-local identities seems to have been considerable. For example, when local bronze industries emerged although they exhibited considerable local innovation they still adopted broader patterns of deposition through the adoption of hoarding.

Inherent in this situation, where the world beyond daily existence mattered considerably, was a tension between the significance of local and non-local identities, which had to be managed and resolved. It is argued that, for the later Prehistoric Period, practices of deposition, associated with burial and also with metalwork, were related to this.

During the Bronze Age the deliberate giving up of apparently valuable objects was a culturally prescribed and meaningful way to deal with objects (Fontijn 2002, p.275). Whether placed in a grave, singly or in hoards, we are dealing with biographies of objects in which a life of circulation ended in deliberate deposition, where a useable object was sacrificed. This situation was repeated during the Anglo-Saxon Period when high-status burials were accompanied by valuable grave goods including brooches, beads and even imported glass vessels from France (Chapter 6).

TIME AND CONTINUITY OF DEPOSITION

A feature of deposits is that they were often structured: specific object types ended up in specific places. For this to happen there must have been general agreement amongst the population that the landscape of the Isle was structured in such a way that certain kinds of places were appropriate for depositing particular types of object. This implies that other environmental elements were not considered the right place to deposit objects. The systems of selective deposition seem to have been based on shared, cultural understanding of the landscape. This understanding was reproduced by every new deposit. The system must therefore have been profoundly traditional. People repeatedly visited specific types of places in the landscape in order to carry out specific types of deposition. Taking the later Bronze Age as an example, throwing a spear into a bog leaves nothing but a memory in the mind of the observer. In the absence of permanent markers, for which there is no archaeological evidence, there existed a collective memory for the traditional location of deposition. To an outsider there would be nothing to indicate the long-term history of deposition in a fen. Yet particular locations, such as between Little Thetford and Barway (Barrowclough forthcoming), were selected time after time for such actions. The repeated use of the same places must have been deliberate: such places were meaningful and historical, and imbued with memory.

It is impossible to recapture archaeologically what it was that made some places culturally appropriate locations for deposition. But, we may attempt to understand the mechanism by which knowledge was transmitted through the generations within the community by way of ethnographic analogy. These sources confirm the existence of comparable natural sacrificial sites, with usage over equally large spans of time as those in, for example, the Bronze Age (Mulk 1997) through to Iron Age and Roman at Haddenham. Key to the transmission of such knowledge in non-literate society is myth and folk tale. Küchler (1987) and Rowlands (1993) both make the point that in the transmission of cultural knowledge there is a tension between continuity and change. In order to memorise particular fens and rivers as historical locations for deposition people must have drawn upon mental templates to create a mental map (Rowlands 1993, p.141; see also Gell 1992, pp.190–205).

In the case of bronze deposition on the Isle we see evidence for the interplay between continuity and change. In the Fens surrounding the island deposition of metalwork took place throughout the whole of the Bronze Age. The historical practice of deposition defines the wet context of the Fens as a particular zone in the landscape. This continuity is set against changes that took place during the Bronze Age. In particular one can point to the shift from burial deposition to metal deposition in the Fens dated to the Middle Bronze Age. This seems to have been associated with the acquisition of new forms of martial identity evidenced by, for example, the shields deposited at Coveney and the spears in the Wilburton and other hoards (Chapter 4). This form of identity continued into the Iron Age with the construction of defended hillforts such as Wardy Hill, Coveney and the warrior burial at Soham (Chapter 5), and ended with the Anglo-Saxon burials with swords and shields in Ely (Chapter 6).

Continuity and change were in tension. In this context the Little Thetford flesh-hook may be re-interpreted as an attempt to break with the past. It reflects, in its structure and components, a deliberate attempt to differentiate past from present as a way of claiming new status positions associated with feasting rituals. These went hand in hand with attempts at naturalising these new positions by claiming bonds with former occupiers of the land. This is most clear in the practice of hoarding where the large quantities of Middle Bronze Age metalwork continues an earlier tradition of deposition begun in the Early Bronze Age, if not before.

THE REPRODUCTION OF ISLAND SOCIETY THROUGH OBJECTS AND SITES

We have seen that imported objects were important throughout the history of the island for the reproduction of society. Through examples from the Bronze Age and Anglo-Saxon Period we have established that depositional practices were conceptually linked to imported artefacts. The strangeness and foreignness of the import is something that required a response among the people of the Isle who acquired it; the object needed to be recontextualised. This required practices suppressing strangeness, relocating the artefact within island society, enabling its comprehension (see Barrett 1999, p.23). These might involve practices that ignored the dependency to which the imported object testified, and realigned the object with the moral order at home (Bloch and Parry 1989). Artefacts, as carriers of histories of long-distance exchange, so often ended up in deposition, that we may assume that deposition was one way to achieve this.

The particular way in which deposition achieved this is unclear from the archaeology. The local landscape is the most conspicuous environment from which island communities can derive a sense of belonging (Gerritsen 2001, pp.125-26). Placing imported objects in this landscape might therefore be considered a compelling way to realign a foreign idea, symbolised by the object selected for deposition, with the local order at home. Bloch and Parry (1989) state that such practices are widespread. On the basis of ethnographic examples they point out how sacrifice, or transformation, of some representative item was a way to make alien, ambiguous items derived from beyond, morally acceptable at home.

Deposition was about much more than simply recontextualising foreign items. Rather it was about the recontextualising or ordering of specific ideas and values. Many of the objects deposited have far more meanings and qualities than just being exotic. They are about personal statuses and identities, related to life-cycles, social power and special activity (such as participating in long-distance exchange, warfare or religion). They are about communal practices and identities: building barrows or churches, cutting down forest, or digging river channels, or highly specific ideas and values celebrated in ceremonial items, for example the pierced lunate spearheads found in the Wilburton hoard (Chapter 4) or Christian crosses found in the Westfield Farm burials (Chapter 6).

Many of the identities are charged, ambiguous and dangerous. A warrior identity is one that pervades many of the periods we have considered in the earlier chapters, evidence for which is provided by the ritual deposits of weapons found in the later Bronze Age hoards, by the Iron Age warrior burial and hillfort, by swords accompanying burials of the Anglo-Saxon Period and by the castles built and knights stationed on the Isle of Ely from time to time during the Medieval Period. Although meaningful symbols, these weapons also represent a society in which small-scale warfare was endemic, taking place as part of the life-cycle of individuals. Perhaps the best evidence for this comes from excavations at Hurst Lane where an Iron Age skull showed signs of death caused by several blows, and also cuts, to the head (Chapter 5). Other skulls from this site had been separated from their bodies and showed signs of having been 'polished', seemingly part of an island-wide pattern of manipulation of heads reproduced at West Fen Road, Wardy Hill, the Ashwell Site, Trinity Lands and the Prickwillow Road excavations. Taken together it is argued that this may reflect a 'cult of the head' peculiar to the island and practised by its warriors: a potent symbol of island identity. In such circumstances the aggression of the warrior had to be controlled for the good of society. Following the anthropologist Harrison (1995, pp.87, 91) we argue that martial identities were essentially temporary ones up to at least the Medieval Period. They were something on the outer surface that could be worn or shed by wearing or laying down the appropriate paraphernalia in ritualised circumstances.

It is argued, following Fontijn (2002, ch.11), that the practice of weapon deposition in special places and circumstances, originating in the Bronze Age, may well be understood as the reflection of the ritual laying down of such roles. Supra regional *personas* that were constructed through foreign, or foreign-styled, objects (such as swords) may also have been charged, confined ones, at odds with the reality of the island community, who defined themselves as belonging to the people they lived and worked with on a daily basis and their attachment to the local island environment. As time progressed in the Iron Age the practice changed to one of decapitation and burial, but as with Bronze Age metal deposition, it was the foreign, 'outsider', that was ritually deposited, often in the ditches of the hillfort or domestic enclosure. The later development of those practices saw swords and shields buried with high-status individuals, often male but not exclusively, in the Anglo-Saxon Period. Some of these people seem to have been from outside the immediate area, perhaps even from distant lands, but it was not their exoticness that marked them out for burial: instead it was their *personas* as high-ranking individuals that gave them this right.

Deposition, by its very nature, has the quality of coping with ambiguous and circumscribed identities and the values they represent. The meanings of the objects or defeated foe are celebrated and magnified in front of onlookers but deconstructed as well. The ritual ends up in their definite disappearance. In the case of weapons, the paraphernalia signalling identity are laid down, and in the case of the Iron Age the enemy's head is physically severed from the body making the elements of deconstruction tangible. It may be no coincidence that depositional locations, frequently boundaries or thresholds, were themselves often ambiguous in nature as were the objects which were placed in them.

Selective deposition, whether in burials or of metalwork, is a system of maintaining island identity whilst articulating change. As such it is a system for resolving ideological and political tensions stemming from different ideas and values that exist within every society. It is through this mechanism that we can see, in part at least, how society on the Isle was reproduced though time.

CONCLUDING COMMENTS

We have found that an insular identity particular to the Isle of Ely has its origins in the Early Bronze Age, when the boundary between the Isle and the outside world was marked by the ritual and ceremonial placing of the dead in barrows. This concern with the marking of territory separating the Isle from the outside world, which had begun with the Early Bronze Age burial barrows, intensified during the later Bronze Age when metalwork hoards were placed on the causeways leading to and from the Isle. The contents of these hoards frequently contained insular weapons of Wilburton type.

The local concern with the insular and outside world was articulated during the Iron Age through an island-wide cult practice, which focused on the ritual burial of the heads of enemies and foes ceremonially severed from their bodies. This cult of the head reinforced the warrior identity that had evolved in the later Bronze Age both ritually and practically. The siting of the Iron

Age and Romano-British shrine complex atop an Early Bronze Age barrow at Haddenham serves as a physical manifestation of this ideology.

During the Roman Period imperial power suppressed the island's identity, particularly following the Boudican revolt. Nonetheless it was unable to eradicate it altogether. Excavations and fieldwork on the Isle have demonstrated that during this period there was a restricted range of Roman object types, and that those that are found occur in lower numbers than would be expected from excavation of comparable sites elsewhere in the region. In contrast to much of Norfolk and Cambridgeshire there are no Roman villas on the Isle, a fact that is striking when there are so many in the area immediately beyond, for example at Burwell and Isleham. The lack of Roman material culture points to the Isle's silent resistance to the Roman occupation, and a stubborn refusal to adopt a Roman way of life.

The withdrawal of Rome from England allowed the Isle of Ely to once again assert its independence. During the Anglo-Saxon Period there was a resurgence of its ritual and religious insular identity. Evidence provided by the objects that archaeologists have excavated on the Isle reveals the existence of local types, for example an island variant of the dramatic great square-headed brooch type. Buildings were constructed on an equally impressive scale, beginning with the first priory and culminating in the medieval cathedral of Ely. The aim of the building was to make the Christian centre visible and to assert the power and independence of the Church. The island location chosen for the centre reinforces the symbolic separation of the Church from the secular world, and also had a practical defensive purpose. Variously attacked by invading Viking and Norman armies, and laid siege by numerous civil wars and disorders, each have successively reinforced the insular identity of those living on the Isle in opposition to 'outsiders' associated with feelings of both fear and loathing.

The wider lessons we can learn from this study are that individual and social identities are fluid, learnt and cross cut gender, age and status. They are dependent on constant reiteration through both everyday actions and discursive practice that continually recreate and define the boundaries of those groups. It is no longer appropriate to see a direct link between the artefacts that people use, the way they dress, the monuments they bury their dead in, and their 'identity'. Nor should they see 'societies' or 'cultures' as static, isolated and homogenous, when they are in reality constantly in flux, characterised by ambiguity and complexity. Society in general, and identity in particular, are much more complex phenomena that have to be studied with greater subtlety, and with a greater regard for issues of action, interaction and practice. In order to study aspects of communal, *island*, identity, we need to pay more attention to the diachronic contexts in which things are used and the ways in which people use them across different scales of analysis. It is these differences in practice that may serve as the locus for emphasising communal distinctions.

BIBLIOGRAPHY

Alexander, M. 2003. 'A medieval and post-medieval street frontage: investigations at Ely Forehill', *Proceedings of the Cambridge Antiquarian Society* 92, pp.135–82.

Atkins, R. 2011. 'Beaker pits and a probable mortuary enclosure on Land off Stirling Way, near Witchford, Ely', *Proceedings of the Cambridge Archaeological Society* Vol.C, pp.47–66.

Ballantyne, R. 2004. 'Islands in wilderness: the changing Medieval use of the East Anglian peat fens, England', *Environmental Archaeology* 9, pp.189–98.

Barrett, J. 1989. 'Time and Tradition: The Rituals of Everyday Life' in H.A. Nordstrom and A. Knape (eds), *Bronze Age Studies*, Stockholm, pp.113–26.

Barrett, J.C. 1994. *Fragments from Antiquity: an archaeology of social life in Britain, 2900–1200 BC*. Oxford: Blackwell.

Barrett, J.C. 1998. 'The politics of scale and the experience of distance: the Bronze Age world system' in L. Larsson and B. Stjernquist (eds), *The World View of Prehistoric Man* Stockholm: KVHAA Konferenser 40, pp.13–25.

Barrett, J.C. 1999. 'The mythical landscapes of the British Iron Age' in W. Ashmore and A.B. Knapp (eds), *Archaeologies of Landscape: Contemporary Perspectives* Oxford: Blackwell, pp.253–65.

Barrowclough, D. 2005. 'Dancing in time: activating the prehistoric landscape' in M.E. Chester-Kadwell (ed.), *Active landscapes: Palaeolithic to Present. Archaeological Review from Cambridge* 20.1, pp.39–54.

Barrowclough, D. 2007. *Multi-Temporality and Material Culture: An Investigation of Continuity and Change in Later Prehistoric Lancashire*. Oxford: BAR British Series 436.

Barrowclough, D. and Malone, C. 2007. *Cult in Context: reconsidering ritual in archaeology*. Oxford: Oxbow Books.

Barrowclough, D. 2008. *Prehistoric Lancashire*. Stroud: The History Press, pp.19–20, Fig.5.

Barrowclough, D. 2010. 'Expanding the horizons of island archaeology: islandscapes imaginary and real, the case of the dry island', *Shima: The International Journal of Research into Island Cultures* 4.1, pp.27–46.

Barrowclough, D. Forthcoming. 'A later Bronze Age hoard from the Barway to Little Theford causeway on the Isle of Ely', *Proceedings of the Cambridge Antiquarian Society*.

Barth, F. 1992. 'Towards greater naturalism in conceptualising societies' in A. Kuper (ed.) *Conceptualising Society*. London, pp.17–33.

Bede, Ven. 731. *Ecclesiastical History of the English People*. London: Penguin Books.

Beech, M. 2006. in C. Evans and I. Hodder. *Marshland communities and cultural landscapes from the Bronze Age to present day*. The Haddenham Project Vol.2. Cambridge: McDonald Institute Monograph 36, pp.369–96, 435–440.

Bentham, J. 1771. *The History and Antiquities of the Conventual and Cathedral Church of Ely*. Cambridge: Cambridge University Press.

Berleant, R. 2007. 'Paleolithic Flints: Is an Aesthetics of Stone Tools Possible?' *Contemporary Aesthetics* 5.

Bishop, B. 2009. 'The Flints' in A. Connor. 'A fen island burial: excavation of an Early Bronze Age round barrow at North Fen, Sutton'. *Proceedings of Cambridge Antiquarian Society* XCVIII, pp.41–2.

Blair, J. 2005. *The Church in Anglo-Saxon Society*. Oxford: Oxford University Press.

Blake, E.O. 1962. *Liber Eliensis*. London: Royal Historical Society, pp.1–62.

Bleau, J. 1684. *Cambridgeshire*. Amsterdam.

Bloch, M. 1954. *The Historian's Craft*. Manchester: Manchester University Press.

Bloch, M. and Parry, J. 1989. 'Introduction: money and the morality of exchange' in J. Parry and M. Bloch (eds), *Money and the Morality of Exchange*. Cambridge: Cambridge University Press, pp.1–31.

Boilean, J. 1850. 'Proceedings of the meeting of the Archaeological Institute', *Archaeological Journal* 7, p.302.

Bone, P. 1989. 'The development of swords from the fifth to the eleventh century' in Hawkes (ed.), *Weapons of Warfare in Anglo-Saxon England*. Oxford: Oxford University Committee for Archaeology Monograph 21, pp.63–70.

Bonsall, C. 1981. 'The coastal factor in the Mesolithic settlement of North West England' in B. Gramsch (ed.), *The Mesolithic in Europe*. Second International Symposium, Potsdam, April 1978, Report, Veröffentlichungen des Museums für Ur- und Frühgeschichte Potsdam Band 14/15. Berlin: Deutscher Verlag der Wissenschaften, pp.451–72.

Bonsall, C., Sunderland, D., Tipping, R. and Cherry, J. 1986. 'The Eskmeals Project 1981–85: an interim report', *Northern Archaeology* 7 (1), pp.1–30.

Bowman, S. and Needham, S. 2007. 'The Dunaverney and Little Thetford flesh-hooks: history, technology and their position within the later Bronze Age Atlantic zone feasting complex', *Antiquaries Journal* 87, pp.53–108.

Bradley, R. 1990. *The Passage of Arms: an archaeological analysis of prehistoric hoard and votive deposits*. Cambridge: Cambridge University Press.

Bradley, R. 1998. *The Passage of Arms: an archaeological analysis of prehistoric hoard and votive deposits* (second edition). Oxford: Oxbow, pp.99–109, 114–129.

Bradley, R. 2000. *An Archaeology of Natural Places*. London: Routledge, pp.28–32.

Bradley, R. 2007. *The Prehistory of Britain and Ireland*. Cambridge: Cambridge University Press.

Bradley, R. and Edmonds, M. 1993. *Interpreting the Axe Trade*. Cambridge: Cambridge University Press.

Braudel, F. 1972. *The Mediterranean and the Mediterranean World at the Time of Philip II*. London: Collins.

Braudel, F. 1980. *On History*. London: Weidenfeld and Nicolson.

Brown, N. 1988. 'A later Bronze Age enclosure at Loft's Farm, Essex', *Proceedings of the Prehistoric Society* 54, pp.249–302.

Brown, M.A. and Blin-Stoyle, A.E. 1959. 'Spectrographic analysis of British Middle and Late Bronze Age finds (including reprint of 'A sample analysis of British Middle and Late Bronze Age material, using optical spectrometry', *Proceedings of the Prehistoric Society*. Supplement to *Archaeometry* 2, p.66.

Brown, N. and Murphy, P. 1997, 'Neolithic and Bronze Age' in J. Glazebrook (ed.), *Research and Archaeology: A framework for the Eastern Counties, 1. Resource assessment*. East Anglian Archaeology Occasional Paper No.3, pp.12–22.

Briggs, C.S. and Turner, R.C. 1986. 'A Gazetteer of Bog Burials from Britain and Ireland' in I.M. Stead, J.B. Bourke and D. Brothwell, *Lindow Man: the body in the bog*. London: Guild Publishing, pp.181–82.

Britton, D. 1960. 'The Isleham Hoard, Cambridgeshire', *Antiquity* 34, pp.279–82.

Bronk Ramsey C., 2001. 'Development of the Radiocarbon Program OxCal', *Radiocarbon* 43, pp.355–63.

Broodbank, C. 1999. 'The Insularity of island archaeologists: comments on Rainbird's 'Islands out of time'', *Journal of Mediterranean Archaeology* 12(2), p.238.

Bruce-Mitford, R. 1978. *The Sutton Hoo Ship-burial, Volume 2, Arms, Armour and Regalia*. London, British Museum.

Brugmann, B. 2004. *Glass beads from Anglo-Saxon Graves*. Oxford: Oxbow.

Bull, S. 2008. *The Lancaster Roman Cavalry Stone: Triumphant Rider*. Lancaster: Palatine Books.

Burgess, C.B. 1976. 'Britain and Ireland in the Third and Second Millenia B.C: a Preface' in C. Burgess and R. Miket (eds), *Settlement and Economy in the Third and Second Millenia B.C*. Oxford: BAR 33.

Burgess, C.B. 1979. 'The background of early metalworking in Ireland and Britain' in M. Ryan (ed.), *The Origins of Metallurgy in Atlantic Europe: proceedings of the fifth Atlantic Colloquium*. Dublin: Stationery Office, pp.207–14.

Burgess, C.B. 1980. *The Age of Stonehenge*. London: Dent.

Burgess, C.B. 1988. 'Britain at the time of the Rhine-Swiss group' in P. Brun and C. Mordant (eds), *Le Groupe Rhin-Suisse-France-Orientale et la Notion de Civilisation des Champs d'Urnes*. Nemours: Mémoires du Musée de Préhistoire d'Ile-de-France No. 1, pp.559–73.

Bushnell, G.H.S. 1951. OS correspondence.

Bushnell, H.S. and Cra'ster, M.D. 1959. 'Pagan Saxon burials at Ely', *Proceedings of the Cambridge Antiquarian Society* 53, p.57.

Cambridgeshire Archaeological Records. 1956. No.7276. Cambridge: Cambridgeshire County Council.

Canuto, M.A. and Yaeger, J. 2000. *The Archaeology of Communities, a New World Perspective*. London: Routledge.

Carr, R.D., Tester, A. and Murphy, P. 1988. 'The Middle-Saxon settlement at Staunch Meadow, Brandon', *Antiquity* 62, pp.371–77.

Carroll, M.A. and Lang A.T.O. 2008. 'The Iron Age' in R. Adkins, L. Adkins and V. Leitch (eds), *The Handbook of British Archaeology* 2nd edn. London: Constable and Robinson, pp.94–133.

Cessford, C., Alexander, M. and Dickens, A. 2006. 'Between Broad Street and the Great Ouse: waterfront archaeology in Ely', *East Anglian Archaeology* 114.

Cessford, C. and Dickens, A. 2007. 'Ely Cathedral and Environs: recent investigations', *Proceedings of the Cambridge Antiquarian Society* XCVI, pp.161–74.

Chaplin, R.R. 1975. 'The ecology and behaviour of deer in relation to their impact on the environment of prehistoric Britain' in J.G. Evans, S. Limbrey H. and Cleere (eds), *The Effect of Man on the Landscape: the Highland Zone*. Council for British Archaeology Research Report 11, pp.40–2.

Chapman, J. 1998. 'Objectification, embodiment and the value of places and things' in D. Bailey and S. Mills (eds), *The Archaeology of Value, Essays on prestige and the process of valuation*. Oxford: British Archaeological Reports International Series 730, pp.106–30.

Chatwin, C.P. 1961. *British Regional Geology East Anglia and Adjoining Areas*. London: Her Majesty's Stationary Office.

Chester-Kadwell, M.E. 2009. *Early Anglo-Saxon Communities in the Landscape*. British Archaeological Reports British Series 481. Oxford: Archaeopress, p.51, Fig.5.5.

Chester-Kadwell, M. 2012. *A Catalogue of Anglo-Saxon Artefacts in Ely Museum*. Ely: Ely Museum.

Christie, P.M. and Coad, J.G. 1980. 'Excavations at Denny Abbey', *Archaeological Journal* CXXXVII, pp.138–279.

Clark, J.G.D. 1934. 'The classification of a microlithic culture : the Tardenoisian of Horsham', *Archaeological Journal* 90, pp.52–77.

Clark, J.G.D. 1934. 'Recent researches on the post-glacial deposits of the English Fenland', *The Irish Naturalists' Journal* 5, pp.144–52.

Clark, J.G.D. 1937. Excavator's Report, *Proceedings of the Cambridge Antiquarian Society* 37, p.xv.

Clark, J.G.D. 1972. *Star Carr: a case study in bioarchaeology*. Reading, Mass: Addison-Wesley Module in Anthropology 10.

Clark, J.G.D., Godwin, H., Godwin, M.E. and MacFadyen, W.A. 1933. 'Report on an Early Bronze Age site in the south-eastern Fens', *Antiquaries Journal* 13, pp.266–96.

Clark, J.G.D., Godwin, H., Godwin, M.E. and Clifford, M.H. 1935. 'Report on recent excavations at Peacocks' Farm, Shippea, Cambridgeshire', *Antiquaries Journal* 15, pp.284–319.

Clark, J.G.D. and Godwin, H. 1940. 'A late Bronze Age find near Stuntney, Isle of Ely', *Antiquaries Journal* 20, pp.52–71.

Clark, J.G.D., Higgs, E.S. and Longworth, I.H. 1960. 'Excavations at the Neolithic site at Hurst Fen, Mildenhall, Suffolk, 1954, 1957 and 1958', *Proceedings of the Prehistoric Society* 26, pp.202–45.

Clark, J.G.D. and Godwin, H. 1962. 'The Neolithic in the Cambridgeshire Fens', *Antiquity* 36, pp.10–23.

Clarke, J.G.D. 1931. 'A Roman pewter bowl from the Isle of Ely', *Proceedings of the Cambridge Antiquarian Society* 31, pp.66–75.

Clarke, D.L. 1970. *Beaker Pottery of Great Britain and Ireland*. Cambridge: Cambridge University Press, pp.476, 550, Fig.885 and 994.

Clarke, D.L. 1973. 'Archaeology: the loss of innocence', *Antiquity* 47, pp.6–18.

Clarke. D.L. 1977. 'Spatial information in archaeology' in D.L. Clarke (ed.), *Spatial Archaeology*. London: Academic Press, pp.1–32.

Clarke, H. and Carter, A. 1977. *Excavations in King's Lynn 1963–1970*. London: Society for Medieval Archaeology Monograph Series 7.

Cleal, R. 1992. 'Significant form: ceramic styles in the earlier Neolithic of southern England' in A. Sheridan and N. Sharples (eds), *Vessels for the Ancestors: Essays on the Neolithic of Britain and Ireland in honour of Audrey Henshall*. Edinburgh: Edinburgh University Press, pp.286–304.

Clough T. and Cummins, W.A. (eds) 1988. *Stone Axe Studies* 2. London: Council for British Archaeology Research Report 67, pp.219–21.

Clough, T. and Green, B. 1972. 'The petrological identification of stone implements from East Anglia'. *Proceedings of the Prehistoric Society* 38, p.145.

Cobbett, L. 1934. 'A Saxon carving found at Ely', *Antiquaries Journal* 14, pp.62–3.

Coles, J.M. 1962. 'European Bronze Age shields', *Proceedings of the Prehistoric Society* 28, pp.156–90.

Coles, B. 1998. 'Doggerland: a speculative survey', *Proceedings of the Prehistoric Society* 64, pp.45–81.

Connor, A. 2009. 'A fen island burial: excavation of an Early Bronze Age round barrow at North Fen, Sutton', *Proceedings of Cambridge Antiquarian Society* XCVIII, pp.37–46.

Cooney, G. 1998. 'Breaking stones, making places' in A. Gibson and D. Simpson (eds), *Prehistoric Ritual and Religion*. Stroud: Sutton.

Crummy, N. 2011. 'The Metalwork' in R. Atkins 2011. 'Beaker pits and a probable mortuary enclosure on Land off Stirling Way, near Witchford, Ely', *Proceedings of the Cambridge Archaeological Society* Vol.C, pp.47–66.

Cunliffe, B. 2005. *Iron Age Communities in Britain, 4ᵗʰ edition*. Oxford: Oxford University Press.

Daniels, R. 1999. 'The Anglo-Saxon monastery at Hartlepool, England' in J. Hawkes and S. Mills (eds). *Northumbria's Golden Age*. Stroud: Sutton, pp.105–12.

Darby, H.C. 1940. *The Medieval Fenland*. Cambridge: Cambridge University Press, pp.144–46.

Darby, H.C. 1983. *The Changing Fenland*. Cambridge: Cambridge University Press.

Defoe, D. 1727. *Tour Thro' the Whole Island of Great Britain*. London.

Dekker, M. and O'Connell, T. 2009. in S. Lucy, R. Newman, N. Dodwell, C. Hills, M. Dekker, T. O'Connell, I. Riddler and P. Rogers. 2009. 'The Burial of a Princess? The Later Seventh-Century Cemetery at Westfield Farm, Ely', *Antiquaries Journal* 89, p.134.

Dickens, A. and Whittaker, P. in prep. *Palace and Kitchen: excavations at Ely King's School*.

Dickinson, T. and Härke, H. 1992. *Early Anglo-Saxon Shields*. London: Society of Antiquaries.

Dodwell, N. 'The Human Bone' in A. Connor 2009. 'A fen island burial: excavation of an Early Bronze Age round barrow at North Fen, Sutton', *Proceedings of Cambridge Antiquarian Society* XCVIII, p.43.

Douglas, M. 1966. *Purity and Danger. An analysis of concepts of pollution and taboo*. London: Routledge.

Douglas, M. 1994 [1970], *Natural Symbols: Explorations in Cosmology*. London: Routledge, p.162.

Durkheim, E. 1915. *Elementary Forms of Religious Life*. London: Allen Unwin, pp.9-11.

Edwards, D. and Hall, D. 1997. 'Medieval pottery from Cambridge', *Proceedings of the Cambridge Antiquarian Society* 86, pp.153–68.

Edwardson, A.R. 1966. 'Beaker and rusticated sherds associated with red deer antler sockets', *Proceedings of the Cambridge Antiquarian Society* 59.

Evans, J. 1885. 'On a hoard of bronze objects found in Wilburton Fen, near Ely', *Archaeologia* 48, pp.106–14.

Evans, J. 1881. *The Ancient Bronze Implements, Weapons and Ornaments of Great Britain and Ireland*. London: Longmans, p.457.

Evans, J. 1872. *The Ancient Stone Implements, Weapons and Ornaments of Great Britain.* London: Longmans, Green, Reader and Dyer, p.263.

Evans, C. 1984. A shrine provenance for the Willingham Fen hoard, *Antiquity* 58, 212–14.

Evans, C. and Serjeantson, D. 1988. 'The backwater economy of a fen-edge community in the Iron Age: the Upper Delphs, Haddenham', *Antiquity*, 62, pp.360–70.

Evans, C. 2003. 'Power and Island Communities: Excavations at the Wardy Hill Ringwork, Coveney, Ely', *East Anglian Archaeological Report* 103.

Evans, C. and Hodder, I. 1984. 'Excavations at Haddenham', *Fenland Research* 1, pp.32–6.

Evans, C. Hodder, I. 1985. 'The Haddenham Project', *Fenland Research* 2, pp.20–1.

Evans, C. and Hodder, I. 1987. 'Between two worlds: archaeological investigations in the Haddenham Level' in J. Coles and A. Lawson *European Wetlands in Prehistory*, pp.186–91.

Evans, C. and Hodder, I. 1988. 'The Haddenham Project-1987: the Upper Delphs', *Fenland Research* 5, pp.12–13.

Evans, C, Knight, M., and Webley, L. 2007. 'Iron Age Settlement and Romanisation on the Isle of Ely: the Hurst Lane Reservoir site', *Proceedings of the Cambridge Antiquarian Society* XCVI, pp.41–78.

Evans, C. and Knight, M. 2000. 'A Fenland Delta: Later Prehistoric land-use in the lower Ouse Reaches' in M. Dawson (ed.), *Prehistoric, Roman and Post-Roman Landscapes of the Great Ouse Valley.* Council for British Archaeology Research Report 119, pp.89–106

Evans, C. and Hodder, I. 2006a. *A Woodland Archaeology: The Haddenham Project* (I). Cambridge: McDonald Institute Monograph.

Evans, C. and Hodder, I. 2006b. *Marshland Communities and Cultural Landscape: The Haddenham Project* (II). Cambridge: McDonald Institute Monograph.

Evans, J.D. 1973. 'Islands as laboratories for the study of cultural process' in C. Renfrew (ed.), *The Explanation of Cultural Change: models in prehistory*. London: Duckworth, pp.517–20.

Evans, C. 2000. 'Iron Age Forts and Defences' in T. Kirby and S. Oosthuizen (eds), *An Atlas of Cambridgeshire and Huntingdonshire History*. Cambridge: Centre for Regional Studies, Anglia Polytechnic University, 22.

Evans-Pritchard, E. 1939. 'Nuer time-reckoning', *Africa*, 12, pp.189–216.

Evans-Pritchard, E. 1940. *The Nuer*. Oxford: Clarendon.

Febvre, L. and Bloch, M. 1929. *Annales d'histoire économique et sociale*. Strasbourg.

Field, N. and Parker-Pearson, M. 2003. *Fiskerton. An Iron Age timber causeway with Iron Age and Roman votive offerings*. Oxford: Oxbow, pp.179–88.

Fiennes, C. 1698. *Journal of Celia Fiennes*. London.

Fokkens, H. 1999. 'Cattle and martiality: changing relations between man and landscape in the Late Neolithic and the Bronze Age' in C. Fabech and J. Ringtved (eds), *Settlement and Landscape. Proceedings of a conference in Aarhus, Denmark, May 4–7 1998*. Aarhus, pp.35–43.

Fontijn, D.R. 2002. 'Sacrificial landscapes: cultural biographies of persons, objects and 'natural' places in the Bronze Age of the southern Netherlands *c*.2300–600 BC', *Analecta Praehistorica Leidensia* 33/34, p.275.

Fowler, G. 1948. 'Cratendune: A problem of the Dark Ages', *Proceedings of the Cambridge Antiquarian Society* XLI, pp.70–6.

Fowler, G. 1949. 'A Romano-British village near Littleport, Cambs, with some observations on the distribution of early occupation, and on the drainage of the fens', *Proceedings of the Cambridge Antiquarian Society*, XLIII, pp.7–20.

Fox, C. 1923. *The Archaeology of the Cambridge Region*. Cambridge: Cambridge University Press.

Fox, C. 1926. 'A dug-out canoe from S. Wales with notes on the typology and distribution of monoxylous craft in England and Wales', *Antiquaries Journal* 6, pp.121–51.

Fraser, D. 1983. *Land and Society in Neolithic Orkney*. Oxford: British Archaeological Reports 117, pp.235–261.

French, C.A. I. 2000. 'Development of fenland in prehistoric times' in T. Kirby and S. Oosthuizen (eds), *An Atlas of Cambridgeshire and Huntingdonshire History*. Cambridge: Centre for Regional Studies, Anglia Polytechnic University, 4.

Frend, W.H.C. 2000. 'Roman Christianity' in T. Kirby and S. Oosthuizen (eds), *An Atlas of Cambridgeshire and Huntingdonshire History*. Cambridge: Centre for Regional Studies, Anglia Polytechnic University, 45.

Gallois, R.W. 1980. *Institute of Geological Sciences, sheet 173 1:50,000 series, Ely*. Southampton.

Gallois R.W. 1988. *Geology of the country around Ely* Memoir British Geological Survey Sheet 173. London: HMSO.

Gardiner, M. and Greatorex, C. 1997. 'Archaeological excavations at Steyning, 1992-95: Further evidence for the evolution of a late Saxon small town', *Sussex Archaeological Collection* 135, pp.168-70.

Gardiner, R. 1997. *The Story of Ely Cathedral*. Tarrant Monkton: Workshop Press, pp.14–5.

Garwood, P. 1999. 'Grooved ware in Southern Britain: chronology and interpretation' in R. Cleal and A. MacSween (eds), *Grooved Ware in Britain and Ireland*. Oxford: Oxbow Books, pp.145–76.

Geake, H. 1997. *The Use of Grave Goods in Conversion-Period England, c.600–850*. BAR, British Series 261. Oxford: Archaeopress.

Gell, A. 1992. *The Anthropology of Time: cultural constructions of temporal maps and images*. Oxford: Berg, pp.190–205.

Gerritsen, F.A. 2001. *Local Identities. Landscape and community in the late Prehistoric Meuse-Demer-Scheldt Region*. Amsterdam: Free University of Amsterdam.

Gibson, D. 1996. *Excavations at West Fen Road, Ely, Cambridgeshire*. Cambridge: Cambridge Archaeological Unit Report 160.

Gibson, A.M. 2000. *The Walton Basin Project: Excavation and Survey in a Prehistoric Landscape 1993–7*. CBA Research Report 118. York: CBA.

Gibson, A. and Kinnes, I. 1997. 'On the urns of a dilemma: radiocarbon and the Peterborough problem', *Oxford Journal of Archaeology* 16, pp.65–72.

Godwin, H. 1978. *Fenland: its ancient past and uncertain future*. Cambridge: Cambridge University Press.

Gräslund, B. 1987. *The Birth of Prehistoric Chronology*. Cambridge: Cambridge University Press.

Green, H.S. 1980. *The Flint Arrowheads of the British Isles*. Oxford: BAR British Series 75.

Green, B. 1980. 'Two 9th century silver objects from Costessey', *Norfolk Archaeology* 37, pp.351–53.

Green, M. 2001. *Dying For the Gods*. Stroud: Tempus.

Grierson, P. and Blackburn, M.A.S. 1986. *Medieval European Coinage*. Cambridge: Cambridge University Press.

Hall, D. 1992. 'The Fenland Project, Number 6: The South-Western Cambridgeshire Fenlands', *East Anglian Archaeology* 56, p.88.

Hall, D. 1996. 'The Fenland Project, Number 10: Cambridgeshire Survey, Isle of Ely and Wisbech', *East Anglian Archaeology* 79.

Hall, D. and Coles, J. 1994. *Fenland Survey: An Essay in Landscape and Persistence*. London: English Heritage, Archaeological Report 1.

Hall, D. 2001. 'A medieval pottery from Ely, Cambridgeshire', *Medieval Ceramics* 25, pp.2–21.

Hampson, E.M. and Atkinson, T.D. 1953. 'City of Ely' in R.B. Pugh (ed.), *The Victoria County History of Cambridgeshire* IV. Oxford: Oxford University Press, p.34.

Härke, H. 1989. 'Early Saxon weapon burials: frequencies, distributions and weapon combinations' in S.C. Hawkes (ed.) 1989. *Weapons of Warfare in Anglo-Saxon England*. Oxford: Oxford University Cttee for Archaeology Monograph 21, pp.49–61.

Härke, H. 1992. 'Changing symbols in a changing society: the Anglo-Saxon weapon burial rite in the seventh century' in M. Carver (ed.) *The Age of Sutton Hoo*. Woodbridge: Boydell Press, pp.149–165.

Harley, R. *Survey of Ely of 1417*. BL 329, fos10–24v.

Harper, C. 1902. *The Cambridge, Ely and Kings Lynn Road*. Cambridge.

Hariot, T. 1588. *A Briefe and True Report of the New Found Land of Virginia*. Frankfurt.

Harris, E.C. 1989. *Principles of Archaeological Stratigraphy*. London: Academic Press.

Harrison, S. 1995. 'Transformation of identity in Sepik warfare' in M. Strathern (ed.) *Shifting Contexts, Transformations in Anthropological Knowledge*. London, pp.81–97.

Hawkes, S.C. (ed.) 1989. *Weapons of Warfare in Anglo-Saxon England*. Oxford: Oxford University Committee for Archaeology Monograph 21.

Healey, H., Malim, T. and Watson, K. 1998. 'A medieval kiln at Colne, Cambridgeshire', *Proceedings of the Cambridge Antiquarian Society* 87, p.57.

Healy, F. 1988. 'Spong Hill, Part VI: 7th to 2nd Millennium BC', *East Anglian Archaeology*, 39. Norfolk Archaeological Unit, Norfolk Museums Service.

Healy, F. 1991. 'Lithics and pre-Iron Age pottery' in R.J. Silvester, 'The Wissey Embayment and the Fen Causeway', *East Anglian Archaeology* 52.

Hedges, J. and Buckley, D. 1978. 'Excavations at a Neolithic causewayed enclosure, Orsett, Essex, 1975', *Proceedings of the Prehistoric Society* 44, pp.219–308.

Hedges, R.E.M., Clement, J.G., David, C., Thomas, L. And O'Connell, T.C. 2007. 'Collagen turnover in the adult femoral mid-shaft: modelled from anthropogenic radiocarbon tracer measurements', *American Journal of Physical Anthropology* 133/2.

Heichelheim, F.M. 1937. 'Some unpublished Roman bronze statuettes in the Museum of Archaeology and Ethnology, Cambridge', *Proceedings of the Cambridge Antiquarian Society* 37, p.73.

Helms, M.W. 1993. *Craft and the Kingly Ideal: art, trade and Power*. Austin: University of Texas Press.

Helms, M.W. 1988. *Ulysses' Sail. An ethnographic odyssey of power, knowledge, and geographic distance*. New Jersey, p.22.

Henderson, I. 1997. 'Anglo-Saxon sculpture' in C. Hicks (ed.), *Cambridgeshire Churches*. Stamford: Paul Watkins, pp.216–32.

Higbee, L. 1999. 'The animal bone' in P. Whittaker *Archaeological Investigations at the Kings School, Ely*. Cambridge: Cambridge Archaeological Unit Report 343.

Higbee, L. 2003. 'Animal bones' in M. Alexander, 'A medieval and post-medieval street frontage: investigations at Forehill, Ely', *Proceedings of the Cambridge Antiquarian Society*, 170.

Hill, J.D. 2000. in T. Kirby and S. Oosthuizen (eds), *An Atlas of Cambridgeshire and Huntingdonshire History*. Cambridge: Centre for Regional Studies, Anglia Polytechnic University.

Hill, J.D., Evans, C. and Alexander, M. 1999. 'The Hinxton Rings: a Late Iron Age cemetery at Hinxton, Cambridgeshire, with a reconstruction of northern Aylesford-Swarling distributions', *Proceedings of the Prehistoric Society* 65, pp.243–73.

Hines, J. 1993. *Clasps=Hektespennes=Agraffen: Anglo-Saxon Clasps of Classes A-C of the 3rd to 6th Centuries AD*. Stockholm.

Hines, J. 1997. *A New Corpus of Anglo-Saxon Great Square-Headed Brooches*. Woodbridge: Boydell Press for Society of Antiquaries.

Hines, J. 1997. *The Anglo-Saxons from the Migration Period to the eighth century: an ethnographic perspective*. London: Boydell.

Hodder, I. and Shand, P. 1988. 'The Haddenham long barrow: an interim statement', *Antiquity* 62, pp.349–53.

Holmes, R. 1980. *Steeple Gate Ely*. Ely.

Holton-Krayenbuhl, A.P.B. 1984. *The Three Blackbirds. A medieval house in Ely, Cambridgeshire*. Ely: Ely Preservation Society.

Holton-Krayenbuhl, A. 1988. 'Excavations at the Paddock, Ely, Cambridgeshire', *Proceedings of the Cambridge Antiquarian Society* 77, pp.119–23.

Holton-Krayenbuhl, A.P.B. 1997. 'The infirmary complex at Ely', *Archaeological Journal* 154, pp.122–23.

Holton-Krayenbuhl, A. 2000. 'Ely' in T. Kirby and S. Oosthuizen (eds), *An Atlas of Cambridgeshire and Huntingdonshire History*. Cambridge: Centre for Regional Studies, Anglia Polytechnic University, p.79.

Holton-Krayenbuhl, A.P.B. (ed.) 2011. *The Topography of Medieval Ely*. Cambridge: Cambridgeshire Records Society, p.20.

Holton-Krayenbuhl, A., Cocke, T. and Malim, T. 1989. 'Ely Cathedral Precincts: the North Range', *Proceedings of the Cambridge Antiquarian Society*, pp.47–70.

Hunter, J.P.C. 1992 (a). *Archaeological Investigations at Bray's Lane, Ely, 1991*. Cambridge: Cambridge Archaeology Unit, Report 8.

Hunter, J. 1992 (b) *Investigations at Walsingham House, Ely*. Cambridge: Cambridge Archaeological Unit unpublished report A110.

Isbell, W.H. 2000. 'What we should be studying: the 'imagined community' and the 'natural community'' in M.A. Canuto, and J. Yaeger, *The Archaeology of Communities, a New World Perspective*. London: Routledge, pp.243–66.

Jones, J. 1924. *A Human Geography of Cambridgeshire*. London: Sidgwick and Jackson Ltd.

Jones, A.E. 1993. Archaeological excavations at the White Hart, Ely 1991–92, *Proceedings of the Cambridge Antiquarian Society* 82, pp.113–37.

Kenney, S. 1999. *Anglo-Saxon and Medieval Deposits at 2 West End, Ely: An Archaeological Evaluation*. Cambridgeshire County Council Archaeological Field Unit Report Number 164.

Kenney, S. 2002. *Roman, Saxon and Medieval Occupation at the former Red, White and Blue Public House, Chief's Street, Ely*. Cambridgeshire County Council Archaeological Field Unit Report Number 195.

Kingsley, C. 1866. *Hereward the Wake*. Cambridge.

Kirch, P. 1986. 'Introduction: the archaeology of island societies' in P. Kirch (ed.), *Island Societies: Archaeological Approaches to Evolution and Transformation*. Cambridge: Cambridge University Press, pp.1–5.

Klein, R.G. 1989. *The Human Career: Human, biological and cultural origins*. Chicago and London: University of Chicago Press, pp.165–70.

Klindt-Jensen, O. 1975. *A History of Scandinavian Archaeology*. London: Thames and Hudson.

Keynes, S. 2003. 'Ely abbey, 672–1109' in P. Meadows and N. Ramsay (eds), *A History of Ely Cathedral*. Woodbridge: Boydell Press, pp.42–4.

Knowles, D. and Hadcock, R.N. 1971. *Medieval Religious Houses, England and Wales*. London: Longman, pp.266–67.

Kristiansen, K. (ed.) 1985. *Archaeological Formation Processes. The Representativity of Archaeological Remains from Danish Prehistory*. Københaven: Nationalsmuseets Forlag.

Küchler, S. 1987. 'Malangan: art and memory in a Melanesian society', *Man* (N.S.) 22, pp.238–55.

Lahr, M. and Foley, R. 2006. 'A representation of the later stages of human evolution in Stringer', C. *Homo Britannicus*, London: Penguin Books, p.51.

Laing, L. 1981. *Celtic Britain*. London: Paladin.

Leach, E. 1976. *Culture and Communication:the logic by which symbols are connected*. Cambridge: Cambridge University Press.

Leach, E. 1977. 'A View from the bridge' in M. Spriggs (ed.) *Archaeology and Anthropology: areas of mutual interest*. Oxford: British Archaeological Reports Supplementary Series 19, pp.171–73.

Leeds, E.T. 1945. 'The distribution of the Angles and Saxons archaeologically considered', *Archaeologia* 91, pp.1–106.

Lethbridge, T.C. 1927. 'An Anglo-Saxon hut on the Car Dyke at Waterbeach', *Antiquaries Journal* 7, pp.141–46.

Lethbridge, T.C. 1930. 'Bronze Age burials at Little Downham, Cambridge', *Antiquaries Journal* 10, pp.162–64, plate xvii.

Lethbridge, T.C. 1933. 'Anglo-Saxon burials at Soham', *Proceedings of the Cambridge Antiquarian Society* 33.

Lethbridge, T.C. 1935. 'Investigation of the ancient causeway in the fen between Fordy and Little Thetford', *Proceedings of the Cambridge Antiquarian Society* XXXV, pp.84–9.

Lethbridge, T.C. 1953. 'Jewelled Saxon pendant from the Isle of Ely', *Proceedings of the Cambridge Antiquarian Society* XLVI, pp.1–3.

Lethbridge, T.C. and O'Reilly, M.M. 1928. 'Archaeological Notes', *Proceedings of the Cambridge Antiquarian Society* 30.

Lethbridge, T.C. and O'Reilly, M.M. 1933. 'Archaeological Notes', *Proceedings of the Cambridge Antiquarian Society* 34, p.165.

Lethbridge, T.C. and O'Reilley, M.M. 1936. 'Archaeological Notes – Bronze Age', *Proceedings of the Cambridge Antiquarian Society* 37.

Lovgren, S. 2005. 'Neandertal Advance: First Fully Jointed Skeleton Built', *National Geographic News*. March 10, 2005.

Lucas, G. 1996. in Hall, D. 'The Fenland Project, Number 10: Cambridgeshire Survey, Isle of Ely and Wisbech', *East Anglian Archaeology* 79, p.41.

Lucas, G. 1998. *The Iron Age Settlement at Watson's Lane, Little Thetford, Ely, Cambridgeshire.* Cambridge: CAU Report 259.

Lucas, G. 2005. *The Archaeology of Time.* London: Routledge, p.18.

Lucas, G. and Hinman. 1996. *Archaeological Excavations of an Iron Age Settlement and Romano-British Enclosure at Watson's Lane, Little Thetford, Ely, Cambridgeshire. Post Excavation Assessment Report.* Cambridge: Cambridge Archaeological Unit Report 194.

Lucy, S. 2000. *The Anglo-Saxon Way of Death.* Stroud: Sutton Publishing.

Lucy, S., Newman, R., Dodwell, N., Hills, C., Dekker, M., O'Connell, T., Riddler, I. and Rogers, P. 2009. 'The Burial of a Princess? The Later Seventh-Century Cemetery at Westfield Farm, Ely', *Antiquaries Journal* 89, pp.81–141.

Lyell, C. 1833. *Principles of Geology.* London: John Murray.

MacFarlane, C. 1897 [1844]. *The Camp of Refuge.* London.

McKinley, J. 1994. 'The Anglo-Saxon Cemetery at Spong Hill, North Elmham. Part VII: The Cremations', *East Anglian Archaeology* 69.

Malim, T. 2000. 'Neolithic Enclosures' in T. Kirby and S. Oosthuizen (eds) *An Atlas of Cambridgeshire and Huntingdonshire History.* Cambridge: Centre for Regional Studies, Anglia Polytechnic University, p.22.

Malim, T. 2001. 'Place and space in the Cambridgeshire Bronze Age' in J. Brück (ed.), *Bronze Age Landscapes: Tradition and Transformation.* Oxford: Oxbow, p.23.

Malim, T. 2005. *Stonea and The Roman Fens.* Stroud: Tempus.

Malim, T. 2010. 'The environmental and social context of the Isleham hoard', *The Antiquaries Journal* 90, pp.73–130.

Marquardt, W. H. 1978. 'Advances in archaeological seriation', *Advances in Archaeological Method and Theory* 1, pp.257–314.

Maryon, H. 1948. 'A sword of the Nydam type from Ely Fields Farm, Near Ely', *Proceedings of the Cambridge Antiquarian Society* XLI, pp.73–6.

Masser, P. and Evans, C. 1999. *West Fen and St Johns Roads, Ely, Cambridgeshire. An Archaeological evaluation. The Trinity, Carter and Runciman Lands.* Cambridge: Cambridge Archaeological Unit Report.

Mason, H. J, 1973. *The Black Fens.* Providence Press.

Meaney, A. 1964. *A Gazetteer of Early Anglo-Saxon Burial Sites*. London: Allen and Unwin, p.64.

Moore, J. 1685. 'Ely' on the map of 'Cambridgeshire and the Great Levell of the Fenne, *The Shires of England and Wales*: Philip Lea.

Mortimer, R. 2000. *West Fen Road, Ely, Cotmist Field: Assessment Report*. Cambridge: Cambridge Archaeology Unit Report No.362.

Mortimer, R., Regan, R. and Lucy, S. 2005. 'The Saxon and Medieval Settlement at West Fen Road, Ely: The Ashwell Site', *East Anglian Archaeology* 110.

Mudd, A. and Webster, M. 2011. *Iron Age and Middle Saxon Settlements at West Fen Road, Ely, Cambridgeshire: The Consortium Site*. Northamptonshire Archaeology Monograph 2. Oxford: Archaeopress, BAR British Series 538.

Mulk, I.M. 1997. 'Sacrificial places and their meaning in Saami society' in D.L. Carmichael, J. Hubert, B. Reeves and A. Schanche (eds), *Sacred Sites, Sacred Places*. London: One World Archaeology 23, pp.121–31.

Myres, J.N.L. 1977. *Corpus of Anglo-Saxon Pottery of the Pagan Period*. Cambridge: Cambridge University Press.

Mudd, A. 2000. *West Fen Road, Ely, Cambridgeshire. Interim progress report on excavations to March 2000*. Northamptonshire Archaeology.

Needham, S. 1989. 'Selective deposition in the British Early Bronze Age', *World Archaeology* 10, pp.229–248.

Needham, S. 1996. Chronology and periodisation in the British Bronze Age, *Acta Archaeologica* 67, pp.121–40.

Needham, S., Bronk Ramsay, C., Coombs, D., Cartwright, C. and Pettitt, P. 1997. 'An independent chronology for British Bronze Age metalwork: the results of the Oxford radiocarbon accelerator programme', *Archaeological Journal* 154, pp.55–107.

O'Reilly, M.M. 1928. 'Archaeological Notes', *Proceedings of the Cambridge Antiquarian Society* 29, p.105.

Owen, D.M 1993. *The Medieval Development of the Town of Ely*. Ely: Ely Historical Society, p.11.

Parry, S. 2009. in Lucy, S., Newman, R., Dodwell, N., Hills, C., Dekker, M., O'Connell, T., Riddler, I. and Rogers, P. 2009. 'The Burial of a Princess? The Later Seventh-Century Cemetery at Westfield Farm, Ely', *Antiquaries Journal* 89, p.134.

Paterson, W. 1948. 'The earliest known prehistoric industry', *Nature* 161, p.278.

Pestell, T. 2003. 'The afterlife of 'productive' sites in East Anglia' in T. Pestell and K. Ulmschneider (eds), *Markets in Early Medieval Europe: Trading and 'Productive' Sites, 650–850*. Macclesfield: Wingather Press, pp.122–137

Phillips, C.W. 1939. *Britain in the Dark Ages*. Ordnance Survey, Memoir with south sheet 1:1,000,000 (N. Sheet 1938).

Potter, K.R. (trans.) 1976. *Gesta Stephani*. Oxford: Oxford University Press.

Potter, T.W. 2000. 'Roman Fenland' in T. Kirby and S. Oosthuizen (eds), *An Atlas of Cambridgeshire and Huntingdonshire History*. Cambridge: Centre for Regional Studies, Anglia Polytechnic University, p.25.

Powell, T.G.E. 1958. *The Celts*. London: Thames and Hudson.

Preston, J. 1996. 'Ely' in D. Hall, 'The Fenland Project, Number 10: Cambridgeshire Survey, Isle of Ely and Wisbech', *East Anglian Archaeology* 79, p.30.

Pryor, F. 2010. *The Making of the British Landscape: How we have transformed the Land, from Prehistory to Today*. London: Penguin.

Pugh, R.B. 1953. *The Victoria County History of the County of Cambridge and the Isle of Ely*, Vol.4. Victoria County History. Oxford: The Institute of Historical Research, Oxford University Press, pp.30–2.

Rackham in Holton-Krayenbuhl, A.P.B. 1984. *The Three Blackbirds. A medieval house in Ely, Cambridgeshire*. Ely: Ely Preservation Society, p.13.

Rainbird, P. 1999. 'Islands out of time: a critique of island archaeology', *Journal of Mediterranean Archaeology* 12(2), p.217.

Ralph, S. 2007. 'Severed Heads and Broken Pots: Cult Activity in Iron Age Europe' in D. Barrowclough and C. Malone (eds), *Cult in Context: Reconsidering Ritual in Archaeology*. Oxford: Oxbow Books.

Read, B. 2008. *Hooked-Clasps and Eyes: A Classification and Catalogue of Sharp- or Blunt-Hooked Clasps and Miscellaneous Hooks, Eyes, Loops, Rings or Toggles*. Langport: Portcullis Publishing.

Reaney, P.H. 1943. *The Place-names of Cambridgeshire and the Isle of Ely*. Cambridge: Cambridge University Press.

Regan, R. 2001a. *West Fen Road, Ely. Cornwell Field: Assessment Report*. Cambridge: Cambridge Archaeological Unit.

Regan, R. 2001b. *Excavations south of the Lady Chapel, Ely Cathedral, Cambridgeshire. Assessment Report*, Cambridge Archaeology Unit Report 419.

Renfrew, A.C. 1979. 'Discontinuities in the endogenous change of settlement pattern' in C.Renfrew and K.L. Cooke (eds), *Transformations, Mathematical Approaches to Culture*. London: Academic Press, pp.437–61.

Renfrew, C. 2004. 'Islands out of time? Towards an analytical framework' in S.M. Fitzpatrick (ed.) *Voyages of Discovery: the archaeology of islands*. Westport: Praeger, 275–94.

Renfrew, C. and Bahn, P. 1996. *Archaeology: Theory, Methods and Practice*. London: Thames and Hudson Ltd.

Renfrew, C. and Cherry, J.F. (eds), 1986. *Peer Polity Interaction and Socio-Political Change*. Cambridge: Cambridge University Press.

Rex, P. 2004. *The English Resistance: the Underground War Against the Normans*. Stroud: Tempus.

Richards, C. 1996. 'Henges and Water. Towards an elemental understanding of monumentality and landscape in Late Neolithic Britain', *Journal of Material Culture* 1, p.317.

Rincon, P. 2010. *Neanderthal genes 'survive in us'*, BBC NewsChannel 6 May 2010: http://news.bbc.co.uk/1/hi/sci/tech/8660940.stm.

Robinson, B. 2000. *Saxon and Medieval Occupation at St Mary's Lodge, Ely: a recording brief*. Cambridgeshire County Council Archaeological Field Unit, Report 171.

Roe, F.E.S. 1966. 'The battle-axe series in Britain', *Proceedings of the Prehistoric Society* 32, pp.199–245.

Rowlands, M.J. 1993. 'The role of memory in the transmission of culture', *World Archaeology* 25, pp.141–51.

Sahlins, M. 1987. *Islands of History*. Chicago: Chicago University Press.

Salzman, L.F. (ed.) 1938. *The Victoria County History of the County of Cambridge and the Isle of Ely*, Vol.1, Victoria County History. London: The Institute of Historical Research.

Salzman, L.F. (ed.) 1948. *The Victoria County History of the County of Cambridge and the Isle of Ely*, Vol.2, Victoria County History. London: The Institute of Historical Research, pp.29, 264, 266, 259–62, 295–303.

Sheail, G. 2000. 'Geology', and 'Relief and Landforms' in T. Kirby and S. Oosthuizen (eds), *An Atlas of Cambridgeshire and Huntingdonshire History*. Cambridge: Centre for Regional Studies, Anglia Polytechnic University, pp.1–4.

Shennan, I. and Andrews, J. (eds) 2000. *Holocene Land-Ocean Interaction and Environmental Change Around the North Sea*. London: Geological Society, Special Publications 166, pp.275–98.

Smith, A.G., Whittle, A., Cloutman, E.W . and Morgan, L. 1989. 'Mesolithic and Neolithic activity and environmental impact on the south-east fen-edge in Cambridgeshire', *Proceedings of the Prehistoric Society* 55, pp.207–49.

Soberl, L. and Evershed, R.P. 2011. 'Lipid analysis' in R. Atkins, 'Beaker pits and a probable mortuary enclosure on Land off Stirling Way, near Witchford, Ely', *Proceedings of the Cambridge Archaeological Society* Vol.C, pp.47–66.

Speed, J. 1610. 'Cambridgeshire' in J. Speed, *The Theatre of the Empire of Great Britaine*. London.

Spoerry, P. 2005. 'Town and country in the Medieval Fenland' in K. Giles and C. Dyer, *Town and Country in the Middle Ages: Contrasts, Contacts and Interconnections, 1100–1500*. Leeds: Maney Publishing.

Spoerry, P. 2008. 'Ely Wares', *East Anglian Archaeology Report* 122.

Stewart, D.J. 1868. *On the Architectural History of Ely Cathedral*. London, p.207.

Stringer, C. 2006. *Homo britannicus*. London: Penguin Books.

Stringer, C. and Gamble, C. 1995. *In Search of the Neanderthals*. London: Thames and Hudson.

Stuiver, M., Reimer, P.J., Bard, E., Beck, J.W., Burr, G.S., Hughen, K.A., Kromer, B., McCormac, F.G., Plicht, J.V.D and Spurk. M. 1998. 'INTCAL98 Radiocarbon Age Calibration, 24,000–0 cal BP', *Radiocarbon* 40, pp.1041–83.

Swanton, M.J. 1974. *A Corpus of Pagan Anglo-Saxon Spear-Types*. Oxford.

Taylor, A. 1984. 'A Roman stone coffin from Stuntney and gazetteer of similar coffins in Cambridgeshire', *Proceedings of the Cambridge Antiquarian Society* LXXIII, pp.15–21.

Taylor, A. 1980. *The Castles of Cambridgeshire*. Cambridge.

Taylor, A. 2000. 'Roman Religion' in T. Kirby and S. Oosthuizen (eds), *An Atlas of Cambridgeshire and Huntingdonshire History*. Cambridge: Centre for Regional Studies, Anglia Polytechnic University, p.35.

Topping, P. (ed.) 1997. *Neolithic Landscapes: Neolithic Studies Group Seminar Papers 2*. Oxford: Oxbow Monograph 86.

Trump, B. 1962. 'The origin and development of British Middle Bronze Age rapiers', *Proceedings of the Prehistoric Society* 28, pp.80–103.

Trump, D.H. 1959. 'A beaker from Ely', *Proceedings of the Cambridge Antiquarian Society* 52, p.1.

Uchibori, M. 1978. *The Leaving of this Transient World: a study of Iban eschatology and mortuary practices*. Canberra: Australian National University.

Ucko, P.J. 1969. 'Ethnography and the archaeological interpretation of funerary remains', *World Archaeology* 1, pp.262–90.

University Museum of Archaeology and Ethnology. 1906. Cambridge, No. 173.

Ussher, J. 1650. *The Annals of the World*. London.

Vayda, A.P. and Rappaport, R.A. 1963. 'Island cultures' in F.R. Fosberg (ed.), *Man's Place in the Island Ecosystem*. Honolulu: Bishop Museum.

von Hugel, A. 1887. 'Some notes on the gold armilla found in Grunty Fen', *Communications of the Cambridge Antiquarian Society* 6, pp.96–105.

Waller, M. 1994. 'The Fenland Project, Number 9: Flandrian Environmental Change in Fenland', *East Anglian Archaeology* 70.

Webley, L. and Hiller, J. 2009. 'A fen island in the Neolithic and Bronze Age: excavations at North Fen, Sutton, Cambridgeshire', *Proceedings of the Cambridge Antiquarian Society* XCVIII, pp.11–36.

Webster, L. and Backhouse, J. (eds) 1991. *The Making of England: Anglo-Saxon Art and Culture, AD 600–900*. Toronto: University of Toronto Press.

Wentworth Day, J. 1970. *History of the Fens*. EP Publishing.

White Howells, W. 1997. *Getting Here: The Story of Human Evolution*. Washington: Howells House.

Whittle, A.W.R. 1997. 'Moving on and moving around: Neolithic settlement mobility' in P. Topping (ed.), *Neolithic Landscapes*. Neolithic Studies Group Seminar papers 2. Oxford: Oxbow Monograph 86, pp.15–22.

Whittle, A.W.R. 1980. 'Two Neolithics?' *Current Archaeology* 70 and 71, pp.329–34, 371–73.

Whittle, A.W.R. 1999. 'The Neolithic Period' in J. Hunter and I. Ralston (eds.), *The Archaeology of Britain: an Introduction from Upper Palaeolithic to the Industrial Revolution*. London: Routledge, p.63.

Wilde, J. 2011. *Hereward*. London: Bantam Press.

Wilkes, J.J. and Elrington, C.R. (eds) 1978. *A History of the County of Cambridge and the Isle of Ely: Roman Cambridgeshire*. Vol.7. Victoria County History. Oxford: The Institute of Historical Research, Oxford University Press.

Wilkinson, T. and Murphy, P. 1995. 'The archaeology of the Essex coast, Volume 1: The Hullbridge survey', *East Anglian Archaeology* 71.

Williams, G. 2008. *Early Anglo-Saxon Coins*. Shire Archaeology. Botley: Shire Publications.

Wilson, D.M. and Hurst, J.G. 1960. 'Medieval Britain in 1959', *Medieval Archaeology* 4, pp.134–65.

Wymer, J.J. 1977. *Gazetteer of Mesolithic Sites in England and Wales, CBA Research Report 22*. London: Council for British Archaeology, p.27.

Yates, D. and Bradley, R. 2010. 'Still water, hidden depths: the deposition of Bronze Age metalwork in the English Fenland', *Antiquity* 84, pp.324, 405–415.

Yeager, J. and Canuto, M.A. 2000. 'Introducing an archaeology of communities' in M.A. Canuto, and J. Yaeger, 2000. *The Archaeology of Communities, a New World Perspective*. London: Routledge, pp.1–15.

Yorke, B. 2005. *Nunneries and the Anglo-Saxon Royal Houses*. London: Continuum.

INDEX

ABOUT THE AUTHORS

David Barrowclough MA, PhD, FRAS lives in Ely. He is Director of Studies in Archaeology, Tutor and Fellow of Wolfson College, at the University of Cambridge, and is a past editor of the Proceedings of the Cambridge Antiquarian Society.

Kate Morrison Ayres BA (Hons), MA, FRAS is a graduate of Durham University where she read both Archaeology and Museum and Artefact Studies. She is past Curator of True's Yard Museum, King's Lynn and Swaffham Museum in Norfolk and Ely Museum, Cambridgeshire. She is now Project Manager for the development of a new Heritage Resource Centre on behalf of the Milton Keynes Heritage Consortium and Deputy Director at Milton Keynes Museum.